INCLUDING DIFFERENCE

About NAEA

Founded in 1947, the National Art Education Association (NAEA) is the leading professional membership organization exclusively for visual arts educators. Members include elementary, middle, and high school visual arts educators; college and university professors; university students preparing to be art educators; researchers and scholars; teaching artists; administrators and supervisors; and art museum educators—as well as more than 54,000 students who are members of the National Art Honor Society.

NAEA's mission is to advance visual arts education to fulfill human potential and promote global understanding.

NAEA publishes *Art Education*, *Studies in Art Education*, and other professional papers on art education; holds an annual convention; conducts research; sponsors a teacher awards program; develops standards for student learning, school programs, and teacher preparation; and co-sponsors workshops, seminars, and institutes on art education. For further information, visit our website at www.arteducators.org

To order a copy of this book or obtain additional information, contact National Art Education Association: www.arteducators.org or 800-299-8321.

Order No. 322
ISBN 978-1-890160-59-3

INCLUDING DIFFERENCE

A Communitarian Approach to Art Education in the Least Restrictive Environment

Michelle Kraft and Karen Keifer-Boyd

Dedication

This book is dedicated to preservice and practicing art educators who endeavor to create participatory, inclusive classroom communities for learners of all abilities.

Table
OF CONTENTS

Part I: Empowerment Through Inclusion

Part II: Human Empowerment Through the Arts (HEARTS): A Model for an Inclusive Art Class

ACKNOWLEDGMENTS

We would like to express our appreciation to the participants of HEARTS—to both the preservice educators who enrolled in the course to which HEARTS was attached, and to the students in the HEARTS program. It was the collective of those individuals' open minds, their genuine concern for one another, and their heartfelt desire to engage one another that enabled us all to create the fully participatory least restrictive learning community that we feel is embodied in the Individuals with Disabilities Education Act (IDEA). Without their willingness to contribute, the HEARTS program and this book could not have happened.

We also extend our thanks to Texas Tech University (TTU) and to Lubbock Christian University (LCU) for their support in allowing us to offer the unique, cooperative ART 5360/ART 4370 courses that led to the development of the HEARTS program in 2001. The backing of Dr. Melody Weiler (Director of the School of Visual Arts at TTU at that time; currently Vice President for Academic Affairs at Ringling College of Art and Design) and of Dr. E. Don Williams (Dean of the Hancock College of Liberal Arts and Education at LCU in 2001; currently Director of Graduate Studies at LCU) for HEARTS was invaluable. Their encouragement and provision of resources brought about the inter-university collaboration that made HEARTS the rich experience that it was for participants and for the graduate and undergraduate preservice educators enrolled in the course.

Drs. Weiler and Williams have continued to be generous mentors, colleagues, sounding boards, and friends throughout our professional lives.

There are many others who contributed to the success of HEARTS and the completion of this book—both directly and indirectly—and without whose support none of these things would have happened. Dr. Fred Hartmeister (Professor of Education and Law at Texas Tech University), from early on, was most generous in providing his time, expertise, and encouragement to Michelle in the area of education law and policy and legal analysis. Janice Magness, Director of Burkhart Transition Academy for Autism Education and Research at Texas Tech University (and Michelle's next-door neighbor), reviewed and provided professional insight for the development of this book. Karen's 90-year-old mother, Lenore Treat Keifer (1921–2012), and longtime friend (for more than 45 years) Kathy Harransky, contributed their views for a dialogue about a film in Chapter 2. The Life-Run Center for Independent Living and special educator Elizabeth Rojas Turner were great proponents of HEARTS and helped us recruit participants for the program. We thank our husbands, Albert Kraft and Ernest Boyd, for their continual encouragement as we worked to write this book; throughout our professional lives, they have provided support, served as confidants, and endured the reading of developing manuscripts. They are partners in the truest sense of the word.

INTRODUCTION

ncluding Difference: A Communitarian Approach to Art Education in the Least Restrictive Environment is an approach to inclusion that respects and finds value in all humanity. Inclusion in a learning community is the responsibility of all members to find strengths and build capacities in each other within their shared environment. Equality is not an absolute, and access is relative to an individual's needs. A communitarian perspective utilizes the intent of the Individuals with Disabilities Education Act (IDEA) federal regulations for empowerment of all. A communitarian perspective guided the formation of the HEARTS program presented as an example in Chapter 4. While the book aims to prepare preservice art educators, the model that we have developed is useful for current practitioners, too. The book offers strategies for the inclusion of individuals who experience moderate to severe disabilities into the art class community in a fully participatory way.

Special educator Rutherford Turnbull (1991) describes a "communitarian" perspective, a paradigm that—rather than merely compensating for an individual's perceived disability—views all people within a community as *interdependent*, able to contribute in working toward a common good. The communitarian approach to inclusion respects all humanity—regardless of ability or disability—and is aligned with the philosophy behind IDEA. The problem is that inclusion policy is not always implemented at the classroom level according to the intent of the law. Reasons include the following:

1. Fear of extensive modifications for those experiencing severe disabilities (Gerber & Fedorenko, 2006; Sheldon, 1996)
2. Lack of art teacher involvement in the planning process when including students with disabilities (Schiller, 1999; Kraft, 2001; Wexler, 2009)
3. Teacher attitude (Bartlett & McLeod, 1998; Benin & Cartwright, 2006; Derby, 2011; Eisenhauer, 2008; Erickson, 2004; Grigal, 1998; Reid & Knight, 2006)
4. Misunderstanding of the law and its intent (Anderegg & Vergason, 1996; Danforth, 2007; Jaeger & Bowman, 2006; Kauffman & Hallahan, 1995; Kraft, 2001)
5. Lack of preservice education in working with learners experiencing (moderate to severe) disabilities (Allison, 2008; Carrigan, 1994; Guay, 1994; Ripley, 1997)

We believe that in addressing this last reason—lack of preservice education—we can address all the other reasons, too, and better equip art educators to create the least restrictive environment (LRE) for all learners, as envisioned by special education law.

Because teacher attitude and perception are so integral to the successful education of all students within the LRE, it is important that the teacher view all these stakeholders as possessing the ability to contribute to the class environment and, by extension, society at large. IDEA (2004) points out this expectation of participation of all citizens, including those experiencing disabilities, as a goal of education when it says,

> Disability is a natural part of the human experience and in no way diminishes the right of individuals to participate in or contribute to society. Improving educational results for children with disabilities is an essential element of our national policy of ensuring equality of opportunity, full participation, independent living, and economic self-sufficiency for individuals with disabilities. (20 U.S.C. § 1400)

We advocate a paradigm, therefore, that not only provides access to educational opportunity, or works to compensate for perceived shortcomings resultant from disabilities, but that views all students as capable and worthwhile contributors to the class environment.

To this end, we adopt the terminology of "students with different-abilities" or "typical-abilities," as opposed to "disabled students" and "nondisabled students," in order to (a) allow for a person-first perspective that (b) locates abilities within a spectrum that all of us possess at varying levels given our circumstances. Likewise, we often interchange that terminology with "student experiencing (dis)abilities" to emphasize that one's specific (dis)ability is an experience situated within a context that may vary from environment to environment. Our hope is that presenting the concept of disability in this (perhaps) unfamiliar way may allow the reader to reconsider how he or she perceives (dis)ability as something that each of us encounters, rather than to view "disability" as a deficiency within an(other) individual.

Rutherford Turnbull (1991) presents such a paradigm with his *communitarian perspective.* He argues against the notion of "individualistic utilitarianism," which focuses on individual self rather than one's responsibility toward others, as this notion poses particular problems for those experiencing disabilities. He explains,

> We are all interdependent, disabled upon nondisabled, nondisabled upon disabled… In our work as elsewhere we rely on each other… but we still resist that interdependency when faced with employing a person with a disability and a job coach or making reasonable modifications of the workplace, modifications that benefit us all. (p. 19)

The same holds true for the education environment, as well. As a microcosm of society at large, the classroom is the first place in which the communitarian perspective could be advanced.

Likewise, Turnbull (1991) posits that our notion of liberty has too long been tied to the idea of individual advancement and points out "there is no individual freedom without group and community participation" (p. 25). Society's tendency to pit one group's or individual's rights against another creates division and prevents productive and meaningful dialogue. Within the communitarian perspective, there is greater focus upon responsibility, common good, and community. In aligning liberty with community, rather than with rigid autonomy, individuals are free to make choices and empowered to yield that same liberty to others. I (Keifer-Boyd, 2000) also demonstrate this communitarian perspective in my community-based approach to developing art curriculum. Within this approach, I solicited the participation of community members in creating an art curriculum that addresses the community's aesthetic values, interests, and needs. I found that

> participatory processes establish communication among people who formerly had no way to voice opinions to those outside their own sphere. An environment that is neither threatening nor antagonistic will facilitate dialogue. A cooperative environment arises when all participants' concerns are acknowledged and discussed respectfully. (p. 157)

A communitarian perspective also cultivates ownership and commitment through consensus decision making, as well as mutual respect for individual differences.

Similarly, Turnbull points out that the communitarian perspective values the input and choices of all participants and that the involvement of all is necessary and valuable within a true community context. Such a paradigm, we believe, most closely resembles the purposes and philosophy behind education of all learners within the LRE, as envisioned by the special education mandate. Figure 1 illustrates the communitarian perspective as it arises from the joining of the values of respect, empowerment, and participation.

This book, at its most specific level, is directed toward preservice art educators; however, the models, philosophies, resources, and research-based findings that it contains are of fundamental importance to the practicing art educator who is striving to create an inclusive classroom for learners with a variety of (dis)abilities. Likewise, the book's content and strategies may be generalized to educators of a variety of subjects outside of art.

Since a number of studies cited within the book advocate preservice educator courses that include field experiences working with students experiencing moderate to severe disabilities (those whom preservice educators may have less experience in working with), we envision this text proving a valuable resource for such courses. Indeed, an increasing number of universities are offering courses in art education of special populations, both as special topics courses and as a part of the regular art education curricular rotation (The Ohio State University, Texas Tech University, Pacific University, the University of North Texas, the University of Maine, and Lubbock Christian University, just to name a few).

As civil rights legislation, IDEA is rooted in the precepts set forth in the U.S. Supreme Court's decision in *Brown v. the Board of Education* (1954), a case dealing with race and equal protection. In *Brown,* the Court held that "where a State has undertaken to provide an opportunity for an education in its public schools, such an opportunity is a right which must be made available to all on equal terms" (p. 493). Similarly, the LRE mandate in IDEA states that students experiencing disabilities are to be educated alongside their "non-disabled" peers to the maximum extent appropriate and that they are to be removed from the general classroom environment only when they cannot be educated satisfactorily there (2004; U.S.C. 20 § 1412 (a)(5)(A)). Earlier incarnations of special education legislation in the US emphasized an equality-as-access model that has slowly evolved into a more participatory philosophy (Kraft, 2003).

Within a community that strives for liberating equality that is not defined as sameness, sustained interaction with

Figure 1. Diagram of the Communitarian Perspective: Our Theoretical Framework.

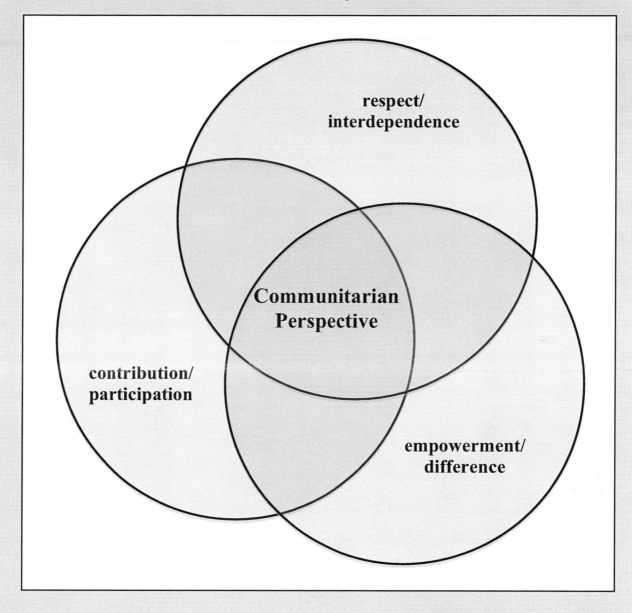

others is promoted through communicative art expression in which each learns to identify strengths in the others. Each person, despite disabilities, has strengths. The different strengths, once identified, can be skillfully encouraged so that individual strengths contribute to the group's goals. Communitarian liberty allows stakeholders to make choices regarding their work and their learning and to take responsibility for those choices and empowers them to actively participate in the educative process in a safe and enabling environment. Communitarian productivity is measured in terms of opportunity to contribute, with the understanding that, in an interdependent community, everyone has contributions to make.

Student teachers' written reflections (responding to each HEARTS session) supported our belief that the best way to remove biases and prejudices is through positive working experiences with people different from themselves. Thus, our book guides the process for creating such experiences in teacher education programs. Since U.S. schools do not fully comply with IDEA federal regulations (Schemo, 2004), it is not a given that inclusive communitarian situations exist to provide such experiences. They need to be created for sustained social change to occur regarding inclusive practices in education.

In our research of inclusion practices, we have found few resources that address the art class environment specifically and none that present the history and philosophy of IDEA dovetailed with a model of inclusion, as we do here. Our book combines concepts related to analysis of the current special education law and case law, issues related to preservice teacher education, and strategies to address the varied needs of a broad spectrum of special populations within the art class setting, an environment that offers unique inclusion benefits and challenges not found in the general classroom. This book contributes to the small but growing body of literature on current special education law and inclusion practices in the art class environment. Likewise, our book will help meet higher education needs at a time when teacher certification programs are reexamining curriculum for integrated and stand-alone courses that meet increasing state expectations for addressing educational diversity, especially in the education of those experiencing (dis)abilities.

To explore the communitarian perspective reflected in IDEA and its practice in the inclusive art class, we organized this book into two sections. The first part, "Empowerment Through Inclusion," provides legal and theoretical ammunition for changing education and attitudes to include students with different abilities. Chapter 1 provides the legal landscape of special education law to harvest for creating an inclusive art education environment. A series of exhibits about pivotal court cases is designed to generate discussion questions to help art teachers use special education law in the US to create inclusive learning environments. Chapter 2 examines empowerment through difference, exploring the value of diversity, as well as stereotypes associated with disabilities that are often advanced through visual culture imagery. It also offers art education approaches for reclaiming what "disability" means, including strategies for assistive technologies. Chapter 3 concludes Part I by providing guidance on how to work collaboratively with stakeholders (e.g., parents, art educators, students, special educators, paraeducators) and by offering inclusion strategies that utilize adaptive technologies and knowledge of diversity from specific case studies.

Beginning with Chapter 4, the second section of the book, "HEARTS: A Model for an Inclusive Art Class," presents one model for a preservice art education course in teaching in the inclusive art class as an example of communitarian theory in practice. Through implementation of communitarian theory, we explore preservice art-educator learning experiences in working with students of all abilities, including those

experiencing moderate to severe disabilities. In Chapter 5, we challenge standardized assessment techniques as ineffective for an authentic understanding of student learning in the inclusive, diverse, communitarian art class. We offer strategies for meaningful assessment approaches as practiced in the HEARTS program and conclude with a discussion of the usefulness of assessment data to further create inclusive education. Chapter 6 draws on previous chapters to highlight how to break through barriers that hinder an inclusive art learning environment. Inclusion practices can increase funding for art education, differentiate curricula, and create a sense of shared responsibility. We use HEARTS as one example of teachers preparing an accessible exhibition of student art, in which they consider both the design and engagement aspects of access. In our HEARTS epilogue, we look back to students' and teachers' reflections on their experience in the HEARTS program for "aha" moments of changes in attitudes toward teaching students experiencing different-abilities and look forward to changes in preservice education.

Throughout the book we provide many resources, some of which are websites. We realize that the Internet is ever changing. If the website address no longer opens to the resource, we recommend that teachers use the Internet Archive Wayback Machine (www.archive.org/web/web.php) to access a site that is no longer available. Paste in the uniform resource locator (URL) in the Internet Archive Wayback Machine, and this archive program will recover the lost site. After introducing the full title of an organization, law, or educational practice, we use its acronym if the acronym is commonly used among educators. As this can be confusing to the preservice teacher, we provide a glossary of acronyms at the end of the book, as well as an index to locate discussions of concepts important to a communitarian approach in art education.

It is our hope that this book provides art educators, preservice art educators, and others working alongside individuals experiencing all levels of abilities with both a philosophical approach and practical, foundational, research-based strategies for teaching in an inclusive class as envisioned by IDEA.

Part I:

EMPOWERMENT THROUGH INCLUSION

Chapter 1

COMMUNITARIAN INTERPRETATION OF SPECIAL EDUCATION LAW TO CREATE INCLUSIVE ART LEARNING ENVIRONMENTS

(Re)Interpretation, (Re)Authorization: Beyond "Normal" Standards

"Maybe in the future we will have art teachers who want to work with the special students," noted one special educator when we told her of our plans to create a preservice program to prepare and motivate art teachers to create inclusive classrooms (E. R. Rojas, personal communication, April 30, 2001). She was pointing to teacher discomfort in creating inclusive classrooms, a challenge that we felt may result from a lack of opportunities, in preservice preparation, to gain confidence and practice strategies for teaching art to a range of differently-abled learners. Practicum experiences that allow preservice art teachers to interact with people experiencing severe disabilities might lessen future resistance to working with them in the art class. Federal mandates in the United States call for inclusion of students who experience disabilities within the art class; however, parents, teachers, and administrators often are not informed on how to interpret U.S. federal law in the practice of teaching and learning in the inclusive art setting.

Therefore, we begin with an examination of special education law in the US through a policy analysis of legislative changes initiated by pivotal court cases. Further, we discuss the idea of inclusion in relationship to visual art national standards so that art educators can design inclusive art curricula that adhere to standards for visual art education recognized as excellent and substantive education by education policymakers at the national, state, and local agency levels.

Inclusion Law: (Non)Reality in Art Classrooms

The passage of the Education for All Handicapped Children Act in 1975 provided legal support for the inclusive education of students experiencing varying levels of disabilities within general classroom settings. Some teachers were (and some even still are) reluctant to teach inclusively; many felt (and still feel) poorly equipped and unprepared to meet the wide range of students' varying (dis)abilities, which may span from gifted and talented to severe disabilities, all in one classroom.

The 1997 incarnation of the Individuals with Disabilities Education Act (IDEA) mandated that state education agencies (SEAs) must disseminate to teachers research-based knowledge on successful teaching practices for improving educational results for students experiencing disabilities (20 U.S.C. § 1453, (c)(3)(D)). However, while SEAs may regularly provide such knowledge and skills to special educators, general and content teachers (including art teachers) are rarely, if ever, made aware of research-based models and strategies for educating students with disabilities in an inclusive class environment. Lack of communication notwithstanding, the right of students experiencing (dis)abilities to be educated alongside their (typically)abled peers, to the maximum extent appropriate, is one of the strongest components of the special education mandate.

In the past, the law and the courts often perceived the art class as a non-academic setting rather than a core subject. As recently as the 1990s, case law concerning least restrictive environment (LRE) described the art class as a "non-academic" environment for inclusion (*Sacramento City Unified School District Board of Education v. Rachel H.* 1994). However, recent interpretations of the special education mandate (since its 2004 reauthorization) regard education in the arts as among the "core academic subjects" (Office of Special Education Programs, 2007; see also IDEA Regulations, 2006, specifically § 300.10). Traditionally, though, the art class has operated as one of the first testing grounds for the inclusion of students who have special educational needs (Schiller, 1999);

the assumption has been that if students experiencing disabilities can succeed in art, then they may be able to succeed in other, academic courses, too. Arnold (1999) believes that the art class has the potential to engage a diverse range of learners in the educative process. Art is open-ended, provides for choice making, involves students in critical thought, may be collaborative, and can be as much process-oriented as it is product-oriented. In this way, the art class offers some unique benefits as an inclusive environment. Art, however, like all subjects, can be poorly taught, too (Hurwitz & Day, 2007). On the other hand, teaching excellence, informed by strategies and models for successful education of all students in the inclusive art class, will also provide the type of inclusive education envisioned by special education law.

New Authorization of the Law: The Individuals With Disabilities Education Improvement Act (IDEA) of 2004

In reauthorizing the Individuals with Disabilities Education Act (IDEA)[1] in 2004, Congress cited the "low expectations" and "insufficient focus on applying replicable research on proven methods of teaching and learning" that have traditionally characterized special education for those with disabilities (20 U.S.C. § 1400 (c)(4)). New changes in IDEA 2004 emphasize, therefore, academic excellence—through teacher preparation and qualifications and through early intervention with students—as well as greater user friendliness through reduction of paperwork, by streamlining the individualized education program (IEP) process, and in adjustments to due process procedures. The U.S. Department of Education points out that

> Enactment of the new law provides an opportunity to consider improvements in the current regulations that would strengthen the Federal effort to ensure every child with a disability has available a free appropriate public education [FAPE] that—(1) is of high quality, and (2) is designed to achieve the high standards reflected in the Elementary and Secondary Education Act [ESEA] of 1965, as amended by the No Child Left Behind Act of 2001 [NCLB]. (Wright, 2005, p. 3)[2]

The historical progression that led to IDEA (in its earliest form of the Education for All Handicapped Children Act [EAHCA] of 1975) laid the foundation for inclusion through strong lobbies of critique. The effects of ESEA and NCLB—though they are not special education laws—are also felt in the current version of IDEA through responses to lobby efforts. (See Figure 1.1 for an overview of the chronology of special education law. The "Knowledge to Empower" section of this chapter discusses each of these laws in greater detail.) Our communitarian interpretation of special education law is informed by this history of critique, especially throughout court cases.

Lawmakers intended NCLB and IDEA as complementary pieces of legislation that "bring together 40 years of segregated educational policies in the US for students with disabilities and for students living in poverty... [to] serve all children without requiring a label to receive supplemental instruction" (Grigorenko, 2008, p. xvii). Laura Chapman (2005, 2007), however, points to what she sees as NCLB's total disregard for schools educating students in poverty-stricken areas. She argues that the 7–13% of funding for educational operating costs that states receive through NCLB is not enough to "offset the impact of poverty on the achievement of students" (2007, p. 26). The problem, she posits, lies in the law's arbitrary standards for student achievement (through testing in math, science, and English), standards so high that 65–85% of schools are expected to fail to meet these by 2014 (Chapman, 2007).

Many art educators expose, too, the devaluing of education in the arts (through the law's language; its overemphasis on math, science, and English; its impact on scheduling for art classes; and its role in diminishing fine arts budgets) by NCLB (Chapman, 2005, 2007; Fehr, 2008; Sabol, 2010). Because of this, art educators such as Dennis Fehr (2008), through the National Education Task Force (NET), have worked to encourage Congress to change wording in the reauthorization of NCLB so that it supports the role of art education in the curriculum. Fehr's proposal offered language that demonstrated the role of arts education in fostering divergent thinking, in including difference, and in developing an engaged citizenry (Fehr, 2008). It also included wording to protect education in the art class from interruption for tutoring in other academic areas, cementing the importance of arts education within the core academic requirements.[3]

Echoing some of NCLB's language regarding "high quality education," IDEA 2004 specifies that personnel must

---

[1] The 2004 Individuals with Disabilities Education Improvement Act is referred to as IDEIA by some, while others have kept with IDEA. Both acronyms are correct, and we have opted to keep with the more familiar IDEA throughout.

[2] As of 2012, both NCLB and IDEA are due for reauthorization, but it is NCLB that is undergoing amendment first. Given President Obama's decision to provide waivers for the most controversial aspects of NCLB (Dillon, 2011), it will be interesting to see what, if any, affect these changes will have on IDEA's next reauthorization.

[3] Sabol's (2010) study indicates that 67% of art teachers say that their art schedules have been affected by NCLB in ways that range from scheduling conflicts to removal of students for remediation in other areas to other complications.

CHRONOLOGY OF SPECIAL EDUCATION LAW

Expansion of Teaching in the Education of Mentally Retarded Children Act of 1958: Appropriated funds for educating teachers to work with students experiencing mental retardation; later expanded to include other differing abilities.

Title VI in 1966: Amendment provided grants for the education of students experiencing disabilities.

Education of the Handicapped Act (EHA) of 1970: Repealed Title VI and created a new law; increased federal subsidies for special education programs.

Section 504 of Rehabilitation Act of 1973: Civil rights law that protected the rights of those experiencing disabilities and prohibited discrimination by federally funded agencies.

Elementary and Secondary Education Amendments of 1974: Provided full educational opportunities to students with special needs, including gifted and talented; provided increased funding to states and further protected rights (due process and confidentiality) for students experiencing disabilities; established National Advisory Council on Handicapped Children and the Bureau of Education for the Handicapped.

Education of All Handicapped Children Act (EAHCA) of 1975: Comprehensive law addressing special educational needs; required states to submit a plan describing compliance procedures and to guarantee a free appropriate public education (FAPE) to students experiencing disabilities.

Individuals with Disabilities Act (IDEA) of 1990: Renamed and replaced EAHCA; included a transition plan on students' individualized education programs (IEPs) by age 16, changed language from "handicapped child" to (person first) "child with a "disability"; separated autism from traumatic brain injury.

IDEA Amendments of 1997: Reauthorization of IDEA; IEP team expanded to include general educator (if appropriate); established procedures for disciplining students experiencing disabilities; instituted changes in procedural safeguards to make system less antagonistic (e.g., mediation as an option); outlined funding formulas; delineated distribution of attorneys' fees and services to students in charter schools; emphasis on raising expectations.

IDEA Reauthorization of 2004: Named the Individuals with Disabilities Education Improvement Act; reduced paperwork and streamlined IEP process (i.e., conditions under which members may be absent and submit information as needed, eased the process for IEP changes); brought law into alignment with No Child Left Behind Act of 2001 in defining "highly qualified teachers" for special education and preservice preparation for content-area teachers; made changes to disciplinary processes to include resolution step; set aside funding for early intervention programs.

Note: This figure is adapted from a similar version that appeared in Keifer-Boyd, K., & Kraft, L. M. (2003). Inclusion policy in practice. *Art Education, 56*(6), 46–53.

Figure 1.1. Chronology of Special Education Law.

have "the content knowledge and skills to serve children with disabilities" (20 U.S.C. §1412(a)(14)(A); see also Kaufman, 2008). In order to achieve this, one purpose of the law is

> To ensure that educators and parents have the necessary tools to improve educational results for children with disabilities by supporting system improvement activities; coordinated research and personnel preparation; coordinated technical assistance, dissemination, and support; and technology development and media services. (IDEA, 2004, 20 U.S.C. §1400(d)(3))

Our goal for this book, then, is that it serve as a guide for art teachers as they work to meet the needs of all of their students, but particularly those who are experiencing disabilities. We focus largely upon those low-incidence populations who are experiencing moderate to severe disabilities, those whose disabilities may prove more challenging in the general art class setting. We emphasize Congress's apparent objective of providing as inclusive an educational experience as possible for students experiencing disabilities, an education that actively includes all learners and allows for self-determination and self-realization. This art education, in keeping with IDEA 2004's expectations of excellence, adheres as closely as appropriate to the National Standards for the Visual Arts.

National Standards and Art Inclusion Policy and Practice

IDEA, as civil rights legislation, focuses upon equality of educational opportunity for students experiencing disabilities. The balance of *equality* of education and *excellence* in education, however, is difficult to maintain as teachers work to meet the wide variance of student learning needs in the inclusive classroom. Equity in education at the expense of excellence is not a worthy goal. To offer an equality of mediocrity would be an unacceptable objective of education, including special education. Rather than art education available only to a few or diluted to accommodate the masses, all students should have equal opportunity for excellence in arts education. Doris Guay (1993) notes that the goals of art education for students with and without disabilities should be the same and should include an emphasis on the acquisition of art skills, art knowledge, and an understanding and valuing of art as an essential part of life. We see the value of art education to be this and more. Art education should also contribute to student understanding of art as a visual form of communication and to the awareness of the possibilities of self-expression through art. Also through art education, students with a wide range of (dis)abilities may critically examine imagery; become divergent thinkers, able to consider multiple solutions to a problem; and may form and critique new ideas about self,

others, and life situations. For example, the film *Profoundly Normal* (Alley, Goldberger, Robinson, & Graeme, 2003) tells the story of Donna Shelby (played by Kristie Alley), a woman who experiences a cognitive development disability. On the day that Donna begins her first job at McDonald's, she relates a story about seeing a career woman in a magazine. She recalls the pretty woman, with her cigarette and briefcase in hand, as she walks happily and confidently to work. From this image drawn from popular culture, Donna dreams of one day working, and she pictures herself with her own briefcase, walking to work, perhaps even taking up smoking. From this magazine ad, Donna has constructed for herself an idea of what working will be like, and the magazine image is a strong representation of Donna's expectations and the romanticism and anticipation that she confers upon the ideas of "work" and "career." In this way, Donna uses the image of a professional woman in an advertisement to re-envision herself as a working woman in a new life situation.[4]

The National Standards for the Visual Arts (NSVA) guides art education policies and practices in the US (National Art Education Association, 1994) and better ensures that all students, including those experiencing disabilities, are provided quality and excellence in their art experiences. Such guidelines, however, and the art teacher's interpretation and practice of them, only go so far in providing the art education envisioned by the NSVA. Our discussion of the NSVA for the inclusive class below, then, is filtered through the lens of our own interpretation of these standards in light of IDEA.

The National Standards for the Visual Arts for the K-12 art class emphasize the development of students' art understanding and abilities for the eventual purpose of creating visual imagery that expresses ideas and emotions and reading such communication in the works of others. To this end, the standards include proficiency in the use of materials, an understanding of symbol systems and visual expression to create meaning, interpretation of histories and societies from the study of visual art within specific cultural contexts, an ability to analyze visual art in relation to other disciplines and contexts, and an ability to think and work critically through ongoing critique of one's own work and the work of others.

With artmaking at the heart of the art class experience, some art educators fear that art may become a "filler" for students experiencing disabilities, a subject valued for what it may offer students therapeutically within a medical/prescriptive model of education (Blandy, 1989; Shakespeare, 2006; Stokrocki, 2004). This therapeutic emphasis overshadows art as a relational experience with the world and as a form of

---

4 Further discussion related to this film also occurs in Exhibit 2.B and Figure 2.2 of Chapter 2.

communication and its role in the sustainability of human life on earth.[5] Meaningful educational benefit is the priority of IDEA and subsequent court cases that have interpreted the law. For example, in *Cypress-Fairbanks Independent School District v. Michael F.* (1995) the court supported an approximation of the state's standards for general education in educating students with special needs. This supports a communitarian notion of inclusion, under the law, in which educational goals for students with different-abilities should closely resemble those of students with typical-abilities.

Knowledge to Empower: History of Special Education Law

The special education mandate in the form of IDEA emerged from a number of contributing factors, including earlier incarnations of special education legislation and key court cases. Prior to the first manifestation of IDEA, in the form of the Education for All Handicapped Children Act of 1975 (EAHCA), it was customary that students with disabilities were educated in segregated settings, often in special schools and at the parents' expense. The right to a free public education was not extended to all students equally. The survey of special education legislation below serves to contextualize the current IDEA and its evolution. (Refer also to Figure 1.1.)

Early Special Education Legislation

In 1954, the landmark civil rights case *Brown v. Board of Education* examined the issue of equal protection under the 14th amendment. The Supreme Court found that states that provide for education for some of its citizens must do so equally for all. While the *Brown* case centered on issues of race, its ruling had far-reaching (albeit slower moving) effects for students experiencing disabilities, too.

The federal government made its first significant contribution to the education of students experiencing disabilities with its passage of the Expansion of Teaching in the Education of Mentally Retarded Children Act of 1958 (Pub. L. No. 85–926). This mandate appropriated funds to prepare teachers to work with students who experienced mental retardation, and the law later grew to include other disabilities (Melvin, 1995). Less than a decade later, in 1966, Congress added Title VI to the Elementary and Secondary Education Act (ESEA) of 1965, already in existence. Title VI provided grants for the education of students experiencing disabilities, a move that Congress viewed as a strong step toward establishing leadership and unity in the area of specialized education (S. Rep. No. 168, 1975). In 1970, Congress signed the amendments to the ESEA into law; these repealed Title VI and originated

a new law, the Education of the Handicapped Act (EHA), which resulted in increased federal subsidies for special education programs and became a framework for later special education legislation (Melvin, 1995; Yell, 1998). The goal of EHA was threefold: (a) to provide a free appropriate public education (FAPE) that would meet students' individual needs, (b) to ensure that the educative efforts made on behalf of students with special needs would be beneficial, and (c) to provide these students and their parents procedural safeguards and due process to protect their interests (Kibbler, 1991).

In 1973, Congress passed the Rehabilitation Act (Pub. L. No. 93–112). Section 504 of this law was a piece of civil rights legislation that protected the rights of those experiencing disabilities and prohibited discrimination by any agency receiving federal funds. This law—rather than focusing upon only the special educational needs of students in K-12 schools—broadly addressed the needs of students, parents, and employees.[6] Regarding educational concerns, Section 504 Regulations state that an appropriate education is one that is "designed to meet the individual educational needs of handicapped persons as adequately as the needs of nonhandicapped persons are met" (§ 104.33). In this way, lawmakers placed as much emphasis on the educational needs of those experiencing different-abilities as on the needs of students who experience typical-abilities.

Congress passed the Elementary and Secondary Education Act Amendments (Pub. L. No. 93–380), in 1974. Like Section 504, the goal of the amendments (which also addressed the needs of gifted and talented students) was to provide full educational opportunity for students with special needs. The new law provided for additional financial assistance to states and further protected the rights of students with disabilities regarding due process and assurance of confidentiality. The Amendments also established the National Advisory Council on Handicapped Children and the Bureau of Education for the Handicapped.

Pivotal Court Cases: *PARC* and *Mills*

In 1972, two landmark cases created the foundation for current special education legislation: *Pennsylvania Association for Retarded Children (PARC) v. Commonwealth of Pennsylvania* (1972; hereafter *PARC*) and *Mills v. Board of Education District of Columbia* (1972; hereafter *Mills*). The resulting decisions for these two cases, with their high profiles and proximity to Congress, once more brought special educational

---

[5] Chapter 2 develops this argument in more depth.

[6] Section 504 is different from IDEA in that the latter is a funded mandate, provides for FAPE in the LRE, requires parental consent for evaluations measures, includes multidiscipline team evaluation every three years, and uses the IEP as its method of delivery (Lindstrom, Tuckwiller, & Hallahan, 2008).

concerns to lawmakers' attention. In *PARC,* the parents of seventeen students experiencing mental retardation sued the school district, stating that it was shirking its responsibility to provide the students with a free appropriate public education. The court's decision in *PARC* mandated that all children who were mentally retarded and between the ages of 6 and 21 must receive a free public education that most appropriately resembles the general education program (Yell, 1998).

In the *Mills* case later that year, parents in Washington, DC, challenged school district procedures that excluded from public schools students who were experiencing disabilities. The court, siding with the parents, established due process procedures for special education for Washington, DC, schools. Following these cases, Congress began work on Public Law 94–142, the Education for All Handicapped Children Act of 1975 (EAHCA), the law that would later become IDEA.

Evolution of IDEA: Toward the Inclusion of Difference in the Least Restrictive Environment (LRE)

Congress passed EAHCA (Pub. L. No. 94–142) on November 29, 1975. Its intended purpose was to "establish in law a comprehensive mechanism which will insure that those provisions enacted during the 93rd Congress are expanded and will result in maximum benefits to handicapped children and their families" (S. Rep. No. 168, 1975, p. 6). Under this law, states that received federal funding were required to submit a plan describing compliance procedures and guaranteeing a FAPE to students experiencing disabilities.

Advancing the IDEA: IDEA of 1990

In 1990, EAHCA was amended and renamed the Individuals with Disabilities Education Act (IDEA), or Pub. L. No. 101–476. Accompanying changes included (a) a transition plan included on the student's individualized education program (IEP) by the age of 16, (b) a change in language from "handicapped child" to the person-first usage "child with a disability," and (c) a distinction of autism (which EAHCA had classified under the category of "serious emotional disturbance" and later under "other health impairments") and traumatic brain injury as separate classes receiving benefits (IDEA of 1990; Yell, 1998).

Closer to the ideal: IDEA Amendments of 1997

The IDEA Amendments of 1997 (Pub. L. No. 105–17) provided even more substantive changes to the law. The Office of Special Education and Rehabilitative Services (OSERS, 1995), in its prospectus for the legislative reauthorization and amendments to IDEA, revealed that during the time of its report, 12% of elementary and secondary students received

special education services. It also reported that, between the 1984–1985 and 1991–1992 school years, high school completion rates among students with disabilities had increased from 55% to 64%. In spite of these educational advances, however, OSERS maintained that problems still existed. These included the inappropriate identification and placement of minority students (notably the over-identification and placement of Black students in overly restricted settings),[7] students with disabilities who were not identified and served by IDEA, and poor results in serving students with learning and emotional disabilities.

On June 4, 1997, President Bill Clinton signed the IDEA Amendments of 1997 (Pub. L. No. 105–17) into law. The amendments restructured the format of the law in an attempt to make it more user friendly. The amendments also (a) expanded the IEP team to include both a special and general educator (if the child would be participating in the general classroom); (b) introduced new procedures for the discipline of students with disabilities that included documented behavioral interventions; and (c) changed procedural safeguards to make the due process less antagonistic to parents, even adding an optional mediation step to the process. Other changes established funding formulas, delineated the distribution of attorney's fees under the law, and addressed concerns regarding identification and serving the special educational needs of children enrolled in private schools.

A bigger IDEA: IDEA 2004

President George W. Bush signed the IDEA 2004 reauthorization (Pub. L. No. 108–446) into law on December 3, 2004. Along with highlighting a reduction of paperwork that allows for exploration of innovative practices in the IEP process, as well as increased ease in altering the student's IEP without the necessity of the IEP team meeting (20 U.S.C. § 1414(d)(3)(D)), the 2004 reauthorization of IDEA aligns the special education mandate with the Elementary and Secondary Education Act, as amended by the No Child Left Behind Act. In doing so, IDEA 2004 emphasizes the need for "highly qualified teachers," stating that special educators must meet state certification requirements and must, if they are teaching at least two core academic subjects, demonstrate competency in those subjects. In addition, all personnel working with students experiencing disabilities, including content area teachers, need to be adequately prepared to serve these populations (20 U.S.C. § 1412(A)). These amendments to federal law resulted in changes in state law, including requirements for preservice preparation for teacher certification. For example, the Pennsylvania State Board of Education (2006)

---

[7] This point is alluded to in Chapter 2 and also appears in King's story and *Profoundly Normal,* which we further discuss in Chapter 6.

revised teacher preparation requirements with an implementation date of January 2011 for all new teachers to have 9 credits or 270 hours of coursework/hours of experience in adaptations and accommodations for diverse learners. Other changes in the law include the earmarking of funds for early intervention, changes to the process for disciplinary actions that result in more than 10 days of suspension, and increased opportunity for mediation during the due process procedures through the addition of a "resolution session" step.

Inclusion and IDEA

Inclusion, a word that does not appear in IDEA, represents a philosophy that arises from the apparent intent of the law when educating students experiencing disabilities in the general classroom alongside their peers who have been designated by the schools as having typical-abilities. In this section, we explore those parts of IDEA that allude to education in the general classroom of students with different than typical-abilities.

FAPE and LRE: The Core of Inclusion

A key component of IDEA is the principle of least restrictive environment (LRE), which mandates that the state must ensure that,

> To the maximum extent appropriate, children with disabilities, including children in public or private institutions or other care facilities, are educated with children who are not disabled, and special classes, separate schooling, or other removal of children with disabilities from the regular educational environment occurs only when the nature or severity of the disability of a child is such that education in regular classes with the use of supplementary aids and services cannot be achieved satisfactorily. (IDEA, 2004, U.S.C. 20 § 1412 (a)(5)(A))

While the concept of LRE has not changed significantly in IDEA since the law's inception in 1975 (Weishaar, 2008), it is important to recognize the relationships among LRE, FAPE, and the IEP. IDEA calls for the determination of the most appropriate education and related services for each student with special educational needs, followed by a decision on the proper placement for providing those services (Kauffman & Hallahan, 1995a). The law defines FAPE as

Special education and related services that—

(A) have been provided at public expense, under public supervision and direction, and without charge;

(B) meet the standards of the State educational agency;

(C) include an appropriate preschool, elementary, or secondary school education in the State involved; and

(D) are provided in conformity with the individualized education program required under section 1414(d) of this title. (IDEA, 2004, 20 U.S.C. § 1401(9))

This definition emphasizes the *appropriateness* of education for the learner experiencing disabilities as *determined by the IEP*. The IEP, therefore, plays a valuable role in the FAPE process. IDEA describes the IEP as the written educational plan that is specifically designed for each child experiencing different-abilities. Among other items, the IEP includes information on (a) the student's current level of performance; (b) a description of the disability and how it affects current involvement in the general curriculum; (c) measurable goals and objectives for enabling the student to be involved in and progress within the general curriculum; (d) a description of the special education, related, and supplementary aids and services and modifications that will be provided for the student to be educated and participate with other students and to be involved in extracurricular and nonacademic activities; and (e) "an explanation of the extent, if any, to which the child will not participate with nondisabled children in the regular class and in the activities described in subclause (IV) (cc)" (IDEA, 2004, 20 U.S.C. § 1414(d)(A)).[8] The IEP is the framework for the education of all students, applicable to the special education setting and the inclusive (art) class setting that honors and capitalizes on difference among students for substantive education.

Because appropriateness is intended to be the determining factor in placement, then, the LRE can be regarded to fall somewhere along a continuum of prospective placements, a sliding scale that is relative to the student's needs. Yell (1998) says of the LRE concept,

> The preferred environment is as close to the general education environment as is appropriate. Depending on what special education services an IEP team determines to be required for students to receive a FAPE, however, the LRE may be a more restrictive setting than the general education classroom. (p. 163)

According to this statement, a student's individual needs may preclude education in the general classroom setting, even with the provision of supplemental aids and services. If that is the case, then a more restrictive setting may be that student's most appropriate—and therefore, least restrictive—learning environment.

---

8 In its use of the words "nondisabled children" here, it is ironic to note that the 1990 IDEA's "person first" philosophy does not appear to extend to the 2004 IDEA's discussion of students whose abilities fall within the "typical" range.

Interpreting FAPE and LRE: The Role of Case Law

Since IDEA's passage, the courts have also been interpreting the mandate. Closely following the 1975 enactment of EAHCA and the 1990 reauthorization as IDEA, a number of court cases addressed concerns regarding FAPE, LRE, and the role of the IEP.[9] While Supreme Court decisions are binding across the US, appellate court decisions are only binding within their areas of jurisdiction, although other circuit courts may choose to adopt another appellate court's decision when confronted with similar cases.[10] Included is a brief survey of some court cases that have interpreted FAPE, LRE, and the IEP, with implications for the inclusive general (art) class.[11] A familiarity with these pivotal cases is important to the art teacher in (a) developing an understanding of how the courts have interpreted issues related to inclusion through case law and (b) how this case law may shape the art teacher's own construction of an inclusive art class under the special education mandate.

While the case of *Board of Education of the Hendrick Hudson Central School District, Westchester County v. Amy Rowley* (1982; hereafter *Rowley*) addressed issues related to a FAPE under IDEA, the three cases that follow focus on the concept of LRE. For each of these cases, the issue is the placement of a student experiencing different-abilities in the general classroom setting alongside his or her peers with typical-abilities. Examination of these LRE issues and their relation to FAPE helps us to better understand the relationship of these two concepts in IDEA.

One court case that adopted and expanded upon the *Daniel R. R. v. State Board of Education* (1989; hereafter *Daniel R. R.*) two-part test was that of *Sacramento City Unified School District v. Rachel H.* (1994; hereafter *Rachel H.*). In this case, the school district offered the family a range of nonacademic placements for Rachel, including art, but excluded her from the core academic subjects, saying that—as with Daniel in the earlier case—Rachel would not receive educational benefit from those classes.

The courts, in interpreting LRE, have examined issues of student behavior on the classroom climate as a whole and have, at times, determined that a student must be placed in a more restrictive setting because of his or her effect on the inclusive classroom environment. In both *Daniel R. R.* (1989) and *Clyde K. and Sheila K. v. Puyallup School District* (1994; hereafter *Clyde K.*), the Fifth and Ninth Circuit Courts, respectively, found that the inclusion of students with disabilities required more restrictive placements than the general classroom in order for *all* students to receive education that was appropriate.

---

9 Since the 1990s, court cases regarding philosophy of placement in the general class setting as a LRE have slowed significantly, those questions having been largely settled by the cases presented here, as well as by others referenced in this chapter.

10 An example of this would be in the case of *Daniel R. R. v. State Board of Education*, a case brought before the Fifth Circuit Court of Appeals (which oversees the states of Louisiana, Mississippi, and Texas) in 1989. As a part of their ruling, they developed what came to be known as the Daniel R. R. two-part test for determining placement of a student in the LRE. In 1994, the Ninth Circuit Court of Appeals (which includes the states of Alaska, Arizona, California, Hawaii, Idaho, Montana, Nevada, Oregon, and Washington) adopted and expanded upon the Fifth Circuit's decision and test in *Sacramento City Unified School District v. Rachel H.* (1994) with its Rachel H. four factor test.

11 The exhibits are the court cases, which can be used as stand-alones for preservice and in-service discussion. We include questions to help facilitate these conversations. In the text of Chapter 1, we also consider the significance of these court case outcomes to the art classroom.

Exhibit 1.A. Amy Rowley: 1982 Legal Case Determines FAPE

Amy Rowley was a student who was deaf and attending Furnace Woods School in the Hendrick Hudson School District, New York. She possessed minimal residual hearing and read lips excellently. Before she began attending elementary school her parents met with school administrators to develop her individualized education program (IEP), and together they agreed that Amy would be placed in a general kindergarten classroom while determinations would be made concerning appropriate aids and services to meet her educational needs. Teachers at the school attended courses in sign-language communication, and a teletype machine was installed in the principal's office to facilitate communication with Amy's parents, who were also deaf. After the trial assessment period ended, the educators determined that Amy would remain in the general kindergarten classroom, and she would be provided with a frequency modulation (FM) hearing aid to amplify the words of her peers and teacher. She successfully completed her kindergarten year.

At the beginning of her 1st-grade year, another meeting was called, as mandated by the EAHCA, to develop a new IEP for Amy. The new plan continued to provide for the hearing aid and also added instruction from a tutor for the deaf for 1 hour per day and speech therapy 3 hours per week. Amy's parents also wanted to add to the IEP a provision for a sign-language interpreter for her academic subjects. Such an interpreter had been in Amy's kindergarten class, but he reported that Amy succeeded without his intervention and that his services were not necessary. Based on that and assessments from those working with Amy in her educational environments, the school district determined that Amy did not require the interpreter. Amy's parents disagreed with this decision and requested a due process hearing as provided for by the special education law. The hearing officer found in favor of the school district, based upon the fact that Amy "was achieving educationally, academically, and socially" without such assistance (*Rowley*, 1982). Amy's parents then brought suit in the U.S. District Court for the Southern District of New York, claiming that Amy had been denied a free appropriate public education (FAPE) as provided for in the law.

Board of Education of the Hendrick Hudson Central School District, Westchester County, v. Amy Rowley eventually made its way to the U.S. Supreme Court, which in 1982 handed down its decision addressing the appropriateness of FAPE. The court stated that FAPE for students experiencing disabilities (a) should be personalized, (b) included supplemental aids and services to allow the student to benefit educationally from instruction, (c) was provided at public expense, (d) must meet state education standards, (e) should approximate the grade level's goals utilized in the state's regular education, and (f) must comply with the student's IEP. The court likewise maintained that FAPE did not require that states maximize the potential of each student with disabilities commensurate with the opportunities provided "nondisabled" students.[1] Instead, the court held that lower courts must give attention to two issues in determining whether FAPE has been satisfied:

1. Has the state conformed to statutory procedures?

2. Is the student's IEP, developed through these procedures, reasonably calculated to enable the student to achieve educational benefit?

The Court stated that if a state (and, by extension, a local school district) has met these two requirements, then it had fulfilled its obligation to FAPE under the mandate. In Amy Rowley's case, the Supreme Court viewed her above-average academic performance as evidence that the school district had fulfilled its obligations for FAPE under IDEA. While the Supreme Court decision had little direct impact on Rowley, who was 10 years old by this time, it has had far-reaching implications for defining FAPE for students with special educational needs since then.

Discussion Prompts and Questions for Applying Rowley to FAPE in the Art Class

1. Describe "appropriate education" for learners with a range of educational needs in an art lesson that you have developed.

2. What supplemental aids and services would help a student who is experiencing moderate to severe disabilities meet the art educational standards and objectives that you have set for this lesson?

---

[1] Indeed this decision was far from unanimous with the Court and remains controversial. Chapter 2 of this book, which addresses issues related to empowerment and disability, shares some of our misgivings related to this binding Supreme Court decision.

Exhibit 1.B. Daniel R. R. 1989 Legal Case Develops a Two-Part Test for the LRE

Daniel was a 6-year-old student experiencing Down's syndrome who was enrolled, at his parents' request, for half the school day in a pre-kindergarten class in his neighborhood school. He spent the second half of his day in an early childhood special education classroom. Not far into the school year, the general classroom teacher reported that Daniel—even with constant attention from herself and the paraeducator—was not participating in class activities and was not mastering any of the skills taught. The IEP team, therefore, decided that the general classroom setting was inappropriate to Daniel's needs, and he was removed from the pre-kindergarten class. However, they determined that Daniel could still receive opportunity for interaction with peers experiencing typical-abilities during during recess and lunchtime (if one of his parents was present).

Daniel's parents referred the matter to a hearing officer who held in favor of the school. They then appealed to the federal district court and later to the Fifth Circuit Court of Appeals. The appellate court held that the school district *did include* the student to the maximum extent appropriate under EAHCA when it removed him from the general pre-kindergarten classroom and provided for inclusion only during recess and lunch. The general classroom was not the most appropriate learning environment for the student, the court held, because the teacher was forced to devote all of her time and attention to him, at the expense of the other students in the class. Additionally, the court pointed out that Daniel received no academic benefit from his placement in the pre-kindergarten class, although he did receive opportunity to interact socially with peers experiencing typical-abilities.

In the case of *Daniel R. R. v. State Board of Education*, the appellate court developed a two-part test to determine compliance with the least restrictive environment (LRE) mandate. The first part was to ascertain whether or not education in the general classroom setting could be satisfactorily achieved with supplementary aids and services. Under this first part, the school would attempt to accommodate a student with special needs in the general classroom setting. Additional considerations under this first part of the test include whether or not the student would receive educational benefit from the placement and the adverse effect of the placement on the other students in the classroom.

Under the second part of the test, the court would determine whether a school, having placed a student in a more restrictive setting, still provided for inclusion to the maximum extent appropriate. This provision could include the continuum of placements, such as recess and lunchtime opportunities to interact with typically-abled peers (as the El Paso school district provided in *Daniel R. R.*). If the school district passed both parts of the test, the court held, then it had fulfilled its LRE responsibility under the law. The Fifth Circuit's *Daniel R. R.* two-part test was so influential that it was adopted in subsequent cases by both the Third and Eleventh Circuit Courts, as well.

Questions for Applying *Daniel R. R.* to Create a LRE in the Art Class

1. Is socialization in a group art project of more educational benefit than socialization at recess and lunch? Why or why not?

2. If you had a student in your art class whom you suspected was not receiving educational benefit from the placement, what steps might you take in seeking help to accommodate his or her special educational needs in the inclusive art class?

Exhibit 1.C. Rachel H. 1994 Legal Case Develops a Four-Factor Test for the LRE

Rachel Holland was an 11-year-old student who experienced moderate mental retardation with an IQ tested at 44. Her parents requested that the district fully include her into the general educational setting, but the district maintained that Rachel's (dis)ability precluded any educational benefit in traditional academic settings. They made a counteroffer with a plan that included Rachel in nonacademic placements—such as art, music, lunch, and recess—and placed her in a special education setting for academic subjects.

Rachel's parents rejected the district's offer and appealed to the state's hearing officer, arguing that Rachel most benefited—both academically and socially—in the general classroom. The district, on the other hand, maintained that Rachel was too severely disabled to benefit from education in the general classroom and that the costs involved to include her would be too prohibitive. The hearing officer sided with Rachel's parents, concluding that the school district had not made adequate effort to educate Rachel in the general classroom as a LRE. The school district appealed to the district court, and the case eventually reached the Ninth Circuit Court of Appeals.

The lower district court, in making its decision in *Sacramento City Unified School District v. Rachel H.* expanded upon the *Daniel R. R.* two-part test to create its four-factor test that included the following questions:

1. How did educational benefit in the general classroom setting, with supplemental aids and services, compare with that in the special education classroom?

2. What were the nonacademic benefits of placement in the general classroom as opposed to the more restrictive setting?

3. What effect does the learner's presence have on the general classroom setting?

4. What are the respective costs associated with various placement options and alternatives?

Using these four questions, the district court held for the parents, finding that the general classroom setting (with supplemental aids and services) was the appropriate placement for Rachel. For the first question, the court found that Rachel did receive substantial educational benefit from placement in the general classroom with modifications according to her IEP. For the second part, related to noneducational benefit, the court—siding with testimony from Rachel's mother and current teacher— found that Rachel evidenced strong nonacademic benefit from education in a general classroom through her friendships, her improved self-confidence, and her enthusiasm for school. In regard to her effect on the teacher and general classroom environment, the third question of the four-factor test, the court found that Rachel was not a distraction in class and was well behaved, requiring only a part-time aide perhaps. For the fourth factor, cost, the court stated that the school district did not offer any persuasive evidence that the costs of educating Rachel in the general classroom setting would create undue financial burden or would be even significantly greater than her education in the special classroom setting. The school district then appealed to the Ninth Circuit Court of Appeals, which affirmed the decision of the lower court.

Questions for Applying *Rachel H.* Toward Educational Benefit in the Art Class

1. What supplemental aids and services to benefit Rachel would be needed in a specific art lesson you might teach (or have taught)?

2. Describe some nonacademic benefits of inclusion that you see as unique offerings of the art class.

Exhibit 1.D. Clyde K. 1994 Legal Case Applies the LRE Four-Factor Test

Clyde and Sheila K.'s son Ryan was a 15-year-old who experienced Tourette's syndrome and attention deficit hyperactivity disorder. He received special educational services while enrolled in inclusive classroom settings at Central Susquehanna Intermediate Unit #16. During this time, his behavioral problems escalated dramatically and included (a) frequently disrupting class by taunting others with profanity and name-calling, (b) insulting teachers with vulgar comments, (c) directing sexually explicit remarks to female students, (d) noncompliance, (e) kicking and hitting classroom furniture, and (f) a number of violent physical assaults on other students and school personnel.

Because of these, Ryan was expelled from school, and his parents and the district agreed that it was no longer safe for him to receive his education in the general classroom environment. The district recommended that Ryan be placed in the Students Temporarily Away from Regular School (STARS) program until he could be safely reintegrated into the general school programs. His parents initially agreed but then changed their minds, requesting a due process hearing on the matter. The hearing officer found that the school district was in compliance with special education law. The parents appealed to the district court, and the case was later appealed to the Ninth Circuit Court of Appeals. Using the *Rachel H.* four-factor test, the appellate court, in the case of *Clyde K. and Sheila K. v. Puyallup School District,* found the following:

1. Ryan did not receive educational benefit from his placement in the general classroom because his disruptive behavior prevented him from learning.

2. Any social benefit that he may have derived from his placement in the general classroom was negligible.

3. His placement in the general classroom had an overwhelmingly negative effect on the learning environment as a whole and on the other students.[1]

In regard to the overarching safety of the classroom environment, the court added that it is the responsibility of school officials "to ensure that students entrusted to their care are kept out of harm's way" (Clyde K., 1994). Since Ryan was receiving little to no educational benefit from his inclusion, and since his presence was detrimental to the safety and education of the other students in the class, the court sided with the district in its decision to remove Ryan from the general classroom.

Questions for Applying Clyde K. to Creating a Safe Environment in the Art Class

1. What are some approaches in art education that help channel disruptions into productive behaviors?

2. What steps must the art educator take to safeguard students pertaining to the particular materials, tools, and media in the art classroom?

---

[1] Since the fourth factor, that of cost, was not relevant to the *Clyde K.* case, the court did not consider it.

Impact of *Rowley* on FAPE and Implications of *Daniel R. R., Rachel H.,* and *Clyde K.* on the LRE

At face value, it may appear that the U.S. Supreme Court—with its statement in *Rowley* that schools were not obligated to maximize the learning of the student with disabilities—provided a loophole through which school districts may settle for mediocrity in providing a FAPE. Certainly, some school districts tried to do just that, but subsequent court cases (*Polk v. Central Susquehanna Intermediate Unit 16,* 1988; *Oberti v. Board of Education of the Borough of Clementon School District,* 1993) held that provision of a FAPE for students experiencing disabilities must be meaningful rather than token in nature.[12] Therefore, the approach to education that is most appropriate to a particular student's individual needs must be determined and outlined in the IEP, including any placement in the general classroom setting. Anderegg and Vergason (1996) and Duquette (1990) state that placement in the regular classroom, however, is not an absolute right because educational appropriateness is always the mitigating circumstance. Ideally, education would involve placement with "nondisabled" peers; but appropriateness should always be the determining factor for placement. Indeed, many court cases have cited the special education mandate's preference for education of students with different-abilities alongside their peers with typical-abilities (*Cedar Rapids Community School District v. Garret F.,* 1999; *Honig v. Doe,* 1988; *Sacramento City Unified School District Board of Education v. Rachel H.,* 1994; *Taylor v. Board of Education,* 1986), still recognizing appropriateness as the deciding aspect of that placement. Likewise, a number of cases (*Capistrano Unified School District v. Wartenberg,* 1995; *Chris C. v. Gwinnett County School District,* 1991; *Honig v. Doe,* 1988; *Mark A. v. Grant Wood Area Educational Agency,* 1986; *Taylor v. Board of Education,* 1986) recognize that the LRE for a given student is a more restrictive educational setting when it comes to most appropriately serving his or her needs.[13] While the *Rowley* case addressed the issue of FAPE at the Supreme Court level, the other three cases discussed here address LRE, specifically the placement of students experiencing disabilities in the general classroom.

The LRE case law in *Daniel R. R., Rachel H.,* and *Clyde K.* reveals that FAPE takes precedence in instances where FAPE and LRE conflict. In *Daniel R. R.,* the court acknowledged the tension between FAPE and LRE, as well as the lawmakers' obvious preference for inclusion; this preference, however, must always be tempered by consideration of the most appropriate educational course of action for the particular student's needs. *Rachel H.* added to this the recognition of nonacademic benefits of inclusion, such as the opportunity for socialization with peers with typical-abilities. This case also demonstrated that while cost can be one consideration in whether or not to include a student experiencing disabilities into the general classroom, it must not be the only consideration. Moreover, the cost of separate special educational classrooms may be greater than assistive technologies and services for inclusion in the art classroom. *Clyde K.* and *Daniel R. R.* both revealed that IEP teams must give attention to the learning environment as a whole when determining an inclusive placement. In addition, in *Clyde K.* the issue was not merely disruptive behavior, but violent behavior within the classroom. In this particular case, the student's sexually obscene remarks, noncompliance, and harassment of and physical assaults on classmates precluded his ability to receive appropriate educative services in the general classroom and so disrupted the general class as to warrant his removal to a more restrictive educative environment.

The implications of these case law examples for the art class are especially relevant. The art class—with its often-semi-structured format and social informality—possesses unique potential for social benefit that is different, or at least not as often available, in the general classroom setting. Because of this social dynamic, however, student behaviors such as those evidenced by Ryan K. may rise more quickly to the forefront. In addition, the art class uses many potentially dangerous tools and materials—such as Exacto knives, scissors, chemicals, and ceramic tools—that may pose a hazard with students whose behavioral disabilities manifest themselves in the form of violent outbursts. The art educator must, therefore, be aware of important case law precedents such as *Rachel H.* and *Ryan K.* in balancing the great potential for learning opportunities in the art class with the concern for student safety.

Implementing Inclusion Policy of the Least Restrictive Environment (LRE)

The federal law IDEA passed into regulatory law, then into state policies and procedures, and then local policy and procedures

---

12 Additionally, the *Rowley* (1982) case also determined that, when a student with disabilities *was* to be educated in the general classroom as the LRE, his or her IEP must be reasonably calculated to enable him or her to achieve passing marks and advance from grade to grade.

13 It is important to view the LRE as a continuum, or sliding scale, which includes full inclusion into all general education activity at one end and full-time residential placement at the other. The LRE that is most appropriate for one student's educational needs may be different from that of another and may include a more restrictive educational setting, such as the segregated special education classroom. While there have been court cases since the 1990s that have addressed issues of LRE, they have not dealt specifically with instances of inclusion and placement of students within the general classroom setting as these court cases have.

before it reached the special education or general education classroom setting. The federal mandate provides directives to state education agencies (SEAs) and local education agencies (LEAs) to set forth policy and procedures for the implementation of IDEA; SEAs and LEAs must adhere to this directive to receive financial assistance through IDEA (2004, 20 U.S.C. § 1412 and § 1413). In this section, we examine the three levels of implementation—federal, state, and local—of the LRE mandate of IDEA as it works its way to implementation at the fourth level, the general (art) classroom level. In doing so, we note special attention is needed by art educators in contributing to the IEP, which determines the most appropriate placement, adaptations, and services for a student experiencing different-abilities. At the classroom level of implementation, we introduce the benefits and barriers of inclusion in the art class, and we return to this topic in Chapter 6.

Federal Level

When Congress passes a federal mandate, accompanying federal regulations for its implementation must be developed. The 34th Code of Federal Regulations (CFR) is the accompanying federal regulations to IDEA. The LRE is defined by 34 CFR in terms identical to those in IDEA, demonstrating a strong congressional preference for the education of students with special needs alongside their "nondisabled" peers (§§ 300.114 and following). As in IDEA, the federal regulations stipulate that removal from the general education environment should occur only when the nature of the different-ability is so severe that it precludes education in that environment. The regulations include a continuum of alternative placements and list these in descending order from least restrictive to most restrictive. They include (a) education in the general classroom, (b) instruction in special classes, (c) instruction in special schools, (d) home instruction, and (e) instruction in residential settings, such as hospitals and institutions (IDEA Reg., 2006, 34 CFR § 300.551 (b)(1)).

As in IDEA, such placements are subject to what is most appropriate to the student's educational needs as defined by the IEP. The federal regulations also stipulate that a group rather than an individual must make placement decisions. This group includes the student's parents along with those who are familiar with the student's educative needs.[14] The placement, which must conform to LRE provisions and is based upon the student's IEP, is evaluated annually and must be as close to the student's home as possible (IDEA Reg., 2006, 34 CFR § 300.116(a)(1)).

After the IEP is in effect, and the student's LRE placement is designated as the general classroom, the regulations provide

that the student's IEP must be made available to the general classroom teacher. Each teacher who works with the student must be informed of his or her responsibilities in implementing the student's IEP and the specific modifications and/or supports necessary as set forth by the IEP (34 CFR § 300.323). The IEP must also include, among other content items, a statement of measurable annual goals and short-term objectives for reaching those goals. These objectives must include strategies for meeting the student's individual educational needs to allow for involvement and progression within the general curriculum (IDEA Reg., 2006, 34 CFR 300.320(a)(4)(ii)).[15]

It is imperative that art educators convey educational goals in their curricula to a student's IEP team in order to solicit their help in recommending strategies to meet these goals. The strategies may require technology assistance and teacher education, which by law may be secured if the IEP includes ways to address art education goals. Thus, art educators need to be proactive, rather than passively informed of their responsibilities by the IEP team who may not otherwise consider the art classroom setting and art education goals.

State Education Agency Level

Subpart B of the IDEA regulations (2006), which addresses the state education agency's (SEAs) and local education agency's (LEAs) responsibilities for maintaining eligibility for federal assistance under the mandate, says that states must file with the Secretary of Education a policy that ensures a FAPE to all children between the ages of 3 and 21 who experience different-abilities. This FAPE must be provided to each student who experiences a (dis)ability that requires special education and related services, even if that student is advancing successfully from grade to grade (34 CFR § 300.101). Additionally, states must file policies and procedures for ensuring education in the LRE and list their continuum of alternative placements available to meet the individual needs of the student (34 CFR § 300.114 and 300.115). Usually called state plans, these plans set the procedures that ensure each teacher involved in the student's education has the opportunity to give input and to request assistance in the implementation of the IEP as set forth in IDEA. The state plans also determine the procedures by which teachers receive relevant information from the IEP regarding the student's instruction, such as objectives, adaptations, and modifications that are appropriate to the student's educative needs in keeping with the federal mandate and regulations.

In addressing the education of the student in the LRE, the Texas State Plan, as one example, states that the term *placement*

---

[14] Chapter 3 focuses on stakeholders who are involved with and affected by the implementation of inclusion policy.

[15] The 1999 version of the IDEA Regulations defined the general curriculum as "the same curriculum as for nondisabled children" in 34 CFR § 300.347 (a)(2)(i).

refers to the instructional program or setting rather than a specific teacher or classroom. If such placement is within the art classroom setting, for example, then it is the art teacher's responsibility "to modify methods, materials, and pacing so that students with disabilities can benefit from instruction in the well-balanced curriculum within the regular classroom" (Texas Education Agency [TEA], 2000, p. 15 of Chapter VII). Art educators who participate in the IEP team can both shape their responsibilities and obtain support in meeting those responsibilities. While attendance at every students' IEP meetings may not be possible, attendance at particular ones are essential for providing excellent education to all students.

Local Education Agency Level

Under the 2006 IDEA federal regulations, local education agencies (LEA; including education service centers, individual school districts/boards, etc.) must "adopt policies and procedures [for implementing the special education mandate] that are consistent with the State's policies and procedures" (34 CFR § 300.224(a)(1)). Many of these LEA policies and procedures, therefore, may be embedded within the SEA's plan. A state plan may provide that its LEAs adopt guidelines for operation that describe responsible individuals, actions, and timelines for complying with IDEA (e.g., see Texas State Plan, TEA, 2000). These guidelines or procedures constitute the steps that the local school district takes in implementing special educational procedures and imbue LEAs with the responsibility of proactive execution of a state plan. A school district's procedures for operation are created within that specific district, according to its policies as set forth by the school board. As such, the district may tailor the document, albeit in keeping with the federal mandate, to meet its needs in reference to its students, demographics, faculty, individual implementation issues, and so forth. Where the IEP is concerned, an LEA's operating guidelines might determine the steps for ensuring the most appropriate curriculum that a student is provided for his or her special educational needs and, for instance, when that curriculum shall focus upon academic competencies or functional skills. Likewise, operational guidelines may specify the procedures through which the content area teacher is provided with relevant portions of an included student's IEP (as provided by the federal mandate) that include information on educational goals and objectives, modifications, and necessary adaptations as appropriate to the student's special educational needs.

Art Classroom Level

The individual school and classroom constitute the final level of implementation in the LRE mandate's organizational structure. Dissemination of IDEA information to this level may occur through regional educational service centers in the form of personnel-development opportunities or through a school district's administrative offices to building principals who then share information regarding law or district policy changes with educators of students experiencing disabilities. Often, however, this information may not be shared equally with the special and content area educators (for those students who are educated full- or part-time in the general classroom setting). Necessarily, those content area educators who teach in inclusive classrooms must be kept abreast of updated information regarding special education, just as those special educators who teach in segregated special education classrooms must have content area knowledge to successfully meet students' needs. Almost prophetic of the 2004 reauthorization of IDEA and its alignment with NCLB, one special education administrator expressed the need for increased sharing of information between special and content area educators, saying, "Teachers who teach special needs [students] need the same kind of training that general ed teachers get—they're doing some type of reading, that *we* need to be included in that reading, and vice versa" (quoted in Kraft, 2001, p. 192). Just as the dissemination of special education policy information is highly important to the successful education of students experiencing disabilities in the inclusive class, so too is the sharing of content area information among general and special educators.

Even for art educators who are more than willing to collaborate with special educators and parents to maximize student success in the classroom, it may be that lack of teacher preparation in working with special populations precludes them from initiating that process (Gerber & Fedorenko, 2006; Kraft, 2001). While the IDEA/NCLB alignment blurs the lines between special and general education, Kaufman (2008) notes that the 2002 *President's Commission on Excellence in Special Education* found that: "Children with disabilities require highly qualified teachers. Teachers, parents, and education officials desire better preparation, support, and professional development related to the needs of serving these children. *Many educators wish they had better preparation before entering the classroom*" (italics added; Kaufman, 2008, p. 42).

One aim of this book is to provide a resource for preservice (and practicing) art educators in creating the inclusive art class. To do this, we share the HEARTS model in Chapter 4 in the second section of this book. The HEARTS program, developed by the authors, was embedded within a college course for preservice art educators and included opportunities for the preservice teachers to teach in an integrated classroom with students of all ages and who have both different and typical abilities. Before demonstrating this HEARTS model, though, Chapter 2 delves more deeply into the communitarian notion that we are empowered by our differences. Chapter 3 continues a closer examination of educators, parents, and students as stakeholders in the inclusive art class.

Chapter 2

EMPOWERED BY DIFFERENCE

At the heart of the communitarian values of equality, liberty, and efficiency[1] is the concept *empowerment by difference*. This concept embraces an inclusive community, which strives for liberating equity that is not defined as sameness. Instead, sustained interaction with each other is promoted through communicative art expression in which each learns to identify strengths and capacities in others. Each person, despite disabilities, has untapped potentials and emergent strengths. The different capacities, once identified, can be skillfully encouraged so that individual strengths contribute to the group's goals. Communitarian liberty is to make choices regarding work and learning, to take responsibility for those choices, and to be empowered to actively participate in the educative process in a safe and enabling environment. Communitarian productivity (i.e., efficiency) is measured in terms of opportunity to contribute, with the understanding that, in an interdependent community, everyone has contributions to make. This inclusive, communitarian perspective corresponds with the purposes and intent of the IDEA federal regulations, which include empowerment, and guided the formation of the HEARTS program,[2] presented in the second half of this book. This chapter offers resources and strategies to empower through difference.

Being Different and Making a Difference

Each person is unique. Preparation for inclusion requires a mindset that recognizes there are differences between disabilities and differences among disabilities. Some differences are visible, such as orthopedic or mobility disabilities, while others are invisible, such as cognitive or biochemical brain challenges that manifest as depression, addiction, or in other ways. There is a range of sensory disabilities through which teachers can help students to build capacity of exceptional strengths in alternative sensory ways of knowing. Differences also arise in relation to the length of time an individual has experienced or been aware of an acquired or congenital disability. Communication strategies need to be informed from sensitive observation of the abilities of each individual. Such a mindset does not see those experiencing disabilities as victims but rather as dignified humans who can contribute to and enrich the world.

Rather than erase perceptions of people as different, as the popular "color blind" slogan suggests is possible and preferable (i.e., to not see racial differences), we need to recognize that people do not share the same physical, psychological, and life conditions. These lived-conditions are combinations of social, environmental, historical, political, physical, and individual experiences. Within the art class, what conditions can we capitalize on in seeking students' educational potentials in our recognition that difference exists? First we must recognize that our focus should not be on the difference between individuals, but rather on what unique differences among the group of students can mingle to support the learning of all. Thus, there are strategies to recognize the strength of differences and ways to share those strengths for

---

[1] These are three values that some education policy researchers cite as highly regarded by culture in the US (Guthrie, 1980; McMillan & Schumacher, 1997).

[2] HEARTS refers to the Human Empowerment through the Arts model that we developed as a case study of the art classroom as a least restrictive environment.

a community of learners in which no one falls between the cracks of the educational goals.[3]

Different and Difference

Our theory of difference is not about delineating differences but about analyzing social differences that challenge the *audism* and *ableism* embraced by dominant culture. Audism is the hegemonic notion of the superiority of hearing speakers. Like other dominant notions, audism manifests in language in common phrases such as gaining voice, speaking out, and breaking the silence. Ableism refers to discrimination and oppression toward those who do not fit social concepts of being able.

Empowerment by difference, as an analytic lens for participatory action research or social justice arts-based research, redefines difference to enact sociopolitical transformation of policies, to redress professional and educational environments, and to rewrite media productions. Art educators need to "build critical alliances across seemingly disconnected categories of difference" (Erevelles & Kafer, 2010, p. 211). Working at the intersections of difference means inclusion, challenging normative constraints that create oppression, building community for solidarity toward social justice across differences and with disability allies, and "engaging in transformative scholarship and praxis" (Erevelles & Kafer, 2010, p. 219).

If we allow our curriculum and pedagogical approaches to accommodate difference between stereotyped categories, such as "normal" students and "disabled" students, we are perpetuating stereotypes of people experiencing various disabilities as fundamentally "different" from what it means to be human. Art educator Alice Wexler (2002) challenges the notion of disability as characterized by damaged people who need to be fixed and instead makes a case through interviews, longitudinal studies, and examples from her participatory observation case study that no matter the different abilities, all can be artmakers who participate in their own empowerment process. "Art helps to build on what is intact rather than remediate what is lost" (p. 340).

De-Centering Normal

We can optimistically and naively believe clinical labels of *dis*abilities are formulated from genuine human concern for best practices and treatments. However, these labels emphasize *disorders* (e.g., a spectrum of behavioral or emotional *disorder*s), *deficits* (in attention), and *impairments* (of sight,

hearing, speech, or movement). Each draws attention to the *lack* of something that does not meet standards of what it means to be a normal human being. Nevertheless, the legal category of disability is necessary "as a civil right for all—the right to be ill, to be infirm, to be impaired without suffering discrimination or oppression (Davis, 2002, p. 1). We agree with philosopher Martha Nussbaum (2010) that a primary goal for all educators is to nurture "rich human relationships, rather than relationships of mere use and manipulation... because democracy is built upon the ability to see other people as human beings, not simply as objects" (p. 6).

Disability when situated in dominant views of normalcy becomes spectacle. This viewpoint does not allow for different perspectives, but holds a superior position of viewing others and creates a disembodied "othering" in which humans are objectified. Spectacle is a worldview of a seeing "eye" as a trope for the patriarchal "I," that which is not seen or labeled but oversees. It is typically considered a *gaze from nowhere* but is, in fact, situated in dominant views of normalcy (Haraway, 1991). Davis (2002) posits a dismodernist mode in which "the ideal is not a hypostatization of the norm (that is, dominant) subject but aims to create a new category based on the partial, incomplete subject whose realization is not autonomy and independence but dependency and interdependence" (p. 30). Dismodernist ethics is founded on the principle that "injustice and oppression of various kinds" disable (Davis, 2002, p. 32).

Wexler (2009) asks, "When does difference and excess become abnormal?... How much are normals willing to change to accommodate difference?" (p. 8). We believe that rather than merely aspiring to accommodate difference we should recognize that we are empowered by difference. If even one of us is denied our humanity, social equity, education, health care, and housing, we

> all bear the burdens of that exclusion in painfully violent ways... [which] means we will have to do the hard but important work of building coalitions across the divides of difference—race, class, deafness, disability, gender, sexuality—where we will then proceed to hold one another accountable in mapping the limits and the possibilities of collective transformative praxis. (Erevelles & Kafer, 2010, p. 219)

Normalcy is a delusion that materializes as exclusion, prejudice, marginalization, discrimination, and oppression. "The body is never a single physical thing so much as a series of attitudes toward it" (Davis, 2002, p. 22). The dichotomy between normality and abnormality is socially constructed and cemented within medical, organizational, legal, and master narratives. It is not easy to crack the bonds that privilege

---

3   Keep in mind that according to disability studies scholar Lennard Davis (2002), "even without the baby boomers, currently 15 to 20% of people in the US have disabilities. Add to this caregivers and family members, and about half the population is dealing with disabilities" (p. 4).

specific modes of communication, ways of knowing, and physiques.

Empowered by Inclusion

Empowerment counteracts "exclusion, marginalization, and circumscribed opportunities" (Patterson, 2010, p. 150). Art educator Laurel Campbell (2005) posits that "the concept of inclusiveness, [is] a pillar of holistic philosophy" (p. 54). Campbell's research since 2003, and in the founding of the Caucus on the Spiritual in Art Education (CSAE)[4]—an issues group of the National Art Education Association (NAEA)—makes the case for spirituality as reflective practice that raises questions about "who we are and who we want to become" (Campbell, 2005, p. 54). Campbell proposes that "art as a manifestation of the spirit brings into focus our commonalities while respecting our unique differences" (p. 54). Campbell argues that we need to consider teaching art as an act of inclusiveness "because art making and art inquiry encompass a variety of experiences involving a multitude of senses… [in order to] learn to accept and include others, ultimately realizing what it means to empathize with others" (p. 55). Aligning with the work of ecologist David Orr (2005), she advocates, "one goal of contemporary holistic education is teaching the acceptance of difference" (Campbell, 2009, p. 128).

Preservice art teachers' written reflections (responding to each HEARTS session) supported our belief that the best way to remove biases and prejudices is through positive working experiences with people different from themselves. Thus, this book guides the process for creating such experiences in teacher education programs. Since most schools in the US do not fully comply with IDEA Federal Regulations (Schemo, 2004), it is not a given that inclusive communitarian situations exist to provide such experiences. They need to be created for sustained social change to occur regarding inclusive practices in education.

21st-Century Visual Culture Portrayals of Difference

When you encounter someone who cannot see, walk, hear, speak, or understand as you do, what do you feel and think? We are affected and informed how to respond, in part, by representations of people in films, songs, artworks, literature, advertising, and other forms of social practices and products. In the recent past, disability studies activists and scholars maintained dominant narratives of disability, which emphasize impairment and abnormality, as a medical model in which cures are sought to repair the disabled body. A medical model of disability with its offshoot of rehabilitation emphasizes lack, deficit, deficiency, degenerate bodies, and inferiority. Disability studies' "preoccupation with *impairment* and *disability*—as a rather bedeviled binary—has now been repeatedly substantiated while also called into question on many fronts" (Brueggemann, 2010, p. 260, emphasis added). Disability studies draw attention to how labels and language matter. Impairment conceptually locates the disability within the individual and is adopted in the medical model of cure and care. A feminist intersectional model of disability displaces a center of normalcy from which all else is judged and instead aligns with a social model of disability that regards difference as valuable and seeks to eliminate social discrimination of difference that has manifested in dominant cultural narratives. Language—that is, the labels we use—continues to create discomfort within and outside of disability studies and in individual identity.

Mitchell and Synder (2003) critique the proliferation of likely well-meaning identity-affirmations in the dramatic portrayal of disabled bodies. Disability metaphors of artificial or incomplete humans are materialized in representations of disabilities in films and literature, which Mitchell and Snyder refer to as a *materiality of metaphor* and *narrative prosthesis*. A social realism critical perspective is that the characterization of a body marked as disabled often is inaccurate and misleading about experiences of disability and perpetuates stereotypical social stigmatizing and unrealistic utopia in which disability is eradicated, overcome, or cured. "A fundamental complaint of disabled critics is not simply that film-makers or 'the media' represent disability in stereotypical, rigid and repetitious ways, but that they fail to recognize the phenomenon of misrepresentation in relation to disability" (Pointon & Davis, 1997, p. 3). Mitchell and Synder do not suggest that it is simply a matter of acceptable and unacceptable representations, but that analysis of disability representations should involve the study of historical contexts of their construction and the consequences of the popular cultural narratives.[5] Such study is important to understand social tropes of disability that are portrayed in fiction through literary and visual metaphor, in that these popular arts reveal the social history of disability and impact how society perceives disability.

Disabling Stereotypes

Materiality of metaphor, therefore, is an awareness of how pervasive linguistic and visual metaphors impact how we interpret our lived experiences. Societal representations of what it means to be human, which involve expectations of human relationships to each other and to the world, draw

---

[4] To subscribe to the CSAE's Listserv® place "SUBSCRIBE" in an e-mail subject header and send to CSAE-subscribe@artedlists.org and post at CSAE@artedlists.org

[5] Peters' (2007) study of the history of the body is a good resource to learn historical contexts of social constructions of corporeality.

from entrenched perspectives in the practices that form the materiality of our existence.[6] "Disabled people are as equally socialised into seeing disability as negative as those who are non-disabled, and their own images of themselves can tend to concentrate upon their own personal triumphs or trage- dies, images for which there is a ready market" (Darke, 1997, p. 14; see also Benin & Cartwright, 2006; Charlton, 2006; Chivers, 2001; Derby, 2011). Recognizing the social tropes or clichés at work in films is a useful place to begin to dis- mantle stereotypes of people with disabilities.

Disability Movie Clichés
- The disabled person dies, inspiring the able-bodied to live their lives to the fullest.
- The disabled person offs him- or herself so as not to be a burden to others.
- Blind people have superhuman hearing and can use echo- location.
- The disabled person was really faking it all along!
- Disability, especially disfigurement, is used to indicate that a character is the villain.
- The disabled person needs able-bodied people to teach him or her that life isn't over.
- People with disabilities can cure themselves through sheer force of will. If you're still disabled after the movie ends, it means you're not trying hard enough.[7]

Are these conventional narratives familiar? We expect that most readers who watch movies could identify many films with each of these storylines.

Just as the Bechdel Test draws attention to a systemic problem of the representation of women in films,[8] the list above of dominant narratives in films of representations of disabilities can generate long lists of films identified by stu- dents. This pedagogical approach shifts analysis away from specific films and toward a discussion of systemic social con- structions. Such investigations would reveal that films from a medical model perspective emphasize "'triumph over tragedy' stories, often with the emphasis on physicality of a 'compen- sating' or fulfilling nature" (Pointon & Davis, 1997, p. 1). A social model critique begins with the premise that "one may

have an impairment (or 'condition') but in the right setting and with the right aids and attitudes one may not be disabled by it" (Pointon & Davis, 1997, p. 2).

The challenge is to identify films that differ from these dominant cultural narratives. This would help change how we think about people with abilities. This is similar to the way artists can and have created narratives that change how we think about the pedagogy and environment of schools. For example, "the effects of poverty, alienation, oppression, cruelty and a stultifying curriculum were well understood and explicated by Dickens [in his novels] and stand in sharp contrast to the scientific contributions of his psychological contemporaries" (Thomas & Glenny, 2005, p. 17). In the next section we suggest strategies for challenging stereotypes of disabilities.

Challenging and Reclaiming (Dis)ability

To generate changes in perceptions of disability as abnormal, art curricula should include viewing and discussing films and other artworks that challenge and reclaim what disability means. With many films readily available online, and increas- ing numbers of old and new film selections available online, students can view selected films individually, in small groups, or as a class. Discussion questions to identify if and how films challenge pervasive disenabling narratives include: Is the disability represented as a medical or social condition that is in need of repair? Or, does the individual or social world sur- rounding the individual change their views and relationship to or within the person experiencing a disability?

Film suggestions include *Rolling* (2007), *Murderball* (2005), and *Pumpkin* (2002), although search engines will locate further resources. See, for example, an online archive lists of films (2005 to 2009) from the annual disABILITIES Film Festival & Speaker Series produced by the Museum of disABILITY History and People located in Buffalo, New York.[9] Even when a full film is not readily available, there are often trailers online—such as for *Monica and David* (2009)[10]—that provide excellent material for discussion to redefine disability as empowered by difference.[11]

Consider films such as *The Other Sister* (1999, PG-13, 130 min.), about a young woman who experiences cogni- tive dissonance yet realizes her dream of becoming a veteri- nary assistant; or *Forrest Gump* (1994, PG-13, 120 min.), the

---

[6] This view is developed in Danforth (2007, 2009).

[7] This list was developed by Disability Movies © 2010–2011 at http://disabilitymovies.com/disability-movie-cliches

[8] The Bechdel Test comprises three questions: Are there two or more women in the film who have names? Do they talk to each other? Do they talk about something other than men? See the FeministFrequency video at www.youtube.com/watch?v=bLF6sAAMb4s that shows a high number of films that do not pass this test and indicates that this is a systemic problem.

[9] The lists of films with synopsis can be found at www.disabilityfilmfest. org/films.html

[10] See the trailer for this film at www.monicaanddavid.com

[11] Disabilities studies scholars Lennard J. Davis and Marquard Smith (2006), in their theme issue on "Disability-Visuality" for the *Journal of Visual Culture*, provide a set of articles that redefine the body and disability in terms of social-justice policies and practices.

story of a man experiencing "educable mental retardation"; or *Flawless* (1999, R, 111 min.), in which Robert De Niro plays a man who begins taking singing lessons after suffering a stroke. These movies are about transformation by overcoming a disability. Films about overcoming a disability by an outside force include *What's Eating Gilbert Grape?* (1994, PG-13, 120 min.), with actors Johnny Depp and Leonardo DiCaprio, in an account of an adolescent who provides support for his younger brother who is experiencing cognitive dissonance. Or, *Charly* (1968, PG, 103 min.), which is a fictional story of a man experiencing cognitive dissonance who becomes a genius after a scientific experiment, and *Rain Man*[12] (1988, R, 140 min.), in which Charlie (Tom Cruise) kidnaps his brother Raymond (Dustin Hoffman), who is characterized as autistic savant, from a residential-living care facility because Raymond inherited their father's fortune. Raymond ("Rain Man") is based on Laurence Kim Peek's way of knowing. Dustin Hoffman met with Peek to learn to perform his way of knowing, experiencing, and interacting with the world. Many descriptions of Peek were written after his death in November 2004, including an essay published by the *Guardian News and Media Press* in London titled: "The Real Rain Man Dies of Heart Attack in Home Town of Salt Lake City, aged 58" (Pilkington, 2009):

> Peek has been called a "mega-savant" for his ability to memorise to the word up to 12,000 books, including the Bible and the Book of Mormon. He could read two pages in about 10 seconds—the right page with his right eye and the left simultaneously with his left eye.
>
> He knew phone books by heart, and could tell you what day of the week a particular date fell upon going back decades. One of his party tricks was to tell strangers the names of the people who used to live next door to them years ago.
>
> At the same time, though, he had deep disabilities and relied on his father Fran for help dressing, brushing his hair and other simple motor skills.
>
> "His legacy can be summed up in one word: inspiration," said Darold Treffert, a psychiatrist at the University of Wisconsin medical school who advised the makers of *Rain Man* and who was close to Peek for the past 20 years. (para. 2-4, 6)

USA Today published an essay titled "NASA Studies Mega-Savant Peek's Brain" (Associated Press, 2004), which describes him as follows:

> The 53-year-old Peek is called a "mega-savant" because he is a genius in about 15 different subjects, from history and literature and geography to numbers, sports, music and dates. But he also is severely limited in other ways, like not being able to find the silverware drawer at home or dressing himself. (para. 5)
>
> When Kim Peek was born, doctors found a water blister on the right side of his skull, similar to hydrocephalus. Later tests showed his brain hemispheres are not separated, forming a single, large "data storage" area. (para. 7)

Similar to Hoffman learning to perform Peek from meeting him, actress Claire Danes consulted and studied with Temple Grandin to learn how to perform as Grandin for the movie, *Temple Grandin* (2010). Dr. Temple Grandin, Associate Professor of Animal Science at Colorado State University, can bring everything she has seen to her mind and search through those images. She explains that she is a "visual thinker" and "thinks totally in pictures" (Grandin, February 5, 2010).[13]

We learn about disability from films. Art education should include learning how to question what is presented in films and how to create films. Exhibit 2.A provides a conversation between a filmmaker and the subject of the film concerning how to convey the experience of sight-less. This scenario can be useful as a catalyst for students to create video trailers to pitch their concepts from a social rather than medical model of (dis)ability.

For another approach to challenge and reclaim what disability means, students could learn about the accomplishments of people with disabilities who have been widely recognized for their significant contributions to society.[14] Art educators might use the short video, "Famous People with Disabilities" (available online; Langtree & Langtree, 2006), which includes visual artists such as Leonardo da Vinci, Michelangelo, Vincent van Gogh, and Claude Monet. The video links to an extensive list with brief descriptions of disabilities that can help develop familiarity with these different ways of experiencing the world. The discussion in Exhibit 2.B

---

[12] A site with quotes from a movie like this one at www.imdb.com/title/tt0095953/quotes of *Rain Man* (1988) is useful for reference during discussion to reflect on the spoken text in relation to the images.

[13] She states this in an interview about the film about herself. See www.youtube.com/watch?v=bnI_Y8PyTHM

[14] Art educator Jennifer Eisenhauer (2007, 2008, 2010) uses autoethnography and visual performative text (i.e., narrative research forms in which writing is a form of inquiry in itself) to give readers insight into living with stigmas of disability labels and popular culture portrayals of people experiencing bipolar conditions.

Exhibit 2.A. Challenging and Reclaiming (Dis)ability

Television-commissioned filmmaker Piers Sanderson, working with October First production company, approached David Bradford regarding his interest to be a subject of a film. Sanderson's concept was to film Bradford "throughout a year as he 'build[s] a mental image bank' of significant places, sights and experiences" before his eyesight fails (Bradford & Hull, 2011, p. 126). In 2006, Bradford was diagnosed with retinitis pigmentosa. Bradford discusses this proposal with John Hull, who had authored *On Blindness* (1995), *In the Beginning There was Darkness (2001),* and other studies. Hull describes that he perceives the filmmakers'

> supposition is that blindness is mainly a state of deprivation, mainly an experience of loss. It follows from this that the life of a blind person will be retrospective, living as much as possible in the past, and treasuring every sighted memory as offering relief in a world now grown dark. (Bradford & Hull, 2011, p. 127)

Hull suggests another film concept: "How about a documentary in which you locate things that mean little to you now, perhaps, but which will loom larger and larger as you enter the safe harbour of blindness" (Bradford & Hull, 2011, p. 127). In response to Bradford's question about what is meant by safe harbour, Hull responds:

> What is it like to be blind? Well, there is the wind blowing through your clothes, the immediate impact of water on your hands, the smells of food, the shape and feel of a woman's body, the loved familiarity of one's own room, the fascination of tiny things like the feel of a cup and the soft hair of a baby—such little things is blindness made of, too small to attract the attention of the large world of light and power… There is no pain, and life can be full of interest and beauty, although it is harder to find and too little to mention. (p. 129)

Bradford finds a dilemma in the premise of the film differing from his approach to blindness that it is

> *more* than a condition of deprivation… I do not believe that the natural response of a person who is told they are going blind is to revel or indulge in the sense they know they are losing… The proposed film is, it seems to me, a celebration of sight, perhaps even a eulogy to sight, rather than an exploration of sight loss. (2011, p. 130)

Because of Sanderson's sympathy to Bradford's concern that the film be authentic to his experience of sight loss, Sanderson is given an opportunity to create a trailer to pitch a different concept that would still "capture the attention of 3–4 million (sighted) viewers" (Bradford & Hull, 2011, p. 130). Art educators might share this scenario and ask students: *What would be your concept or approach to creating a film that is an exploration of sight loss?* Following discussion, students could work in teams to prepare a three-minute trailer with their concept. They could create as machinima[1] or mixed reality[2] or live performance and post online to elicit response and commentary. This is one approach to challenge and reclaim (dis)ability.

---

[1] See http://cyberhouse.arted.psu.edu/322/resources/sl/slmachinima.html for how to get started in creating machinima using virtual worlds as a place to create characters, sets, and performance. A free or inexpensive program such as iShowU can record the activity on the screen of a computer. These clips can be arranged and edited with the audio recorded during the activity or otherwise to make a finished movie that can be posted online in a program such asYouTube® or Vimeo® for educators..

[2] Mixed Reality combines the virtual or digital with material reality.

shifts the focus to the contributions and abilities of people experiencing (dis)abilities. Moreover, reclaiming the meaning of disability from "it isn't necessarily bad to be disabled" to "it is bad to be discriminated against, unemployed, poor, and blocked by bad laws, architecture, and communication" redirects critique (Davis, 2002, p. 5). Following viewing and discussion of films, students would be prepared to create paintings, video, or other forms of artworks to challenge and reclaim what "disability" means.

Disabilities Studies and the Inclusive Art Class

Case study, (dis)ability from feminist perspectives, interviews, and participatory interaction are four approaches for engaging preservice art educators to consider educating varied student populations possessing a range of special educational needs. These strategies should be coupled with opportunities for work alongside students experiencing a range of (dis)abilities (including severe disabilities) to provide the preservice art educator with agency that leads to comfort levels necessary to make and adjust modifications successfully for a student's individual needs, thereby promoting the student's opportunity to actively participate in the classroom community.

Teacher education for preparation to create and sustain an inclusive art classroom setting is critical in equipping educators with an understanding of and strategies for educating learners with special needs (Allison, 2008; Keifer-Boyd & Kraft, 2003; Kraft, 2001). It is important to note that the term *education* carries a different connotation than the term *training*. Draves (2000) points out that training is a "one-way street," with an instructor depositing information into the minds of learners. This portrayal of *training* verses *education* is similar to what Paulo Freire (1990) refers to as a banking model in which teaching is based on the belief that knowledge can be deposited into students, a notion he sought to change toward emancipatory and transformative learning. Education, on the other hand, is multifaceted with interactions and contributions from the learners; teachers and students learn from and share with one another. With a more interactive education (as opposed to training), the preservice art educator has ownership of the learning and is better able to adapt it to various situations and the individuated needs of his or her students once in the classroom. This preparation of the teacher, who in turns prepares the classroom for the integration of a specific student, relative to his or her needs, facilitates a smoother transition from the special education environment to the art classroom. What follows are educative strategies to prepare teachers to create inclusive art classrooms.

Case study inquiry

Engaging preservice art educators in video case studies is a strategy to develop critical reflection concerning teaching diverse student populations. When used as a teaching strategy before entering an inclusive classroom field experience, the preservice art educator may be better equipped for considering modifications in teaching approaches and for creating a class environment to stimulate all students' art learning potentials.

Preservice teachers and practicing teachers in in-service programs, as well as individuals pursuing professional development as art educators, can benefit from examination of video case studies of and by differently-abled individuals. We included video case study as one technique in preparing preservice art educators for the Human Empowerment through the Arts (HEARTS) program described in Part 2 of this book. From these video case studies, we asked students to discuss and develop strategies to:
1. Find strengths in themselves and each other.
2. Identify and overcome obstacles.

3. Build group support structures. The group members can support each other by providing encouragement and by helping with finding and sharing resources and expertise.
4. Work together.

These four areas were further developed in reflection after each HEARTS class session. To prepare for discussion,[15] we asked preservice art teachers to select and watch a film as an

---

Figure 2.1. Discussion Prompts for Student Presentations of Films By, About, or With People Experiencing (Dis)abilities.

(1) Video producer, year, title of video, length of film

(2) A key quote from video

(3) Main points/messages of video

(4) Description of how what you learned from video could be applied to teaching in HEARTS

(5) How the format of the video impacted the message (select one 30-second to 2-minute excerpt to illustrate)

(6) A question for discussion generated from your findings (See Exhibit 2.B for example from a HEARTS student.)

---

assignment outside the class session, which included a differently abled person.[16] Figure 2.2 is an updated video list as example of a range of films from which HEARTS preservice art teachers selected. Figure 2.2 also provides websites that provide extensive lists of films of people experiencing (dis)abilities.[17] Internet searches with key terms can provide

---

[15] See Figure 2.1 for presentation guidelines that HEARTS preservice art teachers followed to prepare their case study portrayals.

[16] "Only in the late 1960s did a more liberal image emerge, one that concentrated on seeing disability as 'differently able'" (Darke, 1997, p. 13).

[17] As mentioned in the introduction to this book, enter the URL of a site in the Internet Archive Wayback Machine (www.archive.org/web/web.php) to access a site listed in this book that is no longer maintained or available. The Wayback Machine archives more than 150 billion Web pages from 1996 to the present.

Figure 2.2. Films Featuring a Differently-Abled Person.

Films

- *Able to Laugh* (1993, documentary, 27 min.)
- *Breathing Lessons: The Life and Times of Mark O'Brien* (1996, documentary, 36 min.)
- *CRUTCH* (2006, performance, 4 min.) at www.crutchdoc.com
- *Disability Culture Rap: Disability Identity and Culture* (2000, documentary, 22 min.) www.diversityshop.com/store/product2.html
- *The Diving Bell and the Butterfly* (2007, PG-13, 1hr 52 min). Trailer at www.imdb.com/video/imdb/vi4122018073
- *Finding Nemo* (2003, G, 100 min.)
- *Flawless* (1999, R, 111 min.)
- *Forrest Gump* (1994, PG-13, 120 min.)
- *King Gimp* (2000, documentary, 39 min.)
- *Monica and David* (2010, documentary, 68 min.)
- *Murderball* (2005, R, 85 min.)
- *My Country: The Civil Rights Movement That Created the Americans with Disabilities Act* (1997, documentary, 60 min.)
- *My Left Foot* (1989, R, 103 min.) Based on autobiography of Christy Brown, an artist experiencing cerebral palsy.
- *Profoundly Normal* (2003, NR, 96 min.)
- *Pumpkin* (2002, R, 113 min.)
- *Rolling* (2007, documentary, 21:25, 19.10, 14.56). Online at www.thirteen.org/rolling
- *Silent Fall* (1994, R, 100 min.)
- *Temple Grandin* (2010, PG, 107 min.)
- *The Collector of Bedford Street* (2002, documentary, 34 min.)
- *The Other Sister* (2000, PG-13, 130 min.)
- *Vital Signs: Crip Culture Talks Back* (1997, documentary, 48 min.)
- *What's Eating Gilbert Grape?* (1994, PG-13, 120 min.)

Multimedia Websites

- *Beyond Affliction* (1998). Companion website to the 4-hour disability history radio program on NPR at www.npr.org/programs/disability
- Exhibitions curated by VSA at www.kennedy-center.org/education/vsa/programs/exhibitions.cfm
- *Freedom Machines* (2005). PBS video and teaching resources at www.freedommachines.com

Websites With Lists or Searchable Databases

- www.aboutdisability.com
- http://disabilityfilms.tripod.com. This site presents a detailed list of 2,500 feature films. It is directed toward teachers, students, and anyone who has an interest in how disability is represented in films. Each category is split into major and minor films.

further resource lists of films of documentaries, life stories, and/or interviews from which students can select for video case study.

After each presentation, we suggest the following questions to facilitate discussion about disability social narratives in artworks. These questions are based in the belief that artworks can be "powerful repertoires of protest, strategic resources for social change, and the (re)construction of individual and relational identities" (Harter, Scott, Novak, Leeman, & Morris, 2006, p. 16). These questions should be facilitated to reveal the complexity and range of interpretations and how we interpret from our own positions or beliefs. For example, the character Tiny Tim in the many film versions of Charles Dickens' (1843) *Christmas Carol* can be interpreted as innocent and feeble, requiring care by others, or as a foil to capitalism, or as central to the mythology that sustains capitalism, or a contributor to social life. Exhibit 2.B provides an example of facilitated discussion of a film using the questions below.

1. What are the ways that exclusion or inclusion is sustained or disrupted?
2. How is the disability marked or signified? For example, is the disability peripheral or important to the story? Is it treated as a strength or a weakness, or a marker of evil or joy?
3. If the filmmaker, actor, writer, or visual artist experiences (dis)abilities, is this relevant to the artwork? "The concept of intersectionality emphasizes that multiple dimensions of identity are operating within and among all people at all times... It is, ultimately, impossible to separate these intersecting identities from one another" (Ostrove & Oliva, 2010, p. 112). Is the person's gender, race, sexuality, or class relevant to the artwork? What are the intersections with disability, and in what ways might the intersectionality of the experiences influence the intent and/or reception of the work? Would race, gender, or class differences among persons with the same or similar disabilities discourage or encourage alliance or identity role modeling?
4. How is disability defined or represented in the film's visual and spoken narrative? How does this differ from ADA definitions?[18] What are some other portrayals in literature, film, visual art, documentaries, or personal experience that broaden this definition or representation?
5. What are concepts of normal and abnormal in the film? For example, is disfigurement from a cultural standard of normal considered a disabled condition?
6. Does the artwork (film or otherwise) provide an empathetic experience to differences in embodied living?

---

[18] See American with Disability Act (ADA) definitions at www.ada.gov/pubs/adastatute08.htm

7. A counter-narrative is "a story that resists an oppressive identity and attempts to replace it with one that commands respect" (Lindemann-Nelson, 2001, p. 6). Is there a counter-narrative that contests entrenched language and ideas of normalcy in a way that begins to dismantle hegemonic discourses and social inequities?

(Dis)ability from feminist intersectional perspectives

As evident in numerous examples throughout history, when people are marginalized they create their own spaces, organizations, and systems of support and recognition. Deaf communities are one such example in that outside these communities the spoken language is the privileged form of communication. Disability culture is a collective identity in which "people with disabilities recognize the fact that they are different people, with diverse backgrounds, and often isolated from others with disabilities. The disability experience brings persons with disabilities together, instilling pride in its members who actively recruit younger generations" (Moore & Jeffries, 2006, para. 2).

Middle- to upper-class, heterosexual, abled-bodied White men in the US have not been marginalized in the dominant social and political sphere. Their history is what is taught in schools. Their artwork is what is collected and shown in museums. Their works are in archival collections. Those outside societal parameters of "normal" (i.e., not a middle- to upper-class, heterosexual, abled-bodied White man) who have worked hard and contributed to society have done so despite the unreceptive, hostile environments of dominant social, political, educational, and economic spheres of patriarchy. For example, Lindsey Patterson studies the history of racism and sexism within an institution for the deaf community and notes:

> While earlier generations of male students may have hoped for "gentle tamers" to join them at the [Gallaudet] college [established to provide higher education for deaf people], the real intrusion of women into this male sphere clearly disrupted men's notion of power and place... Deaf men dehumanized women [as] "freaks of nature..." deriding their aspirations for opportunity and empowerment as unnatural. (Patterson, 2010, pp. 150–151)

Philosopher of science Donna Haraway (1991) re-visions objectivity from feminist perspectives so instead of the patriarchal eye/I *gaze from nowhere*, vision is embodied, situated knowledge in specific contexts of people and place. Therefore, what is believed to be natural and normal is defined *from somewhere*.

Exhibit 2.B. Facilitated Discussion About the Film *Profoundly Normal*

Cary (preservice art educator presenter): I selected the film *Profoundly Normal*, which premiered in 2003, because it deals with what it means to be normal and also intersectionality, two concepts we have been introduced to in class. It is based on a true story of two people with cognitive challenges who fall in love, get married, and have a healthy son. The movie uses an interview style in which the couple and their son respond to questions about their life. Their stories are told through flashback scenes that are not chronological but rather events in their adult life were often interspersed with incidents from their childhood. The couple, Donna and Ricardo Thornton, was also interviewed on *Sixty Minutes* in 2003.

A key quote that stands out to me is when Donna spoke proudly of her job at a fast food restaurant. She describes "working alongside other people, and that made me feel good." I interpreted this to be that people who experience disabilities have the right to live lives with respect and dignity. This was conveyed by Donna's joy in her independence. I selected a clip to show the class when she responds to her friend who asks how will they know what to do. "We're going to tell ourselves. We're going to be free." She rationalizes that she is ready to have her own apartment because from her many years at Forest Haven, "I have seen things that children shouldn't see. I thought to myself. I think what I've seen in my life—what in the world could be worse than that?" When teaching in HEARTS, I want to make sure that students with disabilities are included, working alongside their peers, just as Donna worked and lived alongside "typical" peers in *Profoundly Normal*.

Facilitator: What are the ways that exclusion or inclusion are sustained or disrupted in the film?

Cary: Donna refers to her isolation, exclusion, and confinement to a room for several weeks after a caretaker sexually assaulted her friend. She, herself, was only a young girl and was accused and punished for this crime. In reference to this painful memory she responds in the interview, "I think some things are better to not learn." The film presents the "care" facilities for those with disabilities that in this case ranged from utter neglect to actual molestation. I thought this might be unique to a specific facility or from past times before laws protected people with disabilities, but I was alarmed to see that this is an ongoing issue. This abuse of those with disabilities in so-called learning, development, and care facilities was raised recently in the *New York Times* (Hakim, 2011) in which a 13-year-old boy experiencing autism was killed by a caretaker at the Oswald D. Heck Developmental Center while another was witness to the fatal abuse. "Since 2005, seven of the [nine] institutions [in New York] have failed inspections by the State Health Department, which oversees the safety and living conditions of the residents" (para. 9). The Heck Center had not investigated the fractures and lacerations suffered by residents. "Similar problems can be found across the state. The Broome Developmental Center in Binghamton has been cited for repeatedly failing to protect residents from staff members" (para. 11).

Facilitator: This is alarming and important to bring to our attention. How is the disability marked or signified in *Profoundly Normal*? For example, is the disability peripheral or important to the story? Is it treated as a strength or a weakness or a marker of evil or joy?

Cary: Donna and Ricardo's *difference* was the reason for their institutionalization. She surmises, "I believe that if you do things that normal people do that will make you normal. We got to show the world that we are like everybody else." However, she finds that "they tell us to be normal in all these ways and then they tell us we can't get married." In 1984, she and Ricardo married, going against Social Services rules, and inspired others marked as abnormal who also found love and companionship and wanted to be a couple. Donna explains that they "weren't trying to be inspirational, just trying to be like them [normal people]."

Facilitator: If the filmmaker, actor, writer, or visual artist experiences (dis)abilities, is this relevant to the artwork? Is the person's gender, race, sexuality, or class relevant to the artwork? What are the intersections of gender, race, sexuality, and social class with disability, and in what ways might the intersectionality of the experiences influence the intent and/or reception of the work? Would race, gender, or class differences among persons with the same or similar disabilities discourage or encourage alliance or identity role modeling?

Cary: While the filmmaker and the actors did not experience the (dis)abilities they performed, they studied the real lives they portrayed. Donna's physical appearance marks her as a White person and Ricardo's features mark him as a Black person. This may have been the unspoken reason why Social Services ruled they could not get married. There is a scene after their baby is born when Donna reads a nasty letter they received from someone who did not know them personally. Racism and ableism intersected. When he sees how much the letter has upset her, Ricardo declares to Donna: "We aren't going to read any more letters—good letters or mean letters. We don't need people to tell us about ourselves." That is such an empowering statement and points to Ricardo's strong commitment to their relationship. There are couples who are labeled as 'different' for any number of reasons—whether it's race, social standing, gender, or religious beliefs—and I would imagine that the model of empowerment-by-difference portrayed by the Thornton's here would serve as an inspiration for other couples.

Facilitator: How is disability defined or represented in the film's visual and spoken narrative? How does this differ from Americans with Disabilities Act (ADA) definitions? What are some other portrayals in literature, film, visual art, documentaries, or personal experience that broaden this definition or representation?

Cary: In the Findings and Purposes of ADA Amendments Act of 2008, it states: "In enacting the ADA, Congress recognized that physical and mental disabilities in no way diminish a person's right to fully participate in all aspects of society, but that people with physical or mental disabilities are frequently precluded from doing so because of prejudice, antiquated attitudes, or the failure to remove societal and institutional barriers" (42 U.S.C. § 12101 (a)(1)).[1] This was the case for Donna and Ricardo.

Mel (preservice teacher in the class): This movie, *Profoundly Normal*, is reminiscent of the struggles to "be normal" in the movie *The Other Sister*, starring Juliette Lewis, Diane Keaton, and Giovanni Ribisi.

Cary: Yes, I remember that 1999 movie because I recently watched several excerpts online when deciding which film to present in this class. Others perceived the romance between Carla and Daniel, who also have cognitive challenges similar to Donna and Ricardo, as naive. Carla insists, *"We can take care of each other"* when her mother expresses her fear that Daniel would not be able to take care of her daughter as his wife. Carla says she cannot do many things but she can love.

Facilitator: These are two examples of societal barriers toward fully participating in the institution of marriage. What are concepts of normal and abnormal in your case study of a film, Cary?

Cary: You would not know right away that Donna or Ricardo had a disability. It is through communication that their mental differences in processing information become visible. Therefore, cultural standards of communication are the disabling conditions.

Facilitator: Does the film provide an empathetic experience to differences in embodied living?

Cary: When Donna learned that she was pregnant, I wanted to cry because the joy in creating a family with her husband is shattered when she is asked by Social Services to consider that she may give birth to a disabled child or not be able to give her child a normal life.

Syd (preservice teacher in the class): When she missed her stop and rode the bus to the end of the line and then had to walk four miles to work, it reminded me of being in a foreign country and not being able to speak the language or read the signs.

Facilitator: That's an interesting observation, Syd, especially because IDEA acknowledges that disability is a natural part of human existence. I think we can all think of instances where we were in an environment in which we did not feel capable or fully able. Now, Cary, a counter-narrative is "a story that resists an oppressive identity and attempts to replace it with one that commands respect" (Lindemann-Nelson, 2001, p. 6). Does *Profoundly Normal* offer a counter-narrative that contests entrenched language and ideas of normalcy in a way that begins to dismantle hegemonic discourses and social inequities?

Cary: There is counter-narrative about cognitive disability because Ricardo, as a father, supports and encourages his son to learn. For example, Ricardo has a flashback to when he was asked, as a child, to name three cities and could not, and because of his silence was labeled as disabled and institutionalized. He tells his son, "You never know what they are going to ask." Ricardo was teaching from his own life lesson. This raises a question that I'd like to discuss with the class: How can we design our art curriculum so students can learn and teach from their life experiences? And how can we prepare all students to be comfortable, and even find opportunity, when the unexpected occurs?

---

[1] See American with Disability Act (ADA) definitions at www.ada.gov/pubs/adastatute08.htm

A feminist approach to ableism/ability/able-bodied privilege raises questions regarding the identity and cultural conceptions of disability. The intersection of feminist theory and disability studies, which have intertwined in the past 20 years, offers perspectives that de-center concepts of normalcy. Philosopher Susan Wendell (1989) introduced a feminist theory of disability from her observation that:

> some of the same attitudes about the body which contribute to women's oppression generally also contribute to the social and psychological disablement of people who have disabilities. In addition, feminists are grappling with issues that disabled people also face in a different context: Whether to stress sameness or difference in relation to the dominant group and in relation to each other; whether to place great value on independence from the help of other people, as the dominant culture does, or to question a value-system which distrusts and devalues dependence on other people and vulnerability in general; whether to take full integration into male dominated/able-bodied society as the goal, seeking equal power with men/able-bodied people in that society, or whether to preserve some degree of separate culture, in which the abilities, knowledge and values of women/the disabled are specifically honoured and developed. (p. 104)

Wendell brings to our attention how women viewed from a patriarchal hierarchy are perceived as flawed-disabled, and thus this perception dis-enables. Girls and women "are at a higher risk of physical, sexual, and emotional abuse" than men, as are people experiencing disabilities (Wilson, 2011, p. 231). According to the United Nations' (2006) campaign against violence toward women "surveys conducted in Europe, North America, and Australia have shown that over half of disabled women have experienced physical abuse, compared to one-third of non-disabled women" (para. 8). In the United States, "it's estimated that 90% of people with developmental disabilities will be sexually assaulted over the course of their lives—and children with any type of disability are almost twice as likely to experience sexual abuse as non-disabled children—but only 3% of the assaults will ever be reported (Davis, 2000)" (Baladerian, 2006, para. 1).

A politics of difference is at the intersection of disability, gender, race, and class. Disability is "always already inflected by other categories of difference in ways that differ by culture location and historical context" (Burch & Kafer, 2010, xviii). Transnational feminist theory and scholarship has challenged the Whiteness of disability studies and focused on the intersectionality of disability, race, class, and gender (Erevelles & Kafer, 2010).

Nirmala Erevelles, previously a special education teacher and in 2010 an Associate Professor of Education and Instructional Leadership, Policy, and Technology Studies at the University of Alabama, notes that "it is now a well-known fact in educational research that low-income students of color are disproportionately overrepresented in special education classrooms" (Erevelles & Kafer, 2010, p. 208; see also Reid & Knight, 2006). African Americans, particularly male students, are labeled with cognitive disorder and mental retardation and in 2005 comprised 33% of students in special education while only constituting 17% of the public school population (Kunjufu, 2005; Skiba, Poloni-Staudinger, Simmons, Feggins-Azziz, & Chung, 2005). Erevelles calls attention to the lack of acknowledgement that "these labels are often attached to these students by dubious means usually fueled by race and class prejudice. These students, who are certainly part of the disability community even though they have reasons to shun the label, seldom graduate and many ultimately join the prison industrial complex" (Erevelles quoted in Ervelles & Kafer, 2010, p. 209). Intersectional analysis of difference challenges a phenomenological sociology of deviance. Intersectionality considers the social construction of disability intertwined with the social construction of gender, race, class, and sexuality. Historical conceptions of femininity/masculinity intersect with conceptions of disability. Power, privilege, and oppression connect ableism to sexism, racism, and classism.

We urge art educators throughout the K-12 art curriculum to introduce artists who make art about and out of their experiences as persons with disability intersected with gender, race, and class. Works of art relevant to all students focus on the experience of acquiring a changed identity due to injury or other sudden change in abilities or from new life experiences. Today, these works and stories are accessible via the Internet, such as on the U.S. website of the Mouth and Foot Painting Artists (MFPA). This international, for-profit association was formed in 1956 and is "wholly owned and run by disabled artists to help them meet their financial needs. Members paint with brushes held in their mouths or feet as a result of a disability sustained at birth or through an accident or illness that prohibits them from using their hands" (MFPA, 2003, para. 1). The National Institute of Art & Disabilities hosts a site with portfolios of artwork and artist bios. Infinitec.org includes a gallery of artists who use the potentials of assistive technology. Additionally, there are several links to sites of exhibitions, organizations, and artists whose artworks concern disability culture and identity. Some excellent sites include National Arts and Disability Center (NADC, 1998–2011), International Guild of Disabled Artists and Performers (Patston, 2011), and Art of Possibility® Studios (Oberlander, 2011).

Passion Works, in Athens, Ohio, emphasizes the "embodied experience of difference" in a vocational employment program involving 160 adults, referred to as clients, whose "disabilities ranges from moderate to profound" (Harter et al., 2006, p. 7). In a study by Lynn Harter, a professor of communication studies, with four doctoral students, they describe how, for the "client artists, the experience of disability emerges, in part, from inhabiting a body that becomes a site of struggle over the meaning of 'difference'" (Harter et al., 2006, p. 12). Passion Works is an exemplar art education program that holds similar values and practices as the HEARTS program in "recognizing the salience of each other's (dis)similarities and interdependence" (Harter et al., 2006, p. 19). The researchers (Harter et al., 2006) learned from Passion Works about "respect for embodied differences" (p. 22) that challenge "hegemonic constructions of 'normal,' constructions that sediment into social formations that maintain walls of exclusion" (p. 13).

Mark Leeman and Lynn Harter, involved with Passion Works, have engaged with an organization that supports people with disabilities called Ikamva Labantu in Cape Town, South Africa, "to support art ventures across the nations-states" (Harter et al., 2006, p. 22). There are examples throughout the world of counter-narratives of disability. Preservice art teachers in the US can stretch the borders of their future classroom with use of social media to develop art projects with counter-narratives that sustain difference.[19]

Interview insights

Similar to the research approaches by Harter et al. (2006), preservice art teachers can gain knowledge from interviews with those who have worked alongside people experiencing disabilities about building inclusive and empowering environments. In the HEARTS program, we invited a panel to respond to questions by the preservice art teachers. For example, we invited a poetry professor who creates word pictures with braille, a school district special education administrator, and a parent of a child experiencing severe disabilities. If in-person visits are not feasible due to time and cost considerations, we have found that use of Skype® or Google Hangout® for Internet mediated face-to-face (f2f) real-time discussion works well. We sought professionals as guests to our classes who could help "people in dominant groups… to figure out how to share resources and power, give up their prejudices and beliefs in their own superiority, and be flexible in relation to others" (Ostrove & Oliva, 2010, pp. 108–109). Furthermore, this approach introduced preservice teachers to alliance building with support networks that situate education as a community endeavor beyond the boundaries of a

classroom, a school, or a district. Guests might come from the local school district or organizations whose mission is to build alliances across differences of identity, or they might be seasoned art educators who practice inclusion.[20]

If time differences make real-time connectivity difficult, a blog can be set up for students to ask questions to a professional. For example, Douglas Blandy at the University of Oregon responded to questions from the HEARTS preservice art teachers regarding barrier-free accessible exhibition planning. The insights that were gained from these interviews shaped the HEARTS exhibition.

Participatory engagement

Role-play and simulations, through which preservice art educators may temporarily (and in a very cursory way) experience a "disability" while engaging in a learning activity or creating art, may help them develop empathy and consider modification and accommodation strategies in working within an inclusive art class (Allison, 2008). Allison notes that such techniques enable art educators to think and plan critically for their art activities, lesson delivery, and assessment and critique strategies so that they may include all learners in a fully participatory way. However, there are limits to this approach if the focus is on what a person can't do and because each person and each difference is unique. Moreover, unless we spend time with those who are different from us, can we even begin to simulate the experience for insights and abilities to accommodate, bypass, and compensate for obstacles that present themselves in art learning activities in the K-12 art classroom?

The value of interpersonal engagement in building alliances across differences of identity cannot be overstated. It is necessary to work with people different from oneself to develop successful alliances "grounded in effective communication, mutual respect, and a recognition that identities are complicated" (Ostrove & Oliva, 2010, p. 106). When rapport is developed between educators and students with (dis)abilities, then insights arise from informal conversations.

Visual arts enable a form of dialogue that is not remediation but mediation. Communication with performative, material, and technological aesthetic forms mediates in a

---

[19] This premise is developed further in Keifer-Boyd (2012).

[20] Art educators could use the National Art Education Association Special Needs in Art Education Issues Group (SNAE) Listserv as a way to network with other art educators about working with students experiencing disabilities and to ask seasoned teachers to share their experiences and respond to questions posted by new art teachers. Also, this is a good resource to find and invite experienced art teachers to present, via social networking media or in person, in preservice art education courses. Subscribe by sending an e-mail to SNAEsubscribe@artedlists.org with the word SUBSCRIBE in the subject line and then post to SNAE@artedlists.org

tangible way what we feel, know, or imagine. Such participatory engagement is inclusion.

Empowered With Assistive Technologies

As the art teacher introduces an art lesson, students watch an animated figure, projected on a large screen from a computer system, use hand configurations, body positions, movement, and facial expressions to translate spoken language into American Sign Language (ASL).[21] Students learn ASL to communicate with each other and, thereby, better remember what is said from an embodied form of communication. This computer-generated interpreter is one of more than "29,000 assistive technology devices available" since 2009 (Simpson, McBride, Spencer, Lowdermilk, & Lynch, 2009, p. 172). Every year, researchers working with designers continue to develop ways to empower learners through use of assistive technology devices (ATD), which increase, maintain, or improve functional capabilities of people with disabilities.

Assistive technology, which enables communication and learning, is necessary for inclusive or "universal design[22] for learning (UDL) classrooms" (Simpson et al., 2009, p. 172). While in this chapter we discuss some of the types of technology available, in Chapter 3 we focus on the stakeholders involved in identifying appropriate assistive technology to promote agency and learning among students with different-abilities. If the student's individual education program (IEP) includes the need for specific assistive technology solutions, then according to IDEA, as a federal law, the school district is required to provide what is listed in the IEP. Solutions range from low-tech, low-cost options—such as grips (e.g., pencils in a thick kneaded eraser or Styrofoam ball), fasteners (e.g., Velcro), non-skid material, extensions (sticks, rods), and holes or pockets in tables for placing paint or water containers—to high-tech devices such as screen readers, voice activation, touch screens, braille or other modified keyboards, and switches (e.g., button, sip/puff).

In an interview with Nina Kasper, who has taught for 9 years in an elementary school in Miami, Florida, she describes how technology made a difference for one child:

> One of our most severely involved students is just learning to hit the switch to make something happen. Generally, some other kid comes along while she is at the computer and hits the switch. And then she comes

alive.... A severely involved child with a switch toy soon draws a crowd of five children who are interested in working the switch to see what happens. There is definitely social interaction. (Brett & Provenzo, 1995, p. 121)

An example of how technology can help children with *different-abilities* communicate and grow with the child, Sharon Ely (2000) describes how her son

> started using a "two picture" communication board at about 18 months of age. By age five years, his communication board had become a "book," consisting of several pages. From there he went with an electronic device, the Touch Talker by Prentke Romich, at age 6½. (p. 6)

Ely (2000) goes on to describe how her son at age 16 "works very hard to use his own voice, along with his communication device" (p. 6). She explains that

> whether or not an individual gets a piece of equipment (for example, a communication device purchased by the school) depends not only on how the Individualized Education Plan was written, but also on families' knowledge that laws do exist to support education and the use of assistive technology to access that education... It has been my experience that appropriate assistive technology can make the difference between: 1) general education placement verses special education placement; 2) being a participant or "doer" verses an observer on the sidelines; and 3) becoming an independent, productive member of society versus a dependent, unemployed member of society. (p. v)

Ely's advice shows that an important responsibility of the art educator is to be involved with the team that develops the child's IEP. The art educator must communicate learning goals and projects and ask about or suggest assistive technologies. It is important for the art teacher to conduct an analysis of the activities that are important learning events in the art curriculum. Activity analysis identifies the physical, cognitive, psychological, and interpersonal aspects of an activity. These can overlap or be distinctive. For example, for some students cognitive speed may be fast while mobility of hand movement with a keyboard or mouse may not be fast. For many students there is a need for immediate feedback to avoid frustration and to be productively involved in a group working on a project together.

Assistive technology also refers to the use of the Internet to find information, resources, and network with others. Exhibit 2.C provides selected useful sites to review in preparation for an inclusive art classroom.

---

[21] A team of faculty and students at DePaul University's School of Computer Science created Paula, a computer-generated interpreter who translates spoken English into American Sign Language (ASL). See http://asl.cs.depaul.edu (Simpson et al., 2009).

[22] Universal design is further discussed in Chapter 6 of this book.

Exhibit 2.C. Assistive Technology Information, Resources, and Networks

- Disability Studies (Tusler, 2011) readings at www.aboutdisability.com/bib.html#Anchor-Disability-8050

- Art, Disability & Expression Exhibit of VSA Arts (Moore, Stephanie, & Jeffries, Chris, 2006). This online exhibit shows some of the best examples of the vital artistic, political, and cultural expression of the disability community (www.vsarts.org/prebuilt/showcase/gallery/exhibits/disability).

- The companion web site to the 4-hour disability history radio program, *Beyond Affliction: The Disability History Project* (Laurie Block & Jay Allison, co-producers, Straight Ahead Pictures, National Public Radio, 1998), contains excellent primary source material (www.npr.org/programs/disability).

- Disability History Dateline: An extensive, searchable database of events in disability history developed by Paul Longmore at San Francisco State University's Institute on Disability (http://bss.sfsu.edu/disability/dateline.html).

- Disability-Research Discussion List: Maintained by Mark Priestly at the University of Leeds, this list focuses on disability research—both theoretical and practical from a social model perspective. To join, e-mail JISCmail@JISCmail.ac.uk with the following message: join disability-research your name. Past messages are available in a searchable archive at www.jiscmail.ac.uk/cgi-bin/wa.exe?S1=disability-research

- Disability Social History: A resource developed and maintained by Steve Dias and Pat Chadwick on disability history (www.disabilityhistory.org).

- *Disability World*: An archive of the bimonthly web zine by Barbara Duncan and Rosangela Berman-Bieler in English and Spanish focusing on an international perspective of independent living and disability. It has a strong arts and culture section plus international politics with a distinct point of view (www.disabilityworld.org).

- DS-HUM List: An electronic mailing list maintained by Mike Gill at the University of Maryland discussing disability in the humanities. Archives are available to subscribers.

- JFA E-mail Network (Justice for All): An electronic newsletter by Fred Fay with the latest news, legislative alerts, and current problems in the disability community. To subscribe send a message to majordomo@jfanow.org with the following in the body of the message: subscribe justice.

- Computer Assistive Technology Demonstration at http://videos.disabled-world.com/video/185/computer-assistive-technology-demonstration

Technologies to Support Difference

Many familiar technologies that are available to those with computers and Internet access enable accessibility to plentiful resources, communication, expression, self-representation, community, and experiences not possible prior to the mid-1990s. As early as 1995, Eugene Brett and Eugene D. Provenzo Jr. stated:

> We believe that the real significance and excitement of hypermedia as an enabling technology is how it fosters the notion of inclusion for all individuals. A model such as the CyberSpace Museum is exciting because it can be used by virtually anyone—with or without disabilities. (p. 132)

More than 15 years later, this utopian view and, indeed, what most people could have imagined has been surpassed by reality with the proliferation of social hypermedia in the participatory architecture of the Web used by museums, organizations, and individuals. Some examples of strategies and technologies include the following:

- Readings can be scanned and the electronic text can be read aloud using human sounding synthetic speech.[23]
- Internet browsers and other programs enable text or image to be enlarged on the computer screen and for printed materials.
- Hyperlinks can be created for clarification to reduce reading difficulty.

---

[23] For example, Kurzweil 3000 is a program that has been refined over the years with enhanced versions to enable digital text to be heard.

- Concept maps or other graphic organizers[24] including Web tabs, anchors to sections of larger documents, or menu options with roll-over descriptors of contents can be used to structure the learning environment with specific steps to complete an art education activity at the learner's own pace and to facilitate reading in small chunks for those with attention and focus challenges.[25]

- Media Access Generator (MAGpie) is free, do-it-yourself captioning, subtitling, and audio-description software for digital multimedia developed by the CPB/WGBH National Center for Accessible Media (NCAM)—available to download at http://ncam.wgbh.org/webaccess/magpie

- Free-to-use social media offer ways to interact with material on the Internet that facilitates learning. For example, Diigo® is a free-to-use Internet application that expands the functionality of Web browsers. Diigo enables a group to share bookmarked websites and to post notes or to annotate and highlight text on any website, simulating how one might use a physical highlighting marker on printed text in which each person uses a different color highlighter on the same text. Diigo also provides a forum, for invited members to a group, to initiate new topics. Questions and clarifications can be developed in the forum. Diigo also enables the layering of virtual sticky notes on a website, in which, similar to a blog, many can comment on each others' comments. This too provides a way for questions to be raised and explanations to be offered relevant to the learners in the art class.

- Another free-to-use Internet application is VoiceThread®, which enables students to display their artwork and to audio-record responses. This can enable those who have mobility challenges using a keyboard or pen to write about their artwork or those of their peers.[26]

- Some programs, like Read & Write Gold (Texthelp Systems, 2011), highlight each word as a synthetic speaker reads the text aloud and connect to an online spoken dictionary.

- Accessibility Access Keys[27] is a free plug in for the Web-building program WordPress, which enables customized keystrokes to simplify navigation of a website.

Accessible Online Education

Technology and learning in all areas, including art education, increasingly utilize online resources, social media for co-creation and communication, and blogs for students to post their work for public viewing and commentary. However, usability [useABILITY] principles are not the same as accessibility [accessABILITY] principles. While assistive technologies and adaptive devices enable accessibility to online environments, "most sites are not developed to be accessible to users with disabilities" (Jaeger & Bowman, 2005, p. 85). To make these resources, communication forums, and display sites inclusive learning environments there are ADA requirements and resources to help check for ADA compliance.[28] The U.S. government has adopted standards under Section 508 of the Rehabilitation Act[29] that "cover access to electronic and information technology procured by Federal agencies" (Section 508 Homepage, para. 1). "These laws [Section 504 of the Rehabilitation Act, ADA, IDEA] demonstrate a clear intent by Congress to provide equal physical and intellectual access to a wide range of aspects of society,

---

[24] Graphic organizers can be highly structured (Curkovic, 2009) or responsive and animated, such as RSA Animate—Changing Education Paradigms, which is based on Sir Ken Robinson's 2010 presentation on creativity (theRSA.org, 2010).

[25] Educators Ashley Sklyar, Kyle Higgons, and Randall Boone (2007) provide further and specific ideas on how to modify Webquests for students with learning disabilities.

[26] Go2Web20.net is a useful directory of Web tools that offers multimodal approaches to communication for inclusive art classrooms. Also, http://bit.ly/feminist_cyberspaces_wiki is a wiki about feminist teaching with technology with a section on accessibility resources at http://adarocks.wikispaces.com/x+resources+ACCESSIBILITY. Microsoft has an excellent blog post on creating accessible electronic presentations: http://blogs.office.com/b/microsoft-powerpoint/archive/2011/03/01/are-your-presentations-accessible.aspx. See http://en.wikipedia.org/wiki/List_of_free_software_for_audio for a list and links to free audio software and helpful developing multimedia content for differentiated learning.

[27] Accessibility Access Keys can be downloaded for free from http://blog.accessiblefutures.org/?p=9

[28] See the Information Technology Technical Assistance and Training Center (n.d.) at www.ittatc.org and the Alliance for Tech Access (2011) at www.ataccess.org for assistance in evaluating and making websites accessible to all learners and for directories of technologies and technology resource centers particularly helpful to people with disabilities, their families, and educators.

[29] www.access-board.gov/508.htm

including the online environment, for individuals with disabilities" (Jaeger & Bowman, 2005, p. 83).

Accessibility compliance by federal, state, and local government for information and services is regulated by enforcement of Section 508 amendment in 2000 to the U.S. Rehabilitation Act. The NASA Accessibility site (www.nasa.gov/accessibility) provides an overview of the law that sets standards for the removal of barriers that prevent access to information and services on the World Wide Web.

> The Access Board is an independent federal agency devoted to accessibility for people with disabilities. On December 21, 2000, the board issued accessibility standards for electronic and information technology under section 508 of the Rehabilitation Act, as amended. The board also develops and maintains accessibility guidelines for the built environment, transit vehicles, and telecommunications equipment under other laws and enforces design standards for federally funded facilities. (NASA Accessibility, 2009, para. 1)

> Section 508 uses the federal procurement process to ensure that technology acquired by the federal government is accessible. The law also sets up an administrative process through which individuals with disabilities can file a complaint alleging that a federal agency has not complied with the standards. This process uses the same complaint procedures established under section 504 of the Rehabilitation Act (which covers access to federally funded programs and services). Individuals may also file a civil action against an agency to seek injunctive relief[30] and attorney's fees (but not compensatory or punitive damages). (NASA Accessibility, 2009, para. 5)

Electronic-government (e-government) "is the provision of government information and services through the World Wide Web at the local, state, or national level" that enables citizens to be actively involved in the political process (Jaeger & Bowman, 2005, p. 86). The National Council on Disability, an independent federal agency committed to disability policy leadership since 1978, has in recent years advocated for accessibility policies to online resources. With a concern for virtual disenfranchisement of differently-abled persons, the E-Government Act of 2002 in the US "is intended to expand the involvement of citizens, including individuals with disabilities" (Jaeger & Bowman, 2005, p. 89).

Additionally there are support groups. For example, Virtual Ability Island (2011) in the virtual environment of Second Life® is a place to meet with artists with disabilities. The site enables socializing, sharing, and referrals to resources and groups.

The following are questions preservice art teachers should considering when developing or selecting Web resources or utilizing virtual environments as teaching sites:

- Is the content accessible to readers?
- Can discussions also be asynchronistic so that speed in responding is not an issue?
- Are there ways to interact with the content to increase retention and relevancy in learning?[31]

Communitarian Approach Toward Difference

Throughout this chapter, we have provided the theoretical underpinnings of inclusive strategies to prepare preservice teachers to empower by difference. In the words of poet and educator Jenny Corbett (1994), "The denial of difference and impetus to assimilate at all costs carries a high price in terms of human suffering and frustration" (p. 348). We too find assimilationist perspectives dangerous to the well-being of society at large and instead advocate that we can all be empowered by difference. As educators, we can provide an inclusive teaching environment in which students assert their identity by drawing on their experiences in artmaking and take ownership and responsibility for their art production so that it does not oppress others but instead contributes to cultural diversity.

In this chapter, we also have provided several strategies for a paradigm shift to de-center notions of normal, challenge cultural narratives that emphasize cure and care for disabled people, and to create a communitarian inclusive art program that seeks to empower all students. Next, we situate our communitarian approach in the art teaching context of schools in the US.

---

[30] An *injunction* is a court order to stop what is determined a harmful act or condition, or to do something that is considered an equitable remedy. An *injunctive relief* is a legal term for a court ordered rejection of a requested, or previously granted, injunction. An example of an injunctive relief is a request to a court that a differently-abled person is not denied an opportunity that had been denied on the basis it would be harmful to the differently-abled person and/or to others.

---

[31] There are several studies that suggest the use of familiar and assistive technologies can increase motivation, completion of learning activities, communication, and expression for students with disabilities (e.g., Higgins & Boone, 1997; Keifer-Boyd & Kraft, 2003).

Chapter 3

STAKEHOLDERS AND INCLUSION:
Joining Forces for a Communitarian Art Class

While teaching art in the public schools, I (Michelle) recall the collaborative professional relationship I shared with one of the special educators who worked with students experiencing the more severe and profound (dis)abilities at our high school. When transitioning a new student into my art classroom, the special educator might—if he felt that it would be educationally beneficial—visit with me and with the class beforehand. During his visit, he would prepare the class for the new student's arrival by discussing his or her preferences and needs, typical-abilities and different-abilities, and what they as a class might be able to do to help create an environment in which each discovered strengths and capabilities in him- or herself, and others, to achieve learning goals. In other words, a rigid mindset—that there is one right way to learn in the art class—would need to be challenged with ongoing problem solving by listening to and observing each other's ideas in the making.

Meanwhile, these same introductions and conversations were occurring in the special education environment, readying the soon-to-be included student and his or her parents (and other stakeholders as needed: e.g., paraeducators and occupational therapists) for the transition. This preparation and collaboration among stakeholders allowed us, in the art class, to anticipate the opportunity to create an inclusive classroom environment. The special educator responded, in advance, to questions or anxiety that might arise from stakeholders during our period of adjustment as we navigated what it meant to create an inclusive class. This preparation also empowered stakeholders—including all the students—to take ownership of facilitating inclusion.

Depending upon a student's special educational needs, this system—where needed and used—proactively enabled the inclusion of the student experiencing severe disabilities into the art class. I was surprised, therefore, some years later

when I found that the special education teacher had stopped taking these steps when transitioning similar students into the general classroom. He had reluctantly abandoned the approach, explaining,

> [The practice] is not permitted anymore... because of changes in the law in identifying these students in special ed... It's in the IDEA. But *I* feel like, even though a court case determined you can't do that anymore, that it was the most successful way, and I base that solely on experience I've had with students in the past. (quoted in Kraft, 2001, p. 193)

While it is true that confidentiality is an issue in the Individuals with Disabilities Education Act (IDEA, 2004), as well as in other statutes (such as the Family Education Rights and Privacy Act [FERPA], 2010), the IDEA mandate does not address this type of practice directly. Rather, such a decision may be permissible but must be made within the individualized educational program (IEP) team process, with the input of the stakeholders.

This illustrates, however, that one barrier to effective collaboration between special educators and art educators may be stakeholders' misinterpretations of the special education mandate or inclusion policy implementation at their given school or district. In this case, for instance, the special educator's interpretation of the mandate and policy was that he was forced to abandon this method of introduction that he felt had benefited some of his students who were experiencing severe disabilities.[1] Thus, a stakeholder's perception of IDEA and inclusion policy may affect the reality of its implementation, including how stakeholders collaborate with one another.

---

[1] See also the discussion of the MAPS model in the section "Including All Students in Art: Strategies for the Art Class as LRE" in Chapter 4.

Stakeholders in the Inclusive Art Class

Who, exactly, are the stakeholders in the inclusive art class, and how does their investment in and empowerment to practice inclusion policy figure into its successful implementation? Policy analyst Ann Majchrzak (1984) defines a *stakeholder* in two ways: (a) one who is able to contribute to and participate in policy formation or implementation, and/or (b) one who is affected by the policy's implementation. Where input into the decision making of the least restrictive environment (LRE) mandate and inclusion policy implementation in a given art class is concerned, stakeholders include the art educator, the special educator, the paraeducator who accompanies the alter-abled student to the mainstreamed classes, and the parent(s) of the student receiving special educational services.

When we consider the second part of Majchrzak's definition of stakeholder, those who "are affected by policy decisions" (1984, p. 28), the group of stakeholders for the inclusive art class expands to include the students in the classroom—both those who are typically-abled and those who are differently abled. The examination of all of these stakeholders is important to the discussion of successful inclusion strategies in the art class in that these are the individuals who are either shaping, or are shaped by, the implementation of these strategies. The consistent implementation of inclusion policy in the art class as a LRE (and in a way that is aligned with the philosophy and intent of IDEA) may be dependent, in great part, upon stakeholders' common understanding and vision of the mandate's intent and purpose. This common understanding can only be facilitated through communication and collaboration among stakeholders. Within the context of the art class as a LRE, those using a communitarian model (that we see demonstrated in IDEA) value the input and choices of all participants. Moreover, the involvement of all is necessary to achieve equality and liberty, and to realize participatory efficiency, within a true community context. In this chapter, we investigate stakeholders' roles in the inclusive art class, drawing conclusions about the importance of their partnership in creating an inclusive and fully participatory art class for all learners.

Stakeholders Acting on the IDEA of Inclusion Policy

The Art Teacher as Stakeholder

The art teacher, as a "regular education teacher," is one of the individuals responsible for developing and implementing inclusion policy for the student experiencing disabilities whose educational placement encompasses the art class. This policy development and implementation occurs through the art teacher's membership on the student's IEP team (IDEA Regulations, 2006, 34 C.F.R. § 300.321(a)(2)).

Art teachers and IEP involvement: Too much and not enough

Stuart Gerber and Janet Fedorenko (2006) point out the paradox that many art educators face concerning their function on the IEP team. On the one hand, the art class is a popular placement in general education for students with alter-abilities, so art educators may be called upon, more often than most educators, to participate on multiple IEP teams. On the other hand, many art teachers' colleagues may not view them as regular education teachers (even though the law views them as such) because they teach *art*. Perhaps for this reason—at least in part—art teachers' communication with other teachers who share the responsibility of educating the student with special needs may be minimal, occurring only through paperwork (Gerber & Fedorenko, 2006).

Many art educators experience the (actual or electronic) stack of IEPs that accumulate in the highly inclusive art class, as well as the difficulty of remembering each student's special educational modifications—a task that can be especially daunting for the elementary art teacher who may teach every student in the school. Required modifications, while they are theoretically individualized, may also begin to look the same, with such statements as "preferential seating," "cooling-off period," "lengthened test/assignment time," and "instructions delivered in written form" as recurring themes. In cases where the art teacher is omitted altogether from the IEP team and planning for a student's special educational needs, the stated modifications and educational goals in the IEP may bear little resemblance or have any meaning to the goals of the art curriculum. For instance, "preferential seating" means little to the art teacher who is up and about, moving among his or her students as they work. And what, specifically, does it mean to "allow an additional three days to complete" a project if that project is the student throwing a pot on the wheel? When there is a disconnect between IEP modifications and the art class, art educators need to meet with the special educator to discuss how to translate the IEP into the art classroom context. This exchange of information is mutually educative.

Enacting inclusion or reacting in isolation

As Doris Guay (2006b) points out, it is the art educator who is ultimately responsible for student learning in his or her class. This realization may necessitate a paradigm shift in which art educators recognize the need to influence effective implementation of the special education mandate in the unique learning environment of the art class rather than isolated from decisions about students' inclusion in that setting. When teachers face such paradigmatic shifts in approaches to school policy, curricula, and art educational philosophies, a certain amount of dissonance may occur as past practices conflict with newly raised or altered insights (Erickson, 2004).

I (Michelle) encountered this dissonance over 10 years ago when I first came across the *ecological perspective,* a philosophical stance in working with individuals experiencing different-abilities.[2] The ecological perspective considers both the environment and the student's abilities, focusing primarily on factors external to the student, which may be adjusted, rather than on the *defect* as residing within the student (Hallahan & Kauffman, 1995). For me, this way of seeing *special* education precipitated a change in my attitude. No longer did I view a student's disability as precluding certain activities in art; instead, I began to see the learning environment differently and to focus on what the student *could* do if only that environment were adjusted a bit. How might I change the way I have the class discuss and consider art? How might I be able to adjust my mode of presentation, along with students' modes of participation, to facilitate learning? How might I make adjustments in applications of media that could allow for full participation of all learners? Once I viewed the barriers to participation as environmental rather than as inherent within the student and his or her disability, an entirely different approach to and array of potential modifications, adaptations, assistive technologies, and learning enhancements presented themselves—possibilities that became visible only after my paradigm shifted to include this new way of viewing environment-in-disability.[3]

Act I: Enter the art teacher

IDEA Regulations (2006) stipulate that all regular educators who teach a student experiencing disabilities must have access to that student's IEP and be informed of his or her responsibilities in its implementation, including all required special accommodations, modifications, and supports (34 C.F.R. § 300.323(d)). But the statute, in its effort to streamline the

---

2   See "Including All Students in Art: Strategies for the Art Class as LRE" in Chapter 4 for further discussion on the ecological perspective.

3   See Chapter 2 for use of case studies to question assumptions about (dis)abilities and shift perspectives toward enabling art classroom environments as inclusive places of learning. See Chapter 2, in which we advocate for a social model, rather than a medical model, and Chapter 4, in which we discuss ecological perspectives inherent in a social model. Chapter 2 suggests the use of case studies to question assumptions about (dis)abilities, while Chapter 4 discusses how with such a shift of perspectives toward (dis)ability, an ecological perspective seeks to enable art classroom environments as inclusive places of learning.

process and to reduce paperwork, also provides the conditions under which IEP team members, such as the regular educator, may be excused from attending a meeting, even if the meeting involves modification or discussion of his or her subject area (34 C.F.R. § 300.321(e)). The excused participant—in our case, the art educator—must submit in writing, prior to the meeting, input into the IEP's development (34 C.F.R. § 300.321(e)(2)). In doing so, however, the art educator may never have met the student and may not be able to consider optimal strategies in meeting the student's special art educational needs. However, the more clearly the lesson and curricular goals and pedagogical practices are communicated in writing prior to the meeting, the more suitable the strategies in the IEP for the art classroom.

In addition, special education law only requires that a minimum of one regular educator be included on the IEP team for any student who is or may be placed in one or more general education classes as a LRE (2006, 34 C.F.R. § 300.321 (a)(2)). As a stakeholder responsible for implementation of an IEP in the unique academic setting of the art class (with its hands-on emphasis and varied, sometimes even potentially dangerous, media and materials), the art educator must feel empowered to insist, where necessary, that she or he be included and allowed input in all IEP team deliberations that directly affect the student's educational success in the art class. Rather than feeling disempowered, isolated, and devalued, art educators need to develop their agency by having the unique pedagogical processes of the art class included in IEP deliberations. Key to this change is knowing and communicating the value of what art educators contribute to the well-being and creative capacities of students.

The Special Educator as Stakeholder

The special educator, perhaps more readily than the art educator, recognizes his or her role in implementing inclusion policy as opposed to only being affected by it. Unlike the art educator, the special educator has chosen very deliberately, with eyes-wide-open awareness, his or her role as stakeholder in the implementation of IDEA. The special educator, as someone who teaches some content areas in segregated classroom settings, as well as someone who provides support to students included in the regular classroom, also is readily familiar with the varied nuances within the sliding scale of LRE in providing an individualized special education for the student with different-abilities.

Positive trans-actions: The art teacher and special educator

IDEA Regulations (2006), in aligning the law with No Child Left Behind (NCLB, 2001), stipulate that special educators who are responsible for teaching core content areas to students in the special education classroom must be "highly qualified" in those content areas, as well as in the area of special education (34 C.F.R. § 300.18(b)). The special educator does not, however, have to be highly qualified in the content area for any subjects in which he or she provides support, as long as the following is true:

> They are only (1) providing consultation services to other teachers, such as adapting curricula, using behavioral supports and interventions, or selecting appropriate accommodations for children with study skills or organizational skills or (2) reinforcing instruction that the child has already received from a highly qualified teacher in that core academic subject. (U.S. Department of Education, 2007; see also 34 C.F.R. § 300.18)

It is in this capacity that the special educator will work with the art educator for any class that includes a student experiencing alter-abilities. While the special educator must be highly qualified under the law to teach core content areas within the segregated special education classroom setting at the elementary or secondary levels, the art teacher is not required to be a highly qualified special educator to include the student with special educational needs in the general art class setting.

Acting on behalf of students experiencing severe disabilities: Functional curriculum considerations

It is important to note that students experiencing severe disabilities[4] may receive education within a *functional curriculum*. This type of curriculum emerged from applied behavior analysis approaches to special education of individuals experiencing severe disabilities beginning in the mid- to late-20th century.[5] It teaches the student to operate as independently as possible within his or her environment and would include the life skills needed by a student in the current environment in which he or she was functioning, the life skills needed in the student's immediate next educational environment, and the skills the student would need after leaving school to function in vocational, residential, and recreational environments. (Cipani & Spooner, 1994, p. 33)

Emphasis is placed upon self-care skills, behaviors related to communication and socialization, and skills in educational, vocational, and recreational settings.

Even when a student is educated under a functional curriculum, where some special educators give low priority to academic skills, "functional academic skills are indeed part of some students' educational programs" (Turnbull, Turnbull, Shank, & Leal, 1995, p. 288). As art is a form of visual communication, and the National Standards address its communicative and expressive aspects,[6] and as communication is often a component of the functional curriculum, many students experiencing severe different abilities may be able to achieve in an inclusive art class that combines aspects of both the functional curriculum and the standards for visual art. Figure 3.1 demonstrates the connection between the National Standards for Visual Arts (NSVA; National Art Education Association, 1994) in the US and some of the various domains of a special educational curriculum (including the functional curriculum).

For example, functional and adaptive skills in the special education curriculum are often generalizable to other contexts, including making connections between art, culture, and other ideas and disciplines. Likewise, communication and self-help/adaptive domains in special education may include the skills of self-advocacy and decision-making, the same skills that students use in creating, thinking, and communicating about works of art. In this way, the art curriculum—when taught according to the NSVA—may inherently support the student learning outcomes of the (functional) special education curriculum and vice versa.

It is critical, therefore, that the art educator understands *why* a student experiencing severe disabilities has been included in the art class. It is then essential that the art teacher collaborate with the special educator on how to merge aspects of the NSVA with the student's functional curriculum as outlined in the IEP to best meet that student's art educational needs.

Proactive support

To make this collaboration successful, the art educator, depending on a student's level of (dis)ability, may need to rely

---

[4] Turnbull, Turnbull, Shank, and Leal (1995) cite the federal regulations that accompanied the 1990 incarnation of IDEA. These regulations described students with severe disabilities as those "who, because of the intensity of their physical, mental, or emotional problems, need highly specialized education, social, psychological, and medical services in order to maximize their full potential for useful and meaningful participation in society and for self-fulfillment" (34 C.F.R. § 300 and §315.4(d)). The 2006 regulations no longer include this definition.

[5] These late 20th-century approaches were rooted in behavioral psychology from earlier in the century. In 1976, Brown, Nietupski, and Hamre-Nietupski proposed a "criterion of ultimate functioning," which focused on skills that students experiencing severe disabilities would eventually need "to function as effectively and independently as possible in vocational, residential, and social environments" (Cipani & Spooner, 1994, p. 33). The functional curriculum is built on this theory, as well as the ideas of Vincent, Salisbury, Walter, Gruenwald, and Powers (1980) who adapted these ideas to the early childhood special education curriculum.

[6] And also may overlap the functional curriculum in developing students' (motor) skills in working with a variety of media.

Figure 3.1. Connection Between the National Standards for Visual Arts (NSVA) and Special Educational Learning Domains.

National Standards for Visual Arts	Special Educational Learning Domains
1. Understanding visual arts in relation to history and culture	1. (Pre-)Academic/Functional Domain
2. Reflecting upon the merits and characteristics of one's own work and the work of others	2. Cognitive Domain; Communication Domain; Self-help/Adaptive Domain
3. Connecting art to other disciplines	3. (Pre-)Academic/Functional Domain; Cognitive Domain
4. Applying techniques, media, and processes for visual communication	4. (Pre-)Academic/Functional Domain; Cognitive Domain; Communication Domain; Social/Emotional Behavior Domain; Self-help/Adaptive Domain; (Pre-)Vocational Domain
5. Evaluating a range of subject matter, symbols, and ideas	5. (Pre-)Academic/Functional Domain; Cognitive Domain; Communication Domain
6. Understanding functions and structures in which art can be made and perceived	6. (Pre-)Academic/Functional Domain; Cognitive Domain; Self-help/Adaptive Domain; Communication Domain

on the support of the special educator. Knowing the right questions to ask of the special educator may help the art teacher meet the special educational needs of students who are included in the art class as a LRE. Loesl (1999) offers one model for a questionnaire that the art educator may use in communicating with the special educator when a student with special needs is first included in the art class. This form requests information on the student's chronological age, cognitive age, medical conditions and medications, and suggestions for adaptations. Because this strategy may be problematic in some situations,[7] Loesl suggests using this type of form only with students who manifest more severe and profound disabilities to "provide a baseline of expectations for behaviors that may manifest themselves... and the strategies that the special educator has successfully implemented" (p. 60).

Other initial questions for inclusion of students who experience severe disabilities may include the following:

1. *What is the purpose of the inclusion? Is it for academic reasons or for reasons associated with socialization and a functional curriculum?* Knowing the answer to this question will enable the art teacher to formulate realistic curricular goals in meeting a student's needs in the art class. If the student is expected to achieve academic art objectives, then the art teacher may work with the special educator

to develop strategies for achieving those objectives. If, however, the nature of the student's (dis)abilities are severe enough that he or she is included in the art class for socialization rather than academic achievement, then the art teacher is free to construct social roles, situations, and scenarios that will engage the student in appropriate interactions with peers with art as a catalyst; in this case, cognitive achievement of curricular goals in art may not be the focus of the inclusion.

2. *From your observations, which of the student's personal preferences and abilities do you think we can maximize in the art classroom?* This question may begin a discussion on uses of art media and materials with which the student might be most successful. The conversation may also include such questions as: Does the student have any tactile aversions? Is the student able to grasp and/or release? To what extent is the student able to hold art media and control his or her movements (including fine and gross motor skills)? Does the student become fatigued with physical work? Do you feel the student would work better with two- or three-dimensional projects? This type of discussion allows the art educator and special educator to brainstorm on workable modifications, assistive

---

[7] Some potential problems may include those related to the special educator's fear of biasing the art educator by providing such information, concerns regarding confidentiality, and even simply the generation of more paperwork (Loesl, 1999).

technology devices,[8] and other resources for helping the included student with the kinesthetic and creative aspects of artmaking.

3. *May we review together the modifications and adaptations set forth in the student's IEP to see how we might best apply them to the art class?* This type of collaborative review will remind or inform the special educator of the unique educational environment of the art class. Both the special educator and art educator will bring to this discussion different insights based on their own backgrounds and experiences. These shared insights will allow for strategizing how certain special educational requirements may (or may not) be generalized and applicable to the art class and art curriculum objectives in meeting a student's special educational needs.

The Parents as Stakeholders

As with the art educator and special educator, the parent of the child experiencing disabilities is a stakeholder who is both affected by and responsible for the decision making and implementation of special educational policy. IDEA clearly expects that parents will be fully involved in their child's educational progress (Weishaar, 2008). Garten and Murdick (2008) point out that it is through the gateway of the IEP that "parents enter into equal participation with the school to ensure that the student with disabilities is provided… educational opportunity" (p. 337; see also IDEA Regulations, 2006, 34 C.F.R. § 300.112); Downing (2008) describes the student experiencing disabilities and his or her parents as the most critical members of the IEP team. Parents are able to share valuable input concerning their child's typical-abilities and different-abilities from which educators may develop instructional strategies. However, while involvement is provided for by IDEA during IEP formation, it may be that little contact occurs between parents and educators (especially with the art educator) after that. Nevertheless, the art teacher may invite parents to provide contact information on how to be reached, through print or digital means, with news of the art program. Such communication is art advocacy serving multiple purposes.

---

8 IDEA defines assistive technology devices (ATDs) as "any item, piece of equipment, or product system, whether acquired commercially off the shelf, modified, or customized, that is used to increase, maintain, or improve functional capabilities of a child with a disability" (IDEA, 2004, 20 U.S.C. § 1401(1)). Such ATDs may include low-tech devices, such as self-closing scissors and grips for pencils or paintbrushes, or high-tech devices, such as mouth- or head-sticks, voice synthesizers for use with computers, or the various technologies shared in Chapter 2 of this book.

Communication: Interacting versus inaction

Often, routine communication between parents and teachers—in the form of behavior/academic achievement notebooks, parent/teacher conferences, and school open houses—occurs more commonly at the elementary level than at the secondary level. One mother of a student with autism lamented the lack of communication that she had experienced with teachers at the high school level concerning her son's educational progress. She explained:

> I got spoiled in elementary and junior high … We got a notebook, and [the teachers] would write down, everyday, what happened in this notebook, you know? And then, if they had the time, they would call me and tell me what happened that week. Good or bad, I wanted to hear it all.… I would still like to have that notebook. (quoted in Kraft, 2001, p. 314)

The mother noted that, not only was such communication helpful in determining her son's academic progress, but it was also necessary information for his doctor in determining treatment and level of medication—factors that could also impact the student's educational performance. Not only is sharing information beneficial to teachers in implementing their designed interventions, but the parent—as the caregiver of a child with special needs—may welcome and need the support of other adults who are also concerned with his or her child's welfare (Karten, 2005).

Acting together in the interests of the student

Including the parent in the collaborative effort of educating the student with special needs enables the parent to extend educational interventions outside the school setting and into the home (Mostert, 1998). In addition, IDEA regulations (2006) stipulate that parents of, and professionals (including the art teacher) who work with, a student experiencing different-abilities may require training in the use of assistive technologies, where appropriate (34 C.F.R. § 300.6). The parent and art teacher, with the special educator and student, may collaborate to develop adaptations and assistive technologies for creating art that can be implemented in both the classroom and at home (for an example see Exhibit 3.A). Collaboration between educators and parents also allows the parent to share relevant knowledge that can be useful in educational interventions; it empowers stakeholders to share in the support and in reporting the progress of any proposed interventions, as well as in providing feedback (Mostert, 1998).

The Paraeducator as Stakeholder

The instructional aide, or paraeducator, who may accompany the student into the LRE art class functions as a support for the art educator and special educator in serving the special

Exhibit 3.A. Assistive Technologies for Collaboration

Darren, a high school student who experienced severe physical disabilities caused by a traumatic brain injury, was included in Ms. Madison's art class. Darren was nonverbal and possessed limited movement in his arms, though he had some grasping ability in his left hand. It wasn't long before Ms. Madison noticed that Mr. Elwood, the paraeducator who accompanied Darren to art, was making most of Darren's choices for his artwork, selecting his materials for him on a mixed media collage project, arranging the items on Darren's paper, then having Darren glue them down in that arrangement.

"I wonder if there's a way we can get Darren to select his materials and compose them for his art," Ms. Madison commented to Mr. Elwood one day. "How can we have him make these creative choices in a way that we *know* is based on his own personal expression?"

Mr. Elwood thought for a moment, then said, "Darren just got a programmable Chatbox that we use in the special education class, but we were afraid it would get dirty in art class and weren't sure if he'd even need it." He went on to explain that they programmed different phrases for the box, using different programmable overlays for different contexts. Darren, by pressing the buttons, could use the verbal phrases to communicate his wishes, to share greetings, and to respond to simple questions in class.

"So we could change the types of phrases to work for different projects?" asked Ms. Madison. "Like, 'This needs more texture here,' 'I want brighter colors,' or 'I want duller colors'? Then we could get him the materials or colors that he wanted—he could even nod or shake his head to confirm—and you could help him arrange things and adhere them as needed."

Within a week, Mr. Elwood, Ms. Madison, the special educator Ms. West, Darren, and Darren's mom met to discuss how to use the Chatbox so that Darren could complete his own collage. Ms. Madison picked up quickly how the Chatbox worked and discussed with Mr. Elwood and Ms. West how she might best send them phrases that could be programmed for the next art project. Darren's mom, who was already well versed in using the Chatbox, collaborated with Ms. Madison on how its use at home might enable Darren to work on art projects there, something that would be helpful to him physically and in completing his work at his own pace without falling too far behind in the art classroom. Darren's mom, Darren, and Ms. Madison agreed to meet in 3 weeks to see how the assistive technology intervention was working to empower Darren to make artistic choices in his work at home and in the art class.

educational needs of a student. If not properly prepared, however, the paraeducator may become a barrier to inclusion (Gelzheiser et al., 1997; Grigal, 1998; Guay, 1999; Kraft, 2001; Schiller, 1999). A study by Gelzheiser, McLane, Meyers, and Pruzek (1997) indicated that opportunities for social interactions between students who were typically-abled and those who were differently-abled were diminished by the constant presence of a paraeducator. The classroom teacher, too, may not work as readily with the student with special needs if the paraeducator is continuously at the student's side. Some paraeducators may also help the student too much, preventing him or her from completing work to the best of his or her individual ability.

On the other hand, the paraeducator may be helpful in fostering peer interactions, will be knowledgeable of the student's individual (dis)abilities, and can aid in providing for partial participation by fostering and encouraging interdependent autonomy in the art class (Giangreco, Feldman, & Broer, 2001; Guay, 2006b). When properly prepared and orientated to the unique art class environment, the paraeducator may provide support by (a) reinforcing learning for the student experiencing disabilities, (b) individualizing instruction,

(c) recording student performance data and facilitating communication between the special educator and art educator, (d) implementing teacher-designed behavior management plans, and (e) helping the student transition from one task to another (Downing, 2008; Guay, 2006b; Steckelburg & Vasa, 1988).

Doris Guay (2006b) points out that, even though the paraeducator may be working in the art classroom, it is the special educator who defines the paraeducator's major responsibilities. The art educator, however, as the one responsible for all students' learning in the art class, must collaborate with the special educator in communicating expectations and strategies with the paraeducator. The art teacher should not leave the primary role of educating the student experiencing disabilities to the paraeducator; but rather, he or she should partner with the paraeducator as a support in facilitating equitable education opportunities for all students, most notably in including the differently-abled student in a fully participatory way.

Downing (2008), and Giangreco and Broer (2005), describe the overdependence that may occur if one paraeducator is consistently assigned to a specific student. While this arrangement may offer some attractiveness in facilitating familiarity and consistency for the student, the overly dependent relationship that may result could impede the student's interactions with peers and the general classroom teacher and prevent the student from learning to communicate and work with different individuals (Downing, 2008). For this reason, it is advisable to have the student work with a variety of paraeducators.[9] If this cannot be done, then the art educator and special educator and paraeducator may collaborate on strategies that allow the paraeducator to move about the art classroom from time to time, offering help to the class at large. Doing so may foster the individuality of the student experiencing disabilities and will also lessen any stigma that may emerge by having constant adult supervision focused upon one student. In this way, all students in the class may benefit from the aid of the paraeducator, and the student experiencing different-abilities may have a more inclusive, participatory experience in the art class as a LRE.

Stakeholders Affected by the IDEA of Inclusion Policy

The Student Experiencing (Dis)abilities

The stakeholder most affected by inclusion policy is unquestionably the student with special educational needs. The art class as a LRE placement for a student experiencing (dis)abilities is inextricably intertwined with the concepts of free appropriate public education (FAPE) and the IEP, as discussed in Chapter 1. The relationship of these concepts in IDEA requires the determination of the most appropriate education and related services for every student with special educational needs followed by a decision on the proper placement, such as the art class, for providing those services (Kauffman & Hallahan, 1995a). The very definition of FAPE[10] emphasizes the appropriateness of education for the learner experiencing different-abilities as determined by the IEP. This fundamental feature of federal special educational law has remained essentially unchanged since its original enactment in 1975, as has the definition of least restrictive environment.

It is important to remember that LRE refers in large part to educational mode and process and not physical placement alone. Kauffman and Hallahan (1995b) say,

Our interpretation of equal educational opportunity is that students must not be grouped for instruction by caprice or by criteria that are irrelevant to their learning and social development but that they must be grouped by criteria directly related to what they are to learn and how they can be taught most effectively. (p. 165)

Under special education law, it is the *method* of education—as appropriate to the needs of the student—which is of central concern.

Active participation

Guay (1993) notes that in a fully participatory educational process in the inclusive art class, the goals of art education for students with and without (dis)abilities should be the same and should include an emphasis on the acquisition of art skills, art knowledge, and an understanding and valuing of art as an essential part of life. We would also add to this list of goals: (a) an understanding of art as a visual form of communication and (b) the possibilities of self-expression through art along with an appreciation of this communication through the works of self and others.

Echoing Guay's emphasis on the academic goals of art education according to national standards, Blandy (1989) advocates using *culturally* situated education strategies in a way that "allows disabled students to act and appear in a way which is appropriate to persons of their age. 'Special' curriculums and learning activities are restrained by this principle" (p. 10). Such inclusive strategies include ensuring that the learner with special needs is involved in age-appropriate activities and materials within the art classroom (Blandy, Pancsofar, & Mockensturm, 1988). Downing (2008) points to the importance of the teacher's role in orchestrating the class community so that everyone—including the student experiencing severe or multiple different abilities—has a unique role to play, a contribution to make.

In the HEARTS model that we share in Part 2 of this book, we provide some examples in which students experiencing different-abilities, along with typically-abled peers, are each assigned roles within a project or task so that all are actively engaged. For instance, one group of students—which included four high school students who were typically-abled and one high school student with cerebral palsy who used a wheelchair—used a video camera and editing software to create a music video that they called "Chairs." The members of the group planned and shot the video together, and together they selected props and the different types of chairs to include. Each group member appeared in the video, participating in a variety of activities, and each also shot some of the footage. The final video revealed these friends interacting with one another in various campus settings and also showed

---

9   This also allows paraeducators the professional development opportunity of working with different (dis)abilities with a range of students.

10   FAPE includes special education and related services that are provided at public expense, meet state educational standards, are delivered at an appropriate school, and conform to the student's IEP (IDEA, 2004, 20 U.S.C. § 1401(8)). See also Chapter 1.

a number of chairs of different types, all as tools that each of us use in some capacity. The chair also became a metaphor, in general, for the qualities in each person that make us the same as and different from one another.

More than just an act

Anderegg and Vergason (1996) add that normalization is the ultimate goal of education in the general classroom as the LRE. They describe normalization as focusing upon the mastery of foundational adaptive behaviors that enables the individual to be regarded as a wholly involved and functioning member of society. Normalization, they argue, is a closer reflection of the LRE concept than mere placement in that it considers the ends rather than the means. Anderegg and Vergason's normalization view is problematic in that it implies a hierarchy, with those who are typically-abled as the standard. This view is at odds with the communitarian perspective of inclusion, which values difference among stakeholders. We challenge concepts, such as "normalization," "mastery," and "foundational" as having fixed meanings that contradict the situational, individualized nature of education in the LRE

envisioned by IDEA. (See Exhibit 3.B for an example of student empowerment in the IEP process.) Also emphasizing the student's participation in his or her own education, Mostert (1998) supports including the student, where appropriate, in designing his or her special educational intervention:

> First, as with parents, students possess a knowledge of themselves that may well contribute to the success of any professional plan. Understanding the problem from the student's point of view may increase the chances of the student's cooperation. Second, uncovering such knowledge will explicate the student's individual preferences, needs, and perceptions, all of which can easily influence the efficacy of any educational program. Third, including the student in the collaborative process increases the likelihood that the student will be motivated to change out of a sense of ownership and personal responsibility. (pp. 18–19)

Therefore, inclusive education in the LRE must facilitate, to the extent appropriate, self-determination and self-realization to foster the in(ter)dependent living that is envisioned

Exhibit 3.B. Student Empowerment in the Individualized Education Program (IEP) Process

Adam experienced degenerative muscular dystrophy that caused weakness in his arms, often resulting in fatigue during physical activity. At the beginning of his 8th-grade year, he asked to be placed in art class as part of his schedule. He and his mom worked with the special educator to make sure that Mr. Baker, the art teacher, was included in the IEP team meeting at the beginning of the year.

At the meeting, Adam shared with Mr. Baker his concerns for his physical abilities and offered some suggestions that had worked for him in the past in terms of modifications for gripping and holding. "I saw in a catalog some brushes that have special grips that might work," Adam offered. "But there will be times when I just have to rest for a few minutes during work."

"I had planned for us to work in clay during the school year," Mr. Baker said. "What are your thoughts on that?"

Adam replied, "I tried several years ago, when I still had a little more strength, but it wasn't easy. It was so heavy to move around. I don't think I can do that now."

Mr. Baker thought for a moment. "What about pushing? Can you push with some force? Perhaps we can rig up something where you can form shapes in clay by pushing it against another surface."

"It might be easier," Adam replied, "but I'm not sure."

"We could try it, if you'd like to, when we get to that point," Mr. Baker suggested. "If that doesn't work, then I have a clay that air-hardens, rather than fires in the kiln, and it's much less dense and a whole lot lighter in weight than the stoneware we'll be using."

Adam nodded slowly, "Well, let's try it—if neither works, we can come up with an alternative project at that point."

"Yes," Mr. Baker agreed. "The project is about thinking in three-dimensional materials to form metaphors about connectivity. The goals of this project could be met with other materials if needed."

by IDEA.[11] This does not happen by accident, though, and it is a process cultivated by stakeholders implementing the special education mandate. The art teacher may use a number of strategies to facilitate full participation and independent choice making in art. Here are two examples:

1. *Creating scenarios and situations in which individual learners, in small groups, must interact with one another to accomplish a task.* In such groups (which would be rearranged from time to time) each member, according to individual ability where appropriate, would be given a specific role; all roles would be necessary to task completion. For example, a small group of three high school students is designated to load the kiln for the art class. The group includes two typically-abled students, Alex and Jessica, and one student, Cynthia, who experiences Down syndrome and possesses the cognitive age of 8 years old. Alex's assigned task is to carry the green ware to the kiln for bisque firing while Jessica loads the ceramics and places the stilts for the next kiln shelf; Cynthia's role is to hand Jessica green ware, as needed, and to lower the kiln shelves into the kiln. She also places the cone. Each of these tasks is necessary in performing the overarching goal of readying the kiln for firing; students have worked together to achieve the task.

A similar situation may apply to cognitive and affective learning in the art class, as well. In another situation, the class is studying images of war in visual culture. The same group of Alex, Jessica, and Cynthia is provided a folder of several images related to war, including battle front and home front, that they are to categorize under the headings of propaganda, romantic, or documentary; they are also to decide if any images fall into more than one category and why. They will then participate in a class discussion in which they provide reasons for the categorizations of their images. All group members participate in the sorting, but the art teacher has also assigned specific roles to group members: Alex will take notes and synthesize the group's responses in written form, Jessica will share the group's categories orally, and Cynthia will sort the group's choices on the poster board as a visual aid, along with the headings, and display the poster with the categories and images during Jessica's presentation. All three will participate in the question and answer session with the class after their presentation.

2. *Providing students frequent opportunities for choice making in their learning.* This choice making may include choices while a student creates his or her own art, but it may also include the teacher providing a number of options for projects in achieving a particular curricular goal. For example, for a lesson on assemblage, students are provided

three choices for creating their sculptures: (a) a sculpture in-the-round made from scrap pieces of wood that were donated by a local lumber company; (b) a relief sculpture in which students use found objects that they themselves collect; or (c) a small group-created environment that is constructed from cardboard and paper of various weights and types that will be painted a solid color. Students may also be given the option of submitting a proposal for their own alternative idea in creating an assemblage. Providing for a variety of choices in approaching artmaking empowers students, including learners experiencing a range of (dis)abilities, to gravitate toward options that may maximize their individual strengths. It also allows for the ownership and sense of personal responsibility.

The Art Class as a Whole

The typically-abled students comprise the bulk of the stakeholders within the inclusive general classroom setting. In examining education in the art class as the LRE, the question arises as to whether the needs of all students are met or whether the rights of one individual or group supersedes those of any other. Rather than referring to simply a particular classroom or teacher, the term "educational placement" includes the aspects of instructional program or setting (TEA, 2000). If that placement is in the art class, then the art teacher is responsible for providing modifications, according to the identified student's IEP, that will enable him or her to progress educationally. Case law and state-level legislation, which use the term "mainstreaming" over "inclusion," say that it encompasses supplementary aids and services where needed (and specified in the IEP); examples of these may include (but are not limited to) co-teaching, instructional or curriculum modifications and accommodations,[12] special equipment or materials, staff development, and decrease of student-teacher ratio (TEA, 1996, 19 TEC §89.63(c)(1)). Such supplementary aids and services may even be "designed to enrich education in order to enable success of *all* students" (italics added; TEA/ESC 20, 2009, p. 7).

Getting our act together

The emphasis on providing support for both students and teachers here reveals an integrative approach to mainstreaming rather than attention to mere proximity. While the case law in Chapter 1 demonstrated that the education of a student experiencing different-abilities in the regular classroom should not be detrimental to the class as a whole, we may go so far as to say that supplementary aids and services—when

---

[11] See "Self-Advocacy Strategies" in Chapter 4.

[12] A student with special educational needs may not be removed from the general education classroom solely on the basis of necessary accommodations or modifications in the general education curriculum (IDEA Regulations, 2006, 34 C.F.R. §300.116(e)).

Exhibit 3.C. Shared Modifications in the Art Class

Molly, a student experiencing cerebral palsy, was excited about starting photography in her 5th-grade art class. Her art teacher, Ms. Brown, had already talked to Molly's special education teacher about adaptations for Molly's movement in photography, and she had secured funding to buy a tripod and remote shutter release for Molly's use in the art class.

For the portrait assignment, each partner was to photograph the other in various lighting situations. Molly and her partner, Hannah, enthusiastic about the project, finished within the first week. Molly photographed Hannah, and even herself, using the new tripod and remote.

Later in the week, another pair of students—Tyler and Joseph—decided that they wanted to both appear in their photographs together, and they asked Molly if they could borrow her tripod and remote to complete their series of photos. Lance and Abby wanted to try night shots and asked to use the tripod and remote, too.

At the end of the 6 weeks, all of the students used the tripod to photograph their pieces for their digital portfolios. The modification for Molly benefitted the whole class.

applied to the class at large where appropriate—may even result in educational benefits for all students. (For an example, see Exhibit 3.C.) IDEA allows for "permissive use of funds" for initiatives that facilitate learning for all students in the classroom, not just those experiencing disabilities. Such funds, according to IDEA (2004), may be used for

> The costs of special education and related services and supplementary aids and services provided in a regular class or other education-related setting to a child with a disability in accordance with the IEP of the child, even if one or more nondisabled children benefit from these services. (20 U.S.C. § 1413(a)(4))

Extending these types of supports, where prudent and feasible, to typically-abled students in the class may also create a more normative social and educational environment for the student experiencing different-abilities, as well.

The role of the typically-abled student in the inclusive art class is much the same as that before inclusion: All students are in the classroom to learn, and that particular, fundamental role does not change with the integration of students experiencing different-abilities. Still, there are some notable roles that the typically-abled student may fill that may prove to have particular impact on the student experiencing (dis)abilities: that of role model, peer tutor, and friend. Through the fulfillment of these classroom roles, a typically-abled student may provide constructive social interaction with typically-abled and differently-abled peers alike.

Collaboration Among Stakeholders

Schiller (1999) suggests that it is not reasonable, nor is it in keeping with the spirit of inclusion, to expect the general classroom teacher to be involved in educating students experiencing disabilities without any assistance or support. That is why a collaborative process between the special educator

and art educator is beneficial in constructing and enhancing the LRE experience. Grigal (1998) advocates a *transdisciplinary* approach to education that downplays the distinction between general and special education. Through this model, the education of students experiencing disabilities is viewed as a shared responsibility.

Gerber and Fedorenko (2006) cite Friend and Cook (2006) in pointing out several characteristics of collaboration. Collaboration (a) is based on mutual goals, (b) requires equality among participants and depends on equal participation and shared responsibilities among those participants, and (c) is voluntary. It also requires participants to share resources (Gerber & Fedorenko, 2006). Perhaps the most advantageous of the shared resources is shared information. Mostert (1998) points out "a major advantage of habitual, extended collaborative activity is that it provides the potential for access to a great amount of knowledge that might otherwise not be available" (p. 19). To this end, co-planning and co-teaching among collaborators—such as the art educator and special educator—while more demanding in time and coordination, can yield beneficial results in terms of curricular modifications and accommodations that may benefit all students in the class (Gerber & Fedorenko, 2006). As in the examples with Jessica, Alex, and Cynthia, equal participation does not necessarily mean identical, or the same type of, participation. Ripley (1997) and Grigal (1998) acknowledge that initial attempts at collaboration may be difficult, perhaps due largely to different teaching approaches and styles; but time is an essential component of collaboration and must be provided in order for the process to be successful. Given the time and opportunity for collaboration, the benefits to both general and special educators can be great. While the general educator brings content-related knowledge and instructional skills to the table, the special educator brings knowledge on assessment and adaptation, along with a familiarity with a given student's special needs (Gerber & Fedorenko, 2006; Grigal, 1998; Ripley, 1997). The combining of these fields of expertise has the potential to strengthening the instructional process within the inclusive art class.

Interacting to Achieve an Act of Congress

Collaboration that leads to co-planning and co-teaching are at the center of the HEARTS model that we offer in the second section of this book. If students are allowed to see educators (including art teachers, special educators, and paraeducators) work together in teaching students representing all levels of (dis)ability, they may see the divisions blur between these varying levels of ableness. Gerber and Fedorenko (2006) suggest that "the aim of co-teaching is to provide modifications and adjustments that make the curriculum more accessible for all," while co-planning must be equitable and allow for periods of debriefing (p. 168). Planning and teaching lessons together in this way, which allows for joint reflection upon the learning experience, provides the educator team the space for responsive intervention and redirection of accommodations where necessary. Moreover, when art educators and special educators work with students and parents to co-plan, implement, and assess in a systemic way, their participatory action research can be documentation to inform, problem solve, or improve future iterations of learning strategies.

Theory to Practice: Enacting the Act

The "Empowerment Through Inclusion" section of this book, which includes Chapters 1–3, examined the Individuals with Disabilities Improvement Act of 2004 through the theoretical lens of the communitarian perspective that we believe to be the philosophical underpinning of the mandate. To this end, Chapter 1 reviewed special education law in the US though a policy analysis of IDEA, its accompanying regulations, and the case law that has defined, especially, education in the LRE; from this, we drew conclusions about the art class as a unique, inclusive setting for learners of all abilities.

In Chapter 2, we considered the potential of the art class for empowering all learners experiencing a range of (dis)abilities. Through our investigation of the concept of empowerment through difference, the value of diversity, and the stereotypes that are often advanced through our visual culture, we suggested and reflected upon upon approaches for reclaiming what (dis)ability means.

Chapter 3 examined the various stakeholders involved with the inclusive art class, including the art teacher, special educator, paraeducator, parents, and students of all (dis)abilities. We reviewed the role of each stakeholder in enacting the Individuals with Disabilities Education Act (IDEA) for empowering all students—including those experiencing different-abilities—to actively participate in their own art education in collaboration with others.

The second section of this book, "Human Empowerment Through the Arts (HEARTS): A Model for an Inclusive Art Class," shares one example of how the concepts in Part I might be put into effect; Part II represents the practice of the theory. Our HEARTS model is based upon the communitarian approach to inclusion that we see as reflected in the federal mandate and that we have explored in Part I. The second half of the book provides a foundational approach that demonstrates research-based strategies for teaching in the inclusive art class envisioned by IDEA.

Part II:

HUMAN EMPOWERMENT THROUGH THE ARTS (HEARTS):

A Model for an Inclusive Art Class

Chapter 4

STRATEGIES FOR INCLUSION:
Preservice Art Teacher Preparation With the HEARTS Model

While federal mandates call for inclusive classrooms, until preservice programs prepare future art teachers with the knowledge and experience they need to develop such classrooms, change will be either slow or turbulent in the art classroom. This chapter begins by making a case for preservice art teacher experiences with students experiencing (dis)abilities taught alongside students with typical-abilities. We provide a framework for the preservice art education course and the HEARTS program that may serve as a model for designing experience-based courses in art teacher education programs. We also provide additional strategies for inclusion, especially of students experiencing moderate to severe (dis)abilities.

Making the Case for Experiences With Difference in Art Education Preparation

Many educators (Allison, 2008; Carrigan, 1994; Dickens-Smith, 1995; Eraclides, 2000; Erickson, 2004; Forlin, 2010; Loesl, 1999; Schiller, 1999) emphasize the importance of teacher attitude and preparation in successful inclusion in the (art) classroom. For an art teacher to effectively involve a group of learners of varying (dis)abilities in learning about art, he or she must develop a comfort level with his or her role within the LRE. The art educator must also be aware of available supports for instruction within this environment, such as assistive technologies, paraeducators, the individualized education program (IEP) for a given student, in-service training for working with students experiencing disabilities, and the potential collaborative roles of other educators and support staff (e.g., special educator, counselor, occupational/physical/speech therapists, and school diagnosticians).[1] To this end, it

is critical for preservice art educators to learn how to develop and have opportunity to practice strategies for teaching learners with special needs. Early introduction of these strategies may occur at the preservice level, but often teacher education programs (especially secondary programs in a content area) provide only an overview of issues associated with teaching students experiencing (dis)abilties. Rarely do preservice art educators have the opportunity to implement various teaching strategies with learners experiencing moderate to severe disabilities in an inclusive art class setting.

Preservice experiences in working with differently-abled populations affect teacher attitudes toward integrative approaches to education (Allison, 2008; Carrigan, 1994; Cates, McGill, Brian, Wilder, & Andrees, 1990; Dickens-Smith, 1995; Forlin, 2010; Keifer-Boyd & Kraft, 2003). Christine Forlin (1997) conducted a study of preservice teacher education courses in Australia and South Africa that were designed to educate future teachers in working with students with (dis)abilities. The focus of the six-university study was teacher attitudes toward working with students experiencing a wide range of different-abilities. Forlin measured respondents' motivations, reactions, (dis)comfort levels, and (negative) attitudes in working and socially interacting with individuals experiencing different-abilities and noted a causal effect between frequency of associations with those experiencing different-abilities and decreases in discomfort levels. Her study indicated "preservice teachers who had more frequent contact with people with disabilities attributed significantly less discomfort during interactions with them than did those who experienced little contact" (Forlin, 1997, p. 14). Based on these findings, Forlin recommended that preservice teacher education courses in special education be designed to "include direct contact on a regular basis with people with

---

[1] See Chapter 3 for a full discussion of some of these stakeholders' roles in the inclusive art class.

disabilities" (p. 14).[2] Doris Guay (2006a) cites increased demands on art educators in instructing students with "extremely diverse abilities," including severe and multiple disabilities, as schools move increasingly toward full inclusion (p. 8). These increased responsibilities may prove stressful if that art educator has not learned and practiced strategies for inclusion of difference.

Art educators' discomfort in working with students experiencing severe (dis)abilities may stem from a fear that such strategies and modifications may be too extensive. To help alleviate these apprehensions, a preservice program for art educators should include (a) procedures for addressing the needs of more low-incidence populations of students and those experiencing severe or multiple different-abilities; (b) opportunities to interact with students with a variety of needs; and (c) experiences that include collaboration and shared responsibility between stakeholders involved in the education of students with special needs.[3] The HEARTS model[4] that we present in this chapter is based upon these characteristics. With the preparation that such a preservice experience provides, we may have fewer art educators saying, "'Those students will never be able to do more than scribble and be disruptive. The best thing you can do for me is to get them out of my building and we won't have to deal with this at all!'" (Cited in Loesl, 1999, p. 56). There are many examples of art curricula that can incorporate students of all abilities, including that of Lisette Ewing (2000) who successfully designed an art curriculum to meet the needs of nonvisual learners within the regular high school art classroom by considering such factors as materials, environment, experimentation, use of language and critique, and tactilely oriented exhibition.

---

[2] Forlin's results are echoed by others' studies (see Allison, 2008; Keifer-Boyd & Kraft, 2003; Wexler, 2010). Similarly, Carrigan (1994) found that when her art students engaged in prolonged interaction with individuals experiencing moderate to severe mental retardation in an art studio setting, it enabled them to see these individuals as people, with interests, likes, and dislikes—in other words, to develop a relationship. This resulted in an increased level of comfort, decreased anxiety, and (in some cases) a change in attitude among the art students regarding people experiencing severe (dis)abilities. Such examples demonstrate that practicum experiences that enable preservice art teachers to interact with people experiencing severe (dis)abilities might lessen future resistance to working with these individuals in the art class.

[3] The importance of encouraging collaboration between content area educators and special educators, which Ripley (1997) also maintains should be a component of teacher preparation programs, is cited by many art educators (see Cates et al., 1990; Gerber & Guay, 2006; Keifer-Boyd & Smith-Shank, 2006) and is part of the vision of IDEA (Bartlett & McLeod, 1998; IDEA, 2004).

[4] The model that we expand upon here was originally presented in Keifer-Boyd, K., & Kraft, L. M. (2003). Inclusion policy in practice. *Art Education, 56*(6), 46–53.

HEARTS: A Model for Inclusive Art Education

Our belief is that the best way to remove biases and prejudices is through positive working experiences with people with differences. To this end, we designed a course for preservice art educators that included strategies (such as collaboration, modifications, and communication among stakeholders) and built-in opportunities to teach students experiencing moderate to severe different-abilities alongside peers of typical-abilities while adhering to the National Standards for Visual Arts. We present this as one model to help curriculum planners in higher education and school districts to implement change toward inclusive classrooms.

In addition, many states in the US are changing teacher certification requirements (including art teacher certification).[5] The emphasis in the changes in teacher certification will require more teacher preparation concerning diversity (special needs, culture, sexual identities, non-English speakers) and new technologies for communication and learning. The HEARTS model provides an example of how to meet these new teacher certificate accreditation requirements.

The Preservice Art Education Course

Because we wanted students enrolled in our preservice art education programs to benefit from hands-on opportunities to work with learners with a range of abilities in an art classroom setting, the HEARTS program was the nucleus of our team-taught course.

In the HEARTS program, our preservice students act as art teachers and facilitators for students experiencing a variety of abilities, from typically-abled high-school-aged students to students of the same chronological age and older who experienced moderate to severe different abilities. Since most preservice teacher education programs offer field experiences in working with students experiencing mild disabilities, we narrowed our focus to those experiencing moderate to severe (dis)abilities—populations with which preservice art educators may have less experience and, therefore, regard with greater apprehension. Those who did experience these (dis)abilities represented a wide range of special needs, such as cognitive challenges or limitations in mobility, speech, and vision. Some required quiet spaces in which to work, while others needed to move. It was up to our student teachers to be aware of and attend to these varying needs in the art class.

---

[5] See for example the passing of Chapter 49-2 by the Pennsylvania State Board of Education on May 17, 2007, for implementation by January 2011, which requires all new teachers to complete 9 credits of coursework and have 270 hours of experience in adaptations and accommodations for diverse learners.

Approximately one-third of the three-credit course was devoted to the HEARTS practicum, during which our students taught lessons in clay, time-based media, painting, and mosaics and mounted an interactive exhibition of participants' artworks from the HEARTS sessions. The remaining two-thirds of the course was classroom work that laid the groundwork for working in the inclusive art classroom and provided opportunity for debriefing, collaborating, and planning for upcoming HEARTS classes.

Content for and Format of the Class

Our three-credit course met during the summer, for 3 hours per day for 3 weeks. This large block of meeting time proved particularly beneficial once the HEARTS program began as it allowed adequate time for both transport and the art class itself. Students needed to make a 3-week commitment to focus on this course. In addition to the 45 contact hours in the university course, the preservice teachers needed an additional 45 hours outside of class time to read, study, write reflections, write lesson plans, and prepare for teaching. (See Figure 4.1 for the class content and format.)

Class content included instruction on special education law and inclusion (including case law), concepts and strategies related to empowering students through their differences and addressing these differences through multimodal teaching practices, and examination of policy and procedure issues and video case studies as they related to students experiencing disabilities.[6] Below, we outline the topics we studied during the first week of the class in preparation for the implementation of HEARTS.

To begin, we familiarized students with special education law—its history, the "philosophy of independent living" behind it (see "Self-Advocacy Strategies" later in this chapter for this concept, found in IDEA regulations, 2006), the concepts of least restrictive environment (LRE) and free appropriate public education (FAPE) within the law, and the philosophy of inclusion that has arisen from LRE interpretations. We also examined the various stakeholders affected by the inclusive art class environment (e.g., art students experiencing different-abilities, their parents, the art teacher, the art students experiencing typical-abilities, the special educator, the para-educator) and their concerns. With this foundation laid, we finally considered the art class as an inclusive environment, including art's ability to maximize individual differences as a strategy for empowerment.[7]

We then focused upon specific special educational designations—such as visual impairments, autism, hearing loss,

cognitive (dis)abilities, and physical (dis)abilities—and considerations for each of these within the art class. We also examined issues related to policies and procedures in meeting the needs of students experiencing different-abilities within the LRE. We examined how the special education mandate makes its way from the federal level to the classroom level through federal regulations, individual state plans, and local school districts. We invited a special education administrator from a local school district central office to share with us aspects of inclusion of students experiencing (dis)abilities into general class settings from a school district and administrative point of view. She also shared how IEPs are developed and how art teachers can involve themselves in IEP goal setting and strategic planning, seek support for implementation, and collaborate with the stakeholders involved in each IEP.

Before developing the HEARTS curriculum, preservice art educators learned about adaptive technologies for artmaking for differently-abled populations. We investigated special education law as it addresses assistive technologies, and the notion of individuation of modifications for students experiencing (dis)abilities (which, in the case of adaptive technologies, may involve a great deal of trial and error as workable assistive technology solutions are sought for a student's specific needs).[8]

Together, we used the foundational material that the preservice teachers had learned all week to develop the HEARTS curriculum. This included: (a) development of the HEARTS mission statement, (b) development of meaningful goals and objectives for learning that were aligned with the National Standards for Visual Arts, and (c) development of specific lesson plans in clay for the first day of HEARTS that was to follow. Because we knew ahead of time which students who would be attending HEARTS,[9] we were able to anticipate to some extent, as part of this planning, the types of modifications and space concerns that the preservice teachers would need to implement for successful work in clay. This attention to modifications, we told students, would be an ongoing process as we mixed the classes and teachers from session to session. They would be constantly collaborating

---

[6] See Chapters 1–3 for more information on these areas.

[7] See Chapter 2.

[8] See Chapter 2 for resources and technologies for inclusion.

[9] We solicited students through various personal contacts, such as friends, neighborhood group homes, a local center for independent living, and so forth. While it was initially our intent to limit the number and age-range of HEARTS participants, we found that positive response was so great (and we wanted to be inclusive rather than exclusive) that we just couldn't say no. For that reason, we had participants ranging in age from 14 to the upper 60s (cognitive levels varied widely, as well). These larger-than-expected numbers of HEARTS participants, along with the size of our art education class, necessitated two to three separate HEARTS classes for each session, each working in the same media but with some variations in the lessons.

Figure 4.1. The Human Empowerment Through the ARTS (HEARTS) Course Content and Format.

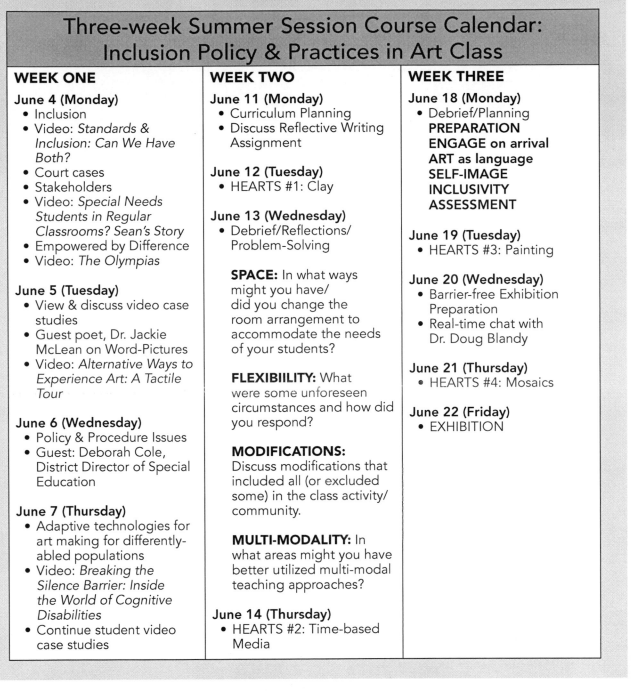

Three-week Summer Session Course Calendar: Inclusion Policy & Practices in Art Class

WEEK ONE

June 4 (Monday)
- Inclusion
- Video: *Standards & Inclusion: Can We Have Both?*
- Court cases
- Stakeholders
- Video: *Special Needs Students in Regular Classrooms? Sean's Story*
- Empowered by Difference
- Video: *The Olympias*

June 5 (Tuesday)
- View & discuss video case studies
- Guest poet, Dr. Jackie McLean on Word-Pictures
- Video: *Alternative Ways to Experience Art: A Tactile Tour*

June 6 (Wednesday)
- Policy & Procedure Issues
- Guest: Deborah Cole, District Director of Special Education

June 7 (Thursday)
- Adaptive technologies for art making for differently-abled populations
- Video: *Breaking the Silence Barrier: Inside the World of Cognitive Disabilities*
- Continue student video case studies

WEEK TWO

June 11 (Monday)
- Curriculum Planning
- Discuss Reflective Writing Assignment

June 12 (Tuesday)
- HEARTS #1: Clay

June 13 (Wednesday)
- Debrief/Reflections/Problem-Solving

SPACE: In what ways might you have/did you change the room arrangement to accommodate the needs of your students?

FLEXIBIILITY: What were some unforeseen circumstances and how did you respond?

MODIFICATIONS: Discuss modifications that included all (or excluded some) in the class activity/community.

MULTI-MODALITY: In what areas might you have better utilized multi-modal teaching approaches?

June 14 (Thursday)
- HEARTS #2: Time-based Media

WEEK THREE

June 18 (Monday)
- Debrief/Planning
PREPARATION
ENGAGE on arrival
ART as language
SELF-IMAGE
INCLUSIVITY
ASSESSMENT

June 19 (Tuesday)
- HEARTS #3: Painting

June 20 (Wednesday)
- Barrier-free Exhibition Preparation
- Real-time chat with Dr. Doug Blandy

June 21 (Thursday)
- HEARTS #4: Mosaics

June 22 (Friday)
- EXHIBITION

and assessing as they learned from HEARTS participants and each other's teaching experiences with them. For that reason, we introduced reflective written assignments following each HEARTS session; using this assessment, we would continually consider what seemed to work well for a class dynamic and for an individual student's needs in the art class setting.[10]

Students in the Class

Because the purpose of our course is to prepare art educators to work with students with a variety of (dis)abilities in the art class through practicum-like experiences, the course is designed with preservice art specialists in mind. However, we believe that any preservice educator who will be working with students with a variety of special needs may benefit from the opportunities to work in a hands-on setting with both

---

[10]   See Chapter 5 for assessment strategies.

students possessing typical-abilities and those experiencing moderate to severe (dis)abilities. In our course, we had both graduate and undergraduate students, both art education majors and elementary generalist education majors who took the course as their fine arts credit.[11] All students were responsible for acting as a lead teacher for one HEARTS session;[12] the other preservice educators would help as instructional support on the days when they were not lead teachers. Our teacher-student ratio for the program varied from 1:4 to 1:16, depending upon the lesson for the day. We balanced HEARTS classes so that each preservice teacher could work simultaneously with students who were typically-abled and differently-abled in every grouping; we also wanted our preservice educators—whether in the capacity of lead teacher or instructional support for the day—to experience working with every special educational difference represented by HEARTS participants.

In searching for HEARTS participants, we sought a balance of gender and of typical-abilities with those experiencing different-abilities. Those invited to participate in HEARTS expressed an interest in art, but most had not taken art classes in grades 9–12 and did not necessarily feel confident in their art skills. (Dis)abilities experienced by HEARTS participants varied; some of these included cerebral palsy, moderate to severe cognitive (dis)abilities, visual (dis)abilities, autism, severe motor (dis)abilities, and different-abilities in hearing.

Planning HEARTS Curriculum

HEARTS mission, program goals, and objectives

Drawing on the readings, lectures, visiting speakers, and video case studies of the first week of the course, the preservice art educators developed the mission statement for HEARTS, along with program goals and objectives (see Figure 4.2).

We felt it important to emphasize goals that provided direction and structure but that were flexible, allowing student teachers' assessments to identify HEARTS participants' "strengths, interests, and expressive modes… [and] students' strong or adequate skill areas and preferred learning" (Guay, 1999, p. 22).[13]

Space considerations

The nature of our studio activities, as well as the nature of HEARTS participants' (dis)abilities, necessitated the consideration of a variety of issues regarding the handling and flexibility of classroom space. For instance, one day a student

---

[11] One elementary generalist major was so moved by her experience with the course and with HEARTS that she changed her major to special education and is now working with elementary students with special needs in the public school.

[12] Time constraints often necessitated two lead teachers for one art class; these individuals would work collaboratively to develop that day's lesson plan and were both tasked with presentation of the lesson to the HEARTS class. In these cases, they acted as team teachers with equal responsibilities for that day's class.

[13] See Guay (1999) pages 22, 23, and 26 for strategies for specific (dis)abilities.

Figure 4.2. Mission and Goals of HEARTS.

Mission Statement: To create a reciprocal learning and nurturing environment accessible to everyone involved using art as a vehicle for a creative and expressive journey of self and others.

Goals:

- To promote positive self-image, self-confidence, and self-expression.

- To encourage a diverse social environment and collaborative interaction in the studio experience.

- To stimulate individual creativity and interest in the visual arts.

- To establish an awareness of each individual's strengths and how everyone can benefit from each other's strengths while enhancing social behavior.

- To increase decision-making skills, cognitive skills, and visual and auditory skills.

- To increase knowledge using technology as a resource for creating art.

- To communicate in clay, painting, video, computer, and mosaic while learning about the materials, tools, technique, and vocabulary of each media.

- To have an informed familiarity with exemplary works of art from a variety of cultures and historical periods.

teacher might be working with paint with a student experiencing visual impairment who required space to spread out and organize materials by touch rather than sight. Another day, that preservice teacher might be working with technology with a student experiencing cerebral palsy that resulted in limitations in controlled movements and necessitated room and certain height specifications to accommodate a wheelchair. For this reason, we professors constantly prompted the preservice educators to assess space concerns as we planned together for individual lessons and classes, collaborating to share observations from previous class experiences.

Flexibility

Together, we and the preservice art educators engaged in what Dewey (1938) refers to as *flexible purposing*, which Taylor, Carpenter, Ballengee Morris, and Sessions (2006) describe as "the value of recognizing new and emergent possibilities for learning and knowing [that are] intrinsic to art education" (p. 129). The need for flexible planning as an ongoing process proved valuable in issues related to art media, space, teaching methods, transport of participants to and from HEARTS, time, exhibition of participants' works, grouping of students for classes, and special educational modifications. HEARTS preservice teachers—through trial and error, debriefing, and reflective writing—developed their awareness of art class flexibility, and identification of emergent possibilities, in meeting a variety of student needs.

Educational modifications

Since 1997, IDEA has provided for the addition of a general educator to the IEP team for the student included in the general class as a LRE, an indication of the strong presumption of inclusion within the law. The involvement of the art teacher in the IEP development process is invaluable because the art class works with materials and functions differently than, say, the English class. The role of the art teacher in aiding the development of the IEP, then, is to consider the student's inclusive role in the art class in regard to such factors as appropriate behavioral interventions, program modifications, and appropriate supplemental aids and services to facilitate learning. The educational modifications to the art curriculum that arise from the IEP process may be necessary to meet the student's physical or cognitive needs. Such modifications are individuated and dictated by what is the appropriate and most effective course of action for the student's unique needs. A teacher's unwillingness to implement modifications or make accommodations for learners with special needs in the art class may have serious ramifications for both the school and the district (Bartlett & McLeod, 1998). All modifications should include the use of age-appropriate materials, expectations, and language (Martin, Jorgensen, & Klein, 1998).

In HEARTS, our debriefing sessions functioned on some level as the IEP team process, in that we shared observations on students' (dis)abilities, our upcoming lessons, and what modifications might be necessary for each student to succeed. In these cases, the informal input of parents and special educators who worked with HEARTS participants proved invaluable and—along with our own observations, our knowledge of art content, and the National Standards for Visual Arts—shaped our implementation of educational modifications in the HEARTS program. Such modifications ranged in nature from rearranging the classroom space according to our students and the given project, presenting information in a variety of formats with attention to multimodal approaches, and using assistive technologies and interventions that enabled students to be as participatory as possible in their artmaking and learning. Specifics on some of these modifications are demonstrated below in the discussion of daily art lessons in HEARTS.

Daily Lessons in HEARTS

The daily lessons in HEARTS included creation of artworks in the media of clay, technological/time-based media, paint, and mosaic (see Figure 4.3). Because of our focus on the communitarian perspective and the art class as an interactive, participatory community, we designed the lessons to address aspects of our selves and others within the concept of community. Lessons were likewise designed to facilitate—even necessitate—interaction among the typically-abled and differently-abled students in HEARTS.

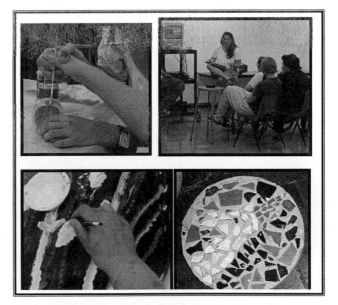

Figure 4.3. HEARTS projects of clay, time-based media, painting, and mosaics.

Clay

The objective for the clay session, titled Molding Relationships, was for students to use hand-building methods to create an object symbolic of their partner's favorite interests. We partnered students experiencing different-abilities with students of typical-abilities, and these pairs interviewed one another to learn about each other's interests and experiences. Each student then, using hand-building techniques, made a clay piece that symbolically represented his or her partner, using information gleaned from the interview.

In planning the clay session, we followed Thunder-McGuire's (1999) advice: "Perhaps the most important contribution an art teacher makes in the special education situation is identifying an individual's idiosyncratic mode of inquiry and interpretative strategies for configuring meaning" (p. 102). For instance, one of the HEARTS participants—Mark[14]—experienced cognitive development comparable to that of a 3-year-old, but, by contrast, had 17 years of life experiences. The preservice art educators found, through reflective observation, that Mark communicated best through action, rather than words, so we partnered to devise ways to engage him in the art class through responsive actions for all aspects of the art lesson. For example, Mark felt empowered to hold the kiln "on" button while Sam inserted the cone between the prongs in the kiln. Similarly, another HEARTS student, Carl, who perceived through hearing and touch (he possessed only slight movement in his fingers and no speech or vision), explored the tiny cone that would control the temperature of the kiln. Each participant had a role in learning about and/or loading the kiln for firing. In this way, all were included in the process of firing the kiln.[15]

Time-based media

Our technology art lessons were titled Get Connected: Cyber Creations; here, our preservice teachers developed three different art lessons involving video and/or computer technologies. For instance, two classes created projects using photo-editing software: one class created still-life drawings of objects that they themselves selected from home as meaningful to them. They next scanned their drawings into the editing software and used various filters and effects to alter the originals. For the other photo-editing lesson, preservice teachers photographed HEARTS participants with a digital camera as participants posed with selected props.[16] Using the editing software, students manipulated their downloaded photographs to create personal visual statements about self. Meanwhile, the third class viewed examples of video art before filming and editing a collaboratively created video that depicted group members' perceptions of self.

Computers are commonplace in high schools of the 21st century, and their integration into the art curricula is expected at the secondary level. We stress in our preservice programs the need to integrate digital technologies in art education and provide preservice teachers with experiences and rationales that will help them secure access in future employment for meaningful contemporary art education. Ironically, HEARTS participants experienced more success with video and computer media than with clay and paint as media, but most of the preservice teachers were less prepared to *teach* digital media, even though they were familiar with the software programs. We recognized, then, that our preservice programs need to provide opportunities for preservice teachers to teach digital/four-dimensional media (e.g., time-based video, animation, or *machinima*)[17] with guided planning and preparation for flexibility to acquire the comfort level with this media that they have in teaching artmaking in two and three dimensions with familiar art materials, such as paint and clay.

Painting

For our painting day, Painting: Painted Feelings, two classes painted on donated cafeteria trays that preservice teachers prepared by spray painting black.[18] For this lesson, students translated selected animal characteristics into form-line abstractions. They could feel the edges of the composition and, with the thick, fast-drying acrylic paint, could physically feel the painting. For one student, who experienced visual impairment, we created a stencil of her chosen animal, the peacock, so she could create her painting to the greatest extent possible on her own. Through touch, she guided the peacock stencil around her tray, filling in with a tactile mixture of paint and glitter. One preservice teacher noted: "I really think that our

---

[14] HEARTS participants' names have been changed to protect their privacy.

[15] At times such as this, and depending upon the nature of a student's (dis)ability, we employed the *principle of partial participation*, which holds that, in spite of the severity of a student's different-ability, he or she is able—perhaps with certain adaptations—to participate in a variety of activities on *some* level; and to this extent the student *should* participate (Sheldon, 1996; see also Blandy, Pancsofar, & Mockensturm, 1988; Guay,1999).

[16] We brought a series of props that expressed individual student interests from information that we gleaned from their interviews for the earlier clay project.

[17] *Machinima* is a new form of artmaking that involves constructions of cultural narratives. The term is derived from combining two words and concepts: machine + cinema, and refers to movies filmed in a simulated virtual world.

[18] We found this to be a good choice for a picture plane because it was durable, had a unique texture for students experiencing visual impairment, and—because each tray was framed with a lip—provided our students experiencing orthopedic disabilities more ease in keeping the paint on the picture plane.

strategies worked and that Miriam had some fun with her independence. Miriam had to have help with getting the colors that she had selected. She was very sure about her colors, and it was really fun to watch her paint" (J. Centofanti, personal communication, June 20, 2001).

We found the stencil modification to work as well for another student experiencing cerebral palsy, which inhibited controlled movements of her hands and arms. Using the stencil, however, she, too, was able to create her own paintings of dolphins. This simple modification to the painting lesson enabled both students (who experienced different-abilities from one another) to be engaged in their own artmaking in as participatory a manner as possible.

In the third painting group, HEARTS participants traced each other's silhouettes, posing before an opaque projector, onto a paper stencil. They used these stencils to arrange their drawings onto a large satin banner that was donated to the program. They then filled their own shapes with symbols (painted with acrylics on fabric)—abstractions of self-identified characteristics—engaging in creative choice making as they created their collaborative composition. One preservice teacher described the project this way:

> Students discussed their painting while working on practice pieces. They talked among themselves and with the teachers about what they were painting and about their decisions (colors, lines, etc.). Claire talked about her choices for colors for the letters in her name, Samantha talked about her yellow rose and whether she should give it more detail, Terri discussed whether she should place another image in the middle of her composition and what it should be. All students… talked about their poses and the outlining. When the images were cut out, the students discussed where to lay the patterns and the placement; after the patterns were transferred everyone discussed the colors to be used and the kind of painting style they would [use] on the images. (D. Maske, personal communication, June 20, 2001)

The preservice teachers of this painting class shared the background of Chuck Close[19]—who lost mobility because of an infection in his spine—with the HEARTS participants. His story encouraged one HEARTS student to use her left hand, rather than her right, through which she had less fine motor control, as an adaptive approach to painting. Another student, confined to a wheelchair, was impressed that Close's canvases were so large and noted that the painting moved rather than the artist. We encouraged her to paint large since the fabric could easily be turned on the table, allowing her to reach all areas.

Mosaics

We entitled our mosaic lesson day Mosaics: Stepping Together, emphasizing students' role as participants within the community at large by creating mosaic stepping stones for a community garden. To prepare, HEARTS students engaged in role-play and a visualization strategy. The first step of the visualization consisted of focus on a specific event, followed by specific questions about the concrete nature of that experience. The preservice teacher who guided the exercise then led students to transform their visual thinking into expressive actions that prepared them to translate the action with its corresponding imagery to making art.[20] Next, we projected on the wall a large video of the garden into which the stepping stones would eventually be placed, telling students about the community members who worked in the garden and their challenge of working in muddy areas; their stepping stones, we told the students, would help these gardeners in their work. Students then stepped on the round stones, which we had placed in front of the video projection, and imagined themselves in the garden, walking on their stones. It was at this moment that Mark—who had, up to this point, communicated only through grunts and monosyllabic, simple responses—spoke passionately his first full sentence that we had heard: "I don't want to get my new shoes muddy!" We realized that this role-playing exercise had stimulated his imagination, and that he could concentrate if he saw himself in the story, developed through the visualization strategy.

After the visualization activity, students created mosaic stepping stones using tiles (donated from stores) to create images derived from what they had visualized and wanted to communicate to the local community. In making the mosaics, some HEARTS students and preservice art educators worked collaboratively. One preservice teacher helped Samantha, a student experiencing cerebral palsy, in drawing a unicorn. Having never drawn a unicorn herself, the preservice teacher had Samantha guide her through the drawing; Samantha made the creative decisions in the drawing and laid the tiles later. The preservice teacher explained,

> The unicorn's horn needed to be silver. She decided later, after we'd laid the tiles in the cement, there wasn't enough contrast with the blue background. We took the silver tiled horn out and replaced it with brown tiles. She was pleased with the results.… It was difficult [in laying the mosaic tesserae] for the piece to land in the right spot or glazed side up, but she never gave up.

---

[19] See Cajori, M. (Producer & Director). (1998). *Chuck Close: A portrait in progress* [Video]. Chicago, IL: Home Vision Arts.

[20] The visualization process is discussed in depth in the book. *Engaging Visual Culture* (Keifer-Boyd & Maitland-Gholson, 2007).

She was excellent in pushing the tiles in. (K. Hembree, personal communication, June 21, 2001)

After display at the HEARTS exhibition, we placed the stepping stones in the Maxey Community Garden, where several of the students worked as part of their school curriculum. One preservice teacher pointed to the students' established relationship with the community garden, noting, "This lesson was especially relevant to the students as they can always visit these mosaics at the garden" (V. Eggemeyer, personal communication, June 22, 2001).

The HEARTS model offers examples of inclusion strategies for working with students representing a range of (dis)abilities in the art class, which dovetail with ideas in Chapter 2 for empowering students through difference. Collaboration, co-planning, and co-teaching are other examples of inclusion strategies. In the section that follows, we provide an overview of additional research-based strategies for meeting the special educational needs of students in the inclusive art class; we also review some benefits of inclusion for all learners.

Including All Students in Art: Strategies for the Art Class as LRE

The McGill Action Planning System (MAPS) Model

Guay (1999) recommends the McGill Action Planning System (MAPS) as an inclusion strategy for students experiencing moderate to severe (dis)abilities, especially at the middle and high school levels. MAPS, which offers both social and instructional supports, involves the following steps but must only be completed if it has been approved by the student's IEP team:

1. Prior to the inclusion of the student identified as having moderate to severe (dis)abilities in the art class, the art teacher visits him or her in the special education classroom (or at his or her residence). This meeting enables the art teacher to meet and observe the student, and his or her teacher or caregiver, to learn about the student's needs, likes and dislikes, abilities, and so forth.

2. After meeting with the student, but before his or her inclusion within the art class, the art educator engages the class in discussion regarding various different-abilities. This discussion may involve the subject of perceptions and expectations regarding (dis)abilities—and even strategies such as role playing and simulations—for the purpose of recognizing similarities and differences among people. The information generated during this discussion is used to introduce the student experiencing severe different-abilities and may be valuable in describing the

student's unique needs and abilities, as well as in identifying possible peer helpers within the art class. These peer helpers later meet with the art and special educators to discuss strategies for welcoming and assisting the new student.

3. After a period of adjustment, these same stakeholders, and the student experiencing different-abilities, meet again to review and discuss assistance strategies. Here, they may reinforce successful strategies as well as identify and make changes to less successful assistance tactics. (Guay, 1999)

A transition program, such as MAPS, empowers the entire class to become involved in the inclusion process. It allows students to explore their own perceptions and attitudes regarding individuals experiencing more severe (dis)abilities, and it provides a constructive framework for attending to those perceptions within the art classroom as the LRE. MAPS also enables all learners to be active participants within the educative process and to take ownership of their own instruction within the inclusive classroom environment. Preparation strategies such as MAPS provide stakeholders a smooth and reciprocal means for transition into the inclusive process.

Ecological Perspective

Hallahan and Kauffman (1995) advocate the adoption of an *ecological perspective*, a strategy that "considers reciprocal effects of child and environment as well as the understanding that problems are not located solely in the child or the environment, but in both" (p. 64). This strategy, therefore, focuses on factors external to the student, which may be adjusted, rather than on the "defect" as residing within the student. Lewis (1993), in considering these ecological factors, offers the "ABC model" in conceptualizing the use of assistive technologies and similar strategies with students experiencing (dis)abilities. Such adaptations, he says, should Augment abilities and Bypass, or Compensate, for (dis)abilities (Lewis, 1993). This approach adheres to the ecological perspective in that it examines the learning environment to the same degree it does the (dis)ability to circumvent barriers to active participation and learning.

Zederayko and Ward (1999) reflect the use of this ABC model in the assistive technology devices that they used for Lisa and Craig, two art students experiencing different-abilities that kept them from gripping art tools, such as pencils and paint brushes. For Lisa, who could only grip for brief periods of time without tiring, the authors designed a wristband with a slot sewn on the back that could hold the pencil or brush. This enabled the student to paint and draw without having to physically grip the tools for artmaking. The same wristband did not work for Craig, however, due to the effects of his cerebral palsy. The authors noted, however, that he was able to slide his arms across his tray and did seem to have some control over the movements of his right arm. From these observations, they designed a drawing tool that consisted of an acrylic-glass base mounted on beads, which allowed the tool to be smoothly pushed back and forth once a pencil or brush was screwed into the small vise.[21] This tool maximized Craig's physical abilities and enabled him to actively participate in his artmaking (Zederayko & Ward, 1999).

Blandy (1989) adds that ecological approaches must also take into consideration the individual student's abilities and the relationship of those abilities to the student's cultural background and significant others within the student's life. He emphasizes art activity that also involves critical self-reflection with questions and tasks that are generated by the student him- or herself. Similarly, Allison (2008) points to the transformational power of personal narrative in its ability to connect people to one another in that, when we hear others' stories, we recognize our own experiences in them.

Principle of Partial Participation

Another inclusion strategy is that of partial participation (Blandy et al., 1988; Guay, 1999; Sheldon, 1996). Karten (2005) emphasizes the important role of concentrating on students' strengths rather than their weaknesses in instilling self-confidence in facilitating learning. Partial participation holds that "regardless of severity of disability, individuals can be taught to participate in a variety of activities to some degree, or activities can be adapted to allow participation" (Sheldon, 1996, p. 116). This strategy is to be used with students who cannot complete all of the steps of a given activity but are able to complete some of them (Blandy et al., 1988). Guay (1999) describes this approach as involving age-appropriate materials and activities and as allowing for assistance with steps of the task that cannot be completed by the student alone, using appropriate prompts or cues.

In Zederayko and Ward's (1999) example in the preceding section, Craig did not engage in his own artmaking until he was outfitted with his drawing tool; instead, he "permitted his aide to complete most of his art projects for him as he sat placidly watching the process" (p. 21). Once he received his drawing tool, the paraeducator's role was minimized to changing the color pen for Craig, while Craig was empowered to fully participate in the drawing process. The authors shared, "Craig felt intense personal achievement with his accomplishments and felt ownership for his drawing. He was so engrossed that he refused to give up his activity long enough

to allow his aide to switch pen colors in the drawing tool" (Zederayko & Ward, 1999, p. 21). In this way, the principle of partial participation enables and empowers the student to take part in the art activity process to the fullest extent possible and validates that student's efforts and abilities.

Task Analysis and Cue Hierarchy

Task analysis and cue hierarchy are often used in tandem as instructional approaches for students experiencing severe disabilities. According to Billingsly, Liberty, and White (1994), task analysis "refers to the process and product of identifying component behaviors" in chains of behavior (p. 82). Once chains of behavior are broken down into steps, these steps can be developed into routines that are taught to the learner until all steps in the routine (and therefore the chain) are mastered. Figure 4.4 is one example of a task analysis chart for an art student experiencing severe (dis)abilities who is included in the elementary school art class for her functional curriculum within the social/leisure domain.

Partial participation can be utilized to the extent that all steps in the chain cannot be mastered. For instance, one chain of behaviors in the art class may be having the student get his or her own paint to begin work. Individual components of this chain may include standing, walking across the room, gripping the paint container and lifting it, gripping then unscrewing the lid, and pouring or squeezing the contents onto a painter's palette. It may be that the student experiencing an orthopedic (dis)ability is able to complete all steps in the task except for the gripping and turning necessary to open the paint container. In this case, the paraeducator, art educator, or a peer may need to aid the student with this one component task while the student him- or herself completes all the other steps.

A specific prompt or cue begins each step of the task chain. That prompt should be developed from a cue hierarchy, which should also include correction procedures. Downing (2008) refers to this hierarchy as "increasing assistance," in which the educator arranges the prompts from "least informative" to "most informative" (p. 65). In this way, the cue that is used for a particular step within a task involves the least amount of intervention possible; cues with a greater amount of intervention are reserved for those steps that a learner fails to master through the lesser cues (Blandy et al., 1988; Downing, 2008). Downing (2008) suggests that it may be necessary, in order to determine which type of cue is the least invasive, to use "graduated guidance"; here, "degrees of physical assistance [are] provided from the most intrusive to least intrusive, with amount of assistance varying within a teaching instance as the student responds and if appropriate" (p. 65). Here are three examples of cue hierarchy, from least invasive to most invasive:

---

[21] Zederayko and Ward (1999) offer detailed illustrations and written instructions for how to create both the wristband and the drawing tool in their article "Art Class: What to Do When Students Can't Hold a Pencil."

Figure 4.4. Completed Task Analysis Chart for Building a Pinch Pot.

Student's Name: _Julie_   Date: _September 1, 2011_

Domain: _Social/Leisure (Art class)_   Teacher: _Ms. Brown_   Grade: _2nd_

Long-Term Goal: _To learn a variety of clay hand-building techniques_

Short-Term Objectives: _The student will correctly create a pinch pot of 2–4" in diameter using clay with 80% accuracy three out of four attempts._

Steps of Task Analysis:

1. Get up from seat.
2. Go to clay area of classroom.
3. Grasp pre-cut portion of clay.
4. Return to work table with clay and place clay on table.
5. Sit down.
6. Roll clay into ball with both hands (Julie may need help with this step).
7. Grasp clay in right hand.
8. Use left thumb and fingers to create depression and form pot.

Instructional Procedure:

Setting: Inclusive art class

Materials: Table, chair, clay table, pre-portioned (and pre-wedged) measures of clay, damp sponge

Procedures: Chain of steps will be presented to Julie concurrently. When verbally prompted to "Get clay and make a pinch pot," Julie will begin the sequence of steps to create her pot. If correct response, praise; if not respond or incorrect, response with verbal prompt "No," followed by repeat of verbal prompt combined with physical prompt. Fade prompts as task mastered.

- Spoken prompt only: The art teacher or paraeducator says, "Go get your paint, James."
- Touch prompt combined with verbal prompt: The art teacher or paraeducator lightly touches the student on the shoulder while saying, "James, go get your paint."
- Hand over hand intervention: The art teacher or paraeducator, says, "Open the paint, James," while aiding the student in opening the jar of tempera paint by placing his or her own hand over the student's and turning the lid with him.

By determining and using the least invasive cue to prompt the student to begin a task, the art educator engages the student experiencing severe different-abilities using the least restrictive stimulus possible.

Kinesthetic and Multimodal Strategies

All students, including those with different-abilities, learn through a variety of modes, including (but not limited to) kinesthetic strategies, oral and auditory means, role-play or other empathetic processes, and tactile and manipulative methods. The art class offers a variety of opportunities for multimodal and kinesthetic learning that may benefit all students.[22]

Karten (2008) points out that some students with special educational needs may be over- or under-sensitive in responding to and processing certain stimuli. For example, art educators working with students experiencing autism may find that these students have difficulty filtering through simultaneous stimuli or respond more readily to imagery rather

---

[22] As we saw in Chapter 2, the use of assistive technology devices may be effective in addressing students' multimodal ways of learning, too.

than spoken or written directives. For this reason, the art educator must consider multiple modalities in designing lessons or tasks for the art class as the LRE.

Kinesthetic and tactile strategies for multimodal learning are easily adaptable to the art class and, in many cases, are an integral part of artmaking. Examples of these include connecting learning to body movement or using a variety of textures, such as working with clay, mixing sand with paint, and drawing or writing with raised glue. By varying the art lesson or activity and addressing a range of modalities and senses, the art teacher will aid students in processing and interpreting information and in communicating with others (Karten, 2005).

Situational Supports as Teaching Strategies: The Role of Peer Instruction and Interaction

The most unobtrusive educational support strategies for students with different-abilities in the art class are *situational supports*, or those that are most obviously available to all students, regardless of (dis)ability. Such inherent educational supports may include space, pacing and time considerations, peer teaching, parent involvement, curriculum and instruction techniques, and available staff assistance (Grigal, 1998). While these supports are often considered "natural" within educational settings, they may require some (re)consideration and adjustment to maximize benefits to learners representing a wide range of (dis)abilities.

For example, instructional pacing that is flexible may benefit all learners within the inclusive art classroom. If an art activity or concept appears too abstract or complex for a student, then it can be broken down into smaller steps to allow for sequenced mastery of objectives (as in the task analysis model).

Peer tutoring can support both typically- and differently-abled students, too (Cates et al., 1990; Gelzheiser, McLane, Meyers, & Pruzek, 1997; Gerber, 2006; Grigal, 1998; Kraft, 2001; Martin, Jorgenson, & Klein, 1998). Peers can provide strong instructional reinforcement and social interaction for one another, which can facilitate active participation in the instruction process as well as enhance the social structure of the classroom community. Gelzheiser, McLane, Meyers, and Pruzek (1997) say that, frequently, it is in the general classroom setting, rather than the special education setting, that teaching strategies that foster peer interaction occur; and this tends to support the claim that inclusive environments offer more opportunity for social integration than do the more segregated special education classrooms. (See Figure 4.5.) However, Gelzheiser et al. also find that general classroom teachers are instrumental in directly teaching social competencies to all students and in fostering peer interaction between typically- and differently-abled students (1997).

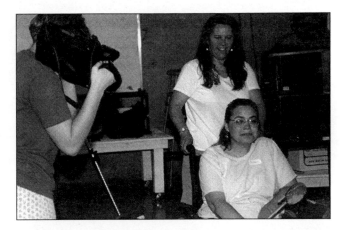

Figure 4.5. Students experiencing typical-abilities and students experiencing different-abilities work in teams on a technology-based art project in HEARTS.

Martin, Jorgensen, and Klein (1998) also discuss the importance of friends and social interaction between all students, including those experiencing (dis)abilities. They share seven conditions essential to the development of friendships for students with special needs:

(1) inclusion in all aspects of community, school, and family life;

(2) access to a method of communication at all times and classmates who understand how to utilize that method;

(3) support that is provided in such a way as to promote self-determination, independence, interdependence, and a confidence in situational supports;

(4) involvement of all students in inclusion and problem-solving processes;

(5) use of age-appropriate materials, expectations, language, and modifications;

(6) involvement of school personnel and family members in cultivating friendships and promoting social activity; and

(7) development of a campus-wide climate of acceptance and "celebration of diversity." (p. 150)

In employing these strategies, schools and classrooms aid in the process of fostering and developing friendships and understanding among all stakeholders within the inclusive classroom.

Self-Advocacy Strategies

Teaching strategies that promote self-advocacy among students, including those experiencing (dis)abilities, address the goals for independent living set forth in IDEA Regulations (2006). These goals include the following:

> Consumer control, peer support, self-help, self-determination, equal access, and individual and system advocacy, in order to maximize the leadership, empowerment, independence, and productivity of individuals with disabilities, and the integration and full inclusion of individuals with disabilities into the mainstream of American society. (IDEA Regulations, 2006, 34 C.F.R. Part 300, App. A)

Lokerson and Joynes (2006) suggest four ways that the art class environment offers opportunities for self-determination, such as:

- Providing for self-expression of personal experience (including the experience of the different-abilities) through art.
- Fostering a safe environment where students are free to discuss their weaknesses and strengths with others.
- Offering constructive criticism and feedback to students that can inform future goals in vocation, volunteerism, or other learning or community experiences.
- Promoting and encouraging independence through positive interventions that allow for and facilitate increased autonomy.

Other strategies to promote self-advocacy and self-determination include: (a) allowing the student to select which works to include in a portfolio for evaluation, (b) providing opportunities for students to make choices regarding their work in the art class, (c) encouraging students' ownership of their own learning by allowing for self-tracking of educational progress, and (d) fostering peer interactions through specific group activities in which all students in the group are assigned a specific role. In these ways, the art class that provides for self-determination and interdependence may directly foster the independent living envisioned by the special education mandate.

Benefits of Inclusion

Successful inclusion provides both academic and nonacademic benefits to students with different-abilities and peers with typically-abilities alike, and IDEA views both types of benefits as valid. For instance, in addition to the *Rachel H.* court

case,[23] the Eleventh Circuit Court of Appeals considered non-academic benefits, such as peer role models, in their decision in *Greer v. Rome City School District* (1991). The court said that, if such benefit is significant, it can be a strong indicator when determining educational placement in the LRE. Behavior modeling by peers is especially important in that it demonstrates age-typical behaviors to students experiencing (dis)abilities. It is important for students of all abilities to interact with people different than themselves; otherwise, the early segregation of students experiencing (dis)abilities from their typically-abled peers may later result in their separation as adults (Mason, 1990). A classroom climate that is integrative and fosters acceptance of difference among its members cultivates respect for such diversity later in life so that it "becomes not only an accepted, but an *expected* part" of both student and adult life (Grigal, 1998, p. 47).

Another benefit of inclusion is shared modifications, which may be extended to typically-abled students as well as those who are differently-abled. Treating students equitably lessens the distinction between students' perceived (dis)abilities, which might otherwise be emphasized in selective provision of modifications. Certainly, there are a number of modifications that are beneficial to students experiencing typical- and different-abilities alike, including: (a) increased time to complete tasks, (b) assignment of peer helpers, (c) presentation of instructions in a variety of different manners (aural, written, etc.), and (d) breaking down tasks into component steps.

Similarly, some resources provided for a student experiencing (dis)abilities in the inclusive art class might benefit the typically-abled students, as well, as we saw with the "permissive use of funds" clause of IDEA (2004) in Chapter 3.[24] Any such resources must be in keeping with the IEP of the student experiencing (dis)abilities, and these may include such high technology assistive technology devices as computer hardware and software or supplemental services, such as the provision of a paraeducator. With this latter provision of a paraeducator, both students with different- and typical-abilities alike may benefit from the increased instructional attention provided by the addition of staff to the inclusive classroom. One study (Ripley, 1997) on collaborative teaching between general and special educators demonstrated improvements in student learning that were linked to increased teacher assistance and reduced pupil-teacher ratio inherent within the collaboration model. In this case, educational services provided for students with different-abilities appear to have had the

---

[23] See Chapter 1.

[24] See also Chapter 6.

residual advantage of enhancing the learning of the inclusive classroom as a whole.

Reflections Leading to Assessment

The combination of the inclusion strategies and the opportunity for experiential preservice art education in the inclusive art class enabled HEARTS preservice teachers and participants to create a fully participatory community. Through these interactions, barriers and stereotypes associated with differences were minimized, and preservice teachers gained confidence in recognizing their students' needs and modifying lessons to accommodate these needs. One preservice educator said after the mosaic lesson, the last lesson in the program,

> I [am becoming] more confident with each student's needs. I can see where a teacher needs to get to know his or her students to be able to adequately modify so the learning process can progress. As a group effort, each teacher [in HEARTS] was able to adapt to the needs of each student. (D. Franklin, personal communication, June 22, 2001)

These observations, and the preservice teachers' abilities to identify needs and modify their lessons in answer to those needs, would not be possible were it not for the ongoing process of assessment embedded within the class. Continual meaningful and authentic assessment was at the nucleus of HEARTS and the successful art experiences of participants and preservice art educators. Chapter 5 provides detailed discussion of the role of authentic assessment in the inclusive art class and shares varied assessment strategies.

Chapter 5

INCLUSIVE ASSESSMENT IN THE INCLUSIVE ART CLASS

Assessment in schools—especially standardized testing—has historically focused on analyzing student outcomes through quantifiable measures. The model of educational efficiency that originated in the Industrial Revolution calls for such standardization when measuring student output. It is based in human capital theory that has economics at its core (Apple, 1995; Kraft, 2006; Levin & Shank, 1970; Welch, 1998). Wilson and Wright (1994) explain, "In a highly bureaucratic and tightly regulated environment all students are expected to master the same objectives, in a similar time frame, under ostensibly uniform conditions, regardless of individual interests or capacity, learning needs, personal circumstances or choice" (p. 227). Changes to this cost-benefit approach to educational efficiency have occurred through the individualized educational requirements of special education law; however, vestiges of the philosophies voiced by Wilson and Wright linger on through No Child Left Behind (NCLB) and states' individual standardized testing practices, which include students experiencing different-abilities.

The communitarian model of efficiency that we advocate and demonstrate in HEARTS offers a different paradigm of efficiency. Communitarian efficiency, or productivity, acknowledges that members of a community may offer contributions in ways that differentiate from capitalist economics of competitiveness (Keifer-Boyd & Kraft, 2003; Kraft, 2006; Turnbull, 1991). For example, when participants in the inclusive communitarian classroom are able to appreciate the diversity of *all* the members, regardless of (dis)ability, then the classroom community becomes richer and more democratic and its members more reciprocal in their investment in one another.

The art classroom has historically been at the forefront of varied and "alternative" assessment practices, such as critique, portfolios, and evaluation of process as well as product.

For this reason, art education has not fully aligned with the educational efficiency aspirations of standardized assessment. Perhaps in part because of this, the art classroom remains a fertile landscape for diverse and meaningful assessment of student learning, allowing for varied forms of data collection. Freedman (2003) points out that art responds to and is shaped by community, and its "products" are often very public, communal responses to private experiences and contextual knowledge. "The primary purpose of... student art is not therapeutic," she explains, "[but] it is social and cultural" (Freedman, 2003, p. 148).

In this chapter, we present meaningful assessment approaches that are a part of the HEARTS program and that can be used to authentically evaluate student learning in the inclusive, diverse communitarian art class. Some of these include qualitative forms of art assessment, such as exhibition and portfolio, but they also include strategies for how these assessments may meaningfully evaluate learning in the inclusive art class, regardless of a student's different-ability. At the end of this chapter, we offer special considerations for the preservice art educator, especially in collecting and sharing the assessment data with other stakeholders in the inclusive education process, such as special educators and parents.

Evaluating and Valuing Difference in the Inclusive Art Class

What constitutes meaningful assessment in the inclusive art class? Robert Sabol (2004), National Art Education Association President from 2010 to 2012, says that assessment, in its most general sense, includes identifying learning goals and purposes, then selecting the methods and procedures for evaluating student attainment of those goals. To accomplish this, teachers make decisions regarding timing, data analysis, and interpretation—and regarding their own responses to these—as part of their assessment decisions; this is done through the selection of criteria for assessment, "the standards to which performances and artifacts will be judged" (Sabol, 2004, p. 5). Beattie (1997) adds that *meaningful assessment* is multilayered and should support student learning objectives. In discussing the needs of learners experiencing different-abilities, Downing (2008) cites Snell (2002) in using the term *authentic assessment* to refer to the teacher's observation of student "performance of real-life tasks in natural contexts" (p. 276). For the assessment to be meaningful, then, it must necessarily be contextual to both the specific art program and to students' particular needs, and it is authentic when it is directed toward meaningful learning tasks (Beattie, 1997, p. 6). Because student learning in the art class does not lie solely in the evaluation of the finished studio product, art teachers often use a variety of indicators and student actions to assess learning, some which may be unrelated to art skills or to the discipline of art (Sabol, 2004). Such indicators—which may include participation, effort, and cooperation in group work—are also life skills necessary to citizenship in community for all students and may also dovetail specifically with the functional curricular needs of the student experiencing severe or multiple disabilities. In the art class environment, teachers routinely employ both process-oriented *formative assessments* alongside product-oriented *summative assessments* to "chart students' intellectual pathways" (Boughton, 2004, p. 589). These varied, meaningful assessments, in their capacity for adaptability, have the potential to provide a rich, expansive story of student learning in the communitarian art class, regardless of the student's individual (special) educational needs.

Connecting Assessment to Learning

For assessment to be meaningful, it must be tied to specific student learning objectives that are tied to life's purposes and events. Sabol (2004) points out that understanding how teachers design and develop art lessons, how they select criteria for evaluation, and how they interpret and review students' learning-outcomes data is tantamount to understanding the role of assessment in art education. Soep (2004a) shows the parallels between the functions of art and assessment in that they both, in some way, try to make evident what had before been undefined. She says, "Artworks function in a larger sense as objects that capture and convey complex meanings.... Both assessors and artists operate in worlds where tensions of translation are inevitable, in the always imperfect action of turning thoughts into things" (p. 579). Thus, artworks as assessments are complex and involve interpretation; but in this way, meaningful art that is authentically assessed mirrors the intricacies and multilayered experiences not only of human learning and knowledge but also of life and community.

When students' art learning centers on real-life experiences, issues, and concerns, this authentic approach calls for an integrated relationship between skills and concepts, as well as between products and processes (Anderson & Milbrandt, 2005; Beattie, 1997; Boughton, 2004; Downing, 2008). Anderson and Milbrandt (2005) advocate a social reconstructionist curriculum that is connected to life purposes and that includes both closed-ended and open-ended assessment methods and objectives that are activist in nature. Closed-ended objectives and assessment methods that are summative may be equated with artworks as completed projects. Open-ended student learning outcomes, however, are often more difficult to assess in that they involve considering a variety of evidences, both formally and informally, as students demonstrate the "acquisition of profound knowledge, webbing, connective understanding (thematically constructed), substantial conversation, and real-world connections" (Anderson & Milbrandt, 2005, p. 15). Both formative and summative assessments are essential in gaining a full understanding of *how* and *what* students are learning in the inclusive art class.

Summative assessment

Formal summative assessments, in which art educators evaluate a final outcome, should be transparent processes. As such, they should include explicitly stated criteria, which may be developed with students as formative assessment, to convey expectations so that students understand *how* they will be evaluated. Likewise, assessment in the inclusive art class should be linked to standards [such as the National Standards for Visual Arts Education (NAEA, 1994) and/or state-defined essential knowledge and skills for art education] so that students are evaluated by these criteria rather than through *norm referenced* methods in which students' artworks are compared to one another (Beattie, 1997).

Ashworth, Bloxham, and Pearce (2010) advocate providing choices to students experiencing (dis)abilities in how they'll present their work for summative evaluation. These authors describe a project in which students experiencing cerebral palsy in an art class were allowed to present performance aspects of their work on pre-recorded video (which allowed for editing) as opposed to live performance; they were also offered the choice of using a video journal as an alternative to a portfolio (Ashworth et al., 2010). Such options may be extended to all students in the inclusive art class, whether their specialized education requires adaptations or not; making these choices available to all students—regardless of (dis)ability—diminishes the possible stigmatization of individualized summative assessment methods.

For instance, during the mosaic project, the preservice teachers allowed HEARTS participants—who represented a range of (dis)abilities—to design their mosaics using the

Figure 5.1. HEARTS students use choice making in how to plan mosaics.

methods that best accommodated their own modes of learning and working. One HEARTS teacher described it this way,

> "For example, some students [who] were strong at revealing their design through drawing were encouraged to sketch out ideas. Others preferred outlining ideas through visual placement of the tiles on the circles of paper." (V. Eggemeyer, personal communication, June 22, 2001; see Figure 5.1)

Preservice teachers did not require all HEARTS students to complete a sketch on paper of their designs before beginning the mosaic; rather, they allowed students to "sketch" their plans through tactile placement of tiles as an alternative where preferred. This flexibility in allowing students to choose their own method of planning addressed the multimodal ways in which students generate ideas to create something meaningful.

When some of the students with different-abilities were unsure of themselves in creating a design, HEARTS teachers provided encouragement while still allowing for personal choice and creativity. HEARTS teacher Debbie Franklin said, "As [the student] placed the tiles where he wanted them, we engaged in feedback with each other. He would ask me where I thought a tile should go, and I would ask him. This helped [him] achieve his own perception and creativity" (personal communication, June 22, 2001). Through opportunity for choice making and self-determination in learning and through summative assessment procedures that are built around and adapted to collaborative and cooperative learning experiences, the art educator may facilitate the creation of and learning in the inclusive communitarian art class.

Formative assessment

Connecting summative assessment methods to formative, in-process assessments provides both the art educator and special educator a richer, more comprehensive, and more accurate picture of student learning in the inclusive art class. Process-oriented assessment may be formal or informal and can include class discussions, critiques, the teacher's own observations, and student sketchbooks or journals. Art teachers often rely as heavily on these evidences of creative thinking and problem solving that are associated with process as they do the final art project in evaluating student learning. Such formative assessments encompass

> not only the physical and cognitive processes related to manipulating media, but also the cognitive processes involved in problem identification, creative thinking, problem solving, synthesis of knowledge, evaluation, and so on. Purposes such as providing students instructional feedback, setting goals for students, and diagnosing students' strengths and weaknesses lend themselves to increased focus on the processes of making art and on the product. (Sabol, 2004, p. 7)

The formative self-assessments of preservice teachers in HEARTS often encompassed formative assessment of student learning outcomes in the program, as well. For example, in the lesson on digital art and time-based media, one preservice art educator who helped to teach a lesson using video reflected,

> I realize it would have been helpful to have utilized a different approach to get the students comfortable with the camera before taping... The one thing I had not fully anticipated was the resistance of the kids to jump into something unfamiliar to them. We did show three clips of video art, but the discussion afterwards was not as productive as it could have been. If I had... planned or had time for some interactive hands-on practice [among students] with the camera itself, that may have made everyone more comfortable. Pairing students together to discuss ideas may have proved more productive, as well. (M. Minnix, personal communication, June 18, 2001)

Another HEARTS student teacher, whose students used technology to create collages, reflected on her in-process assessment of the time-based HEARTS lesson:

> This group was very open to the idea of utilizing technology to create collages. One of the best ideas we incorporated into our lesson plan was taking pictures of individuals as they came in. This was a nice cooperative teacher effort. [Students] were greeted by one student teacher, introduced to props by another, and photographed by another. By using these portraits, the student was motivated to work with the image.

It immediately became a personal reflection. (V. Egg-emeyer, personal communication, June 15, 2001)

Through their reflective teaching journals, preservice art educators in HEARTS reveal that they were continuously engaged in formative assessment of their own inclusive teaching strategies, as well as in how students were (or were not) benefitting from these. This allowed student teachers to set the goals for student learning, to provide feedback, and to assess students' strengths and weaknesses in response to the teaching so that they could maximize participants' physical, cognitive, and affective processes in making art and interpreting visual culture.

Inclusive Assessment for Participatory Democracy

Many of the standardized assessments and educational delivery models that have resulted from Industrial Revolution-inspired educational efficiency movements ignore issues of inequality, which are rooted in differences in class, ethnicity, (dis)ability, and gender (Welch, 1998; see also Knight, 2006; Kraft, 2006). This is why Turnbull's (1991) communitarian approach is important in providing alternative methods of evaluation for students experiencing disabilities—methods that reach beyond measuring productivity in terms of cost-benefit analysis to include broader societal issues, such as personal and community responsibility and empowerment (Kraft, 2006; Welch, 1998; Wexler, 2009).

Freedman (2003) points to the communal aspects of education as among its most important principles. In teaching to foster democratic values in the art class, Keifer-Boyd and Maitland-Gholson (2007) say that students should be educated to

> act on their visual environments in ways that reflect their beliefs and values. One access point is to examine critically the larger systems that encompass their lives—belief systems, patterns of thought, representations of self—that are directly related to the pervasive influx of visual imagery that tells them what to believe, how to think, how to be. (p. 17)

The examples (such as film analysis and diversity exercises to deconstruct stereotypes of (dis)ability) that appear in Chapter 2 of this book aim to do just that in providing for the self-advocacy and contribution of all individuals envisioned by IDEA. Critical inquiry activities encourage students to question the connotations and subtexts of imagery to reveal hidden discrimination. The same application of critical inquiry to assessment practices likewise *exposes* similar discrimination that links student underachievement to individual deficiency rather than to any shortcoming in the assessment method itself (Ashworth, Bloxham, & Pearce, 2010).

The inclusive art class's role in fostering democratic values through authentic instruction and meaningful assessment is strengthened by the art educator's building of community and trust among participants (and by extending that community beyond the classroom to others who may serve as experts and resources). Art educators Carrie Nordlund, Peg Speirs, and Marilyn Stewart (2010) point to the art teacher's responsibility in cultivating a climate of respect to establish the art classroom as a safe place for all learners. This is often achieved through facilitating dialogue by providing open-ended prompts and questions or through journal assignments (Nordlund et al., 2010), the last of which may also be used as formative assessment artifacts and for summative assessment of transformative learning.

Assessing Inclusively

Beattie (1997) advocates an "assessment [that] is equal for all" (p. 7), pointing out that equity concerns the alignment of assessment methods to actual student learning, embedded discrimination within assessment tools, necessary adaptations of assessment instruments, contexts and conditions influencing assessment outcomes, and "proper interpretation of assessment scores" (p. 7). Ashworth et al. (2010) also emphasize accommodation of assessments for students experiencing (dis)abilities, as opposed to the lowering of academic standards, to allow for individual preference in demonstrating learning. In this way, the integrity of educational standards is preserved while allowing for individuated, differential learning as appropriate.

Even where students experiencing multiple or severe different-abilities in the art class are concerned, educational standards and accountability in assessing student progress—as opposed to mere placement for social experiences—is at the heart of the inclusion experience. Downing (2008) advocates linking assessment of students' acquisition of learning objectives to grade-level content area competencies; but she also points to the goals of the functional curriculum, discussed in Chapter 3 of this book, in noting that the curricular goals of students experiencing significant disabilities may not, at face value, appear linked to core academic standards. "Such skills might include making choices, self-care, gross motor development, or self-determination skills" (Downing, 2008, p. 272). However, one study shows that three-fourths of art teachers also consider factors outside stated standards for art education when evaluating student learning, including problem-solving ability, growth and improvement, effort, classroom behavior, initiative and self-motivation, use of previous learning, reflection, synthesis of ideas, and critical thinking (Sabol, 2004). Many of these holistic indicators of student learning are mirrored in the goals of the functional curriculum, too, and Downing (2008) holds that these are more authentically taught within the context of real-world environments. She adds,

> While the focus of the school day should be on academic skills and related to standards expected of all students, these supplementary skills will round out the overall program for a given student. A program that only targets basic skills of daily living is not sufficient and denies the student his or her legal right to access, participate in, and demonstrate progress in the core curriculum. (Downing, 2008, p. 273)

In this way, Downing interweaves the academic curriculum with the functional curriculum, suggesting they are interdependent.

This merging of community life skills with intellectual endeavor resides at the core of authentic instruction and assessment. Art educators Tom Anderson and Melody Milbrandt (2005) posit that the proper aim of authentic assessment is not to ascertain a grade "but to recognize art as a means to understand others and ourselves in the context of community... [This] requires students to think, feel, and become engaged with each other and the larger world, and in doing so... also serve as feedback, as assessment" (p. 15). While there is increasing tension between the "widening participation" in education and the concerns of upholding academic standards (Ashworth et al., 2010, p. 209), casting a wider assessment net may aid art educators in achieving a broader, more holistic picture of student achievement. Later in this chapter, we offer one model of a rubric for portfolio assessment that may be used to evaluate the achievement of learners experiencing a range of (dis)abilities in the art class.

HEARTS Assessment Strategies

Authentic assessment strategies in the HEARTS program included our continuous evaluation of student work and engagement, as well as of our own and our preservice teachers' instruction. Our pedagogy involved identifying and concentrating on students' strengths and aligning those with learning activities that were in keeping with the National Standards for Visual Arts. We worked to provide "opportunities for the person with the disability to be the giver, the provider of enrichment" (Clements, 1999, p. 151). In our instruction and assessment design, we and the preservice art educators sought to understand our students' perspectives of self-advocacy and self-representation in their art processes and outcomes (Keifer-Boyd & Kraft, 2003; see also Ashworth et al., 2010). Anderson and Milbrandt (2005) suggest, "A fundamental aspect of authentic assessment is the student's own reflection.

Self-reflection is a key not only to assessment but also to the individual's process of experience" (p. 35). To leave room for this "process of experience," they advocate teachers' early consideration of learning outcomes within a flexible, but purposeful, framework of instruction (Anderson & Milbrandt, 2005). Keifer-Boyd and Maitland-Gholson (2007) also point to flexibility in curriculum and assessment design, acknowledging that such design must strike a balance between the needs of the learners, the values and beliefs of the community in which the learning takes place, and the content of the discipline. The subject and instruction of art, therefore, must take into consideration the learners' experiences and (dis)abilities, along with their community context.

In HEARTS, we considered art as it reflected social issues like identity, community, and equity, allowing students to take full responsibility for their learning, with teachers' guidance, and to recognize the (personal) power associated with visual symbols and their meaning (Boughton, 2004; Duncum, 2010; Keifer-Boyd & Kraft, 2003; Keifer-Boyd & Maitland-Gholson, 2007; Smith-Shank, 2004). Through the assessment strategies of continual self-reflection, collaborative debriefing, and the HEARTS exhibition and "Find Cards" activity,[1] we engaged in formative and summative evaluations of our students', our preservice art educators', and our own learning and teaching outcomes. In this section, we briefly describe each of these meaningful assessment strategies; we investigate, too, the role of the portfolio as an assessment strategy that allows for flexibility and student self-reflection and empowerment through choice making for students experiencing a wide range of (dis)abilities.

Continual Reflection

In HEARTS, we designed opportunities for continual self-reflection for the range of stakeholders in the program: (a) the HEARTS students who represented a wide range of (dis)abilities, (b) the preservice art education students who served as HEARTS teachers, and (c) ourselves as co-professors of the course in which HEARTS was embedded. This continual self-reflection was important in allowing stakeholders to examine the multi-layered meanings of the art and of the experience of the creative process (Nordlund et al., 2010); likewise, self-understanding, which may be achieved through such reflection, is critical to the development of preservice teachers (Knight, Keifer-Boyd, & Amburgy, 2004). Anderson and Milbrandt (2005) also explain the importance of continuous self-reflection and self-evaluation:

---

[1] See Chapter 6 for a discussion of Find Cards and for examples see Figure 6.2, and http://cyberhouse.arted.psu.edu/322/resources/sl/slmachinima.html

Self-evaluation is empowering: it helps students to become self-regulated learners. Self-reflection, similarly, provides motivation and transformational learning in an environment where personal interests, values, and goals are respected and accommodated. (Anderson & Milbrandt, 2005, p. 36)

As partners in the art education process, all HEARTS stakeholders engaged in self-reflection to assess their own learning and to explore the role of self in relation to one another and the class community at large.

Reflection with HEARTS preservice teachers

One primary aim of HEARTS was full inclusion in the art class as a fully participatory community. Consequently, it was necessary that we (Michelle and Karen) facilitate, and model for our preservice art educators ways to design curriculum and assessment strategies that recognized individual difference and allowed all HEARTS students to "practice negotiation within groups" (Nordlund et al., 2010, p. 40; see also Keifer-Boyd & Kraft, 2003). We did this by allowing for choice-making and challenging assumptions, as Nordlund et al. (2010) advocate and as we posit in Chapter 2 of this book.

Throughout the HEARTS program, we asked the preservice educators to engage in written reflection. We provided specific prompts through which they considered the strengths and weaknesses of their own teaching performance, what they as teachers would have done differently in working with a particular group of students in a particular lesson, and what occurrences within a given HEARTS session might have generated insights or questions. We customized these prompts based upon our own observations of specific HEARTS classes/activities/student outcomes, asking our students how they as teachers,

- Allowed for students' multimodal/multisensory ways of learning within the lesson
- Considered space within the classroom for the activity
- Planned and prepared their lesson for their particular students' needs
- Used media and adaptive technologies
- Assessed their students' needs and interests and learning outcomes

We also asked them to reflect upon how their teaching met the mission and goals of HEARTS and state and national standards for art education. Figure 5.2 provides an example of one set of prompt questions for a written self-reflection—those that we provided after our first HEARTS session, a clay lesson.

Other tools that preservice and practicing art educators might use for self-reflection and self-assessment include peer observation, videotaping teaching and student learning, and journals, diaries, and logs (Beattie, 1997; Freedman, 2003). Insights gleaned from analyzing these forms of collected data can help create a fuller picture of the role of teacher instruction, equity of student learning, and full participation in the inclusive art class community.

Reflection among HEARTS participants

Opportunities for self-reflection and for students to explore identity were embedded within many of the HEARTS lessons and provided one source of assessment. While Soep (2004b) warns against the pitfalls of self-assessment alone (in that some students may self-assess their own work over-negatively and, therefore, remove themselves from artmaking

---

Figure 5.2. Questions for HEARTS Debriefing of Clay Lesson.

Reflective Debrief Questions

SPACE: In what ways might you have/did you change the room arrangement to accommodate the needs of your students? How might the arrangement need to vary for future HEARTS sessions?

FLEXIBILITY: What were some unforeseen circumstances, and how did you respond? What preparation would have helped?

MODIFICATIONS: What modifications did you make to meet certain students' needs in your clay class? Discuss any instances in which, while modifications might even have been made, certain students might not have been included in the class activity/community.

MULTIMODALITY: In what ways did you present information in a variety of ways to meet the needs of all of your students? In what areas might you have better utilized multimodal teaching approaches?

Note: This figure originally appeared in Keifer-Boyd, K., & Kraft, L. M. (2003). Inclusion policy in practice. *Art Education,* 56(6), 46–53.

altogether), Thunder-McGuire (1999) points to the importance of the teacher's role in "identifying an individual's idiosyncratic mode of inquiry and interpretative strategies for configuring meaning" (p. 102). This emphasis on the student's own "interpretive strategies" for making meaning suggests that the student must be empowered to continually self-assess in creating artwork and in interpreting the meaning within the process and final outcome of that creation. Practicing assessment of one's work develops valuable skills that change extrinsic motivation to intrinsic motivation for lifelong development of capabilities; such proficiency in self-assessment also fosters responsibility regarding the work one does and produces.

One example of preservice educators identifying a student's multimodal ways of learning in HEARTS was with Sam, a student who had difficulty verbalizing about new, unfamiliar situations. Once his HEARTS instructors knew of Sam's interests, they could use this context to prompt him to self-assess his art as he worked. For instance, one teacher asked Sam, as she saw him working on his clay sculpture, if he thought that ghosts were scary or nice. "Scary," Sam responded, and he then worked further to incorporate these qualities into his piece (Keifer-Boyd & Kraft, 2003, p. 51). Once the HEARTS teacher helped Sam identify the characteristics that he wanted in his artwork, he was able to assess the expressive qualities of his piece and to modify his work accordingly. Soep (2004b) agrees that such self-reflection and formative, in-process self-assessment is important as a method of "perceiving, interpreting, judging, and transforming one's own projects" (p. 667).

Similarly, the content-based art critique process that internationally renowned artist Judy Chicago applies to her own art practice, and developed into her teaching method, asks regarding the work *during* the creative process,

1. What is your goal with this piece?
2. Start by telling me what you want to express.
3. Let's talk about ways you could do this.
4. How will the viewer understand it?[2] (Keifer-Boyd, 2007)

Collaborative Debriefing

As a form of teacher self-assessment and of planning for effective student assessment, collaborative debriefing is a cooperative equivalent of self-reflection, a way for stakeholders to work in partnership to meet the educative needs of students in the inclusive art class. In HEARTS, we instituted collaborative debriefing among the preservice teachers. It was our hope that this form of group assessment would later carry over into

these student teachers' art classrooms as a technique of working with special educators, parents, and paraeducators in planning for, teaching, and assessing students experiencing different-abilities. Likewise, as our focus was building a fully participatory classroom community, we designed learning activities for HEARTS students that facilitated communication and collaboration among students. Anderson and Milbrandt (2005) say,

> Collaboration may be one of the most effective tools in this difficult process of understanding, constructing, and restructuring community... Learning is actually manifested in relations with others... The teacher's job... is to design tasks that encourage students to discover and take advantage of group heterogeneity so as to build consensus. (p. 27)

Consensus—as opposed to majority rule, or a scenario in which the most vocal, self-confident speakers are heard—is the desired outcome in the inclusive art class in that consensus allows each voice to be heard, thereby enabling difference.

Assessing collaboration among students

The role of assessment among groups of learners in the inclusive art class is twofold: (a) it may be used to empower students to engage in peer assessment with one another, giving them ownership of their own and their peers' learning and (b) it provides the art teacher another type of substantial tool for evaluation, one that assesses student learning outcomes in a setting that is collective rather than exclusive to one person. This latter may allow for observation of transfer and generalization of student knowledge from one (individual) situation to additional, alternative (group) situations. Empowering students to assess their own work through the collaborative development of rubrics, to assess one another's work, and to work cooperatively in groups, includes,

> A process of seeing and responding to the current state of someone else's work, in some cases, offering clear value judgments ('this part is great... here is where it falls apart'); and in other cases, describing or otherwise interacting with the work in a way that is less obviously evaluative, and perhaps [not] even verbalized (e.g., by copying a peer with an admired style). (Soep, 2004b, p. 668)

Collaborative work experiences emerged among HEARTS participants through carefully orchestrated cooperative activities, such as through the introductory interview and clay activity.[3] Eventually, these friend relationships took on lives of their own. One HEARTS preservice teacher commented about the HEARTS students, "Lisa [a typically-abled student]

---

2   Materials from Judy Chicago's 11 teaching projects are available at http://judychicago.arted.psu.edu. (See also Keifer-Boyd, 2003.)

---

3   See Chapter 4 for descriptions of HEARTS activities.

sat next to Meg [a student experiencing visual impairment], and I noticed that she would talk to her and interact in a very quiet way" (J. Centofanti, personal communication, June 19, 2002). In this way, teacher-facilitated interactions between students blurred the lines between (dis)abilities, and, in due time, allowed for organic friendships toward a fully participatory class community.

Collaborative debriefing among HEARTS teachers

We designed the course in which HEARTS was embedded to allow for a day between each HEARTS session for debriefing on the previous lesson and planning for the next. We used student-teachers' written reflections for springboards into discussion on what worked well, what they had noticed about the HEARTS students' individual educational needs, and what they should consider in working with particular students in the next class. Based on these collaborative observations, as we rotated students and designed new lessons with different media, we used this opportunity to plan for space considerations, adaptive technologies, and modifications for lesson delivery and artmaking and to anticipate challenges and how we might address them in the next HEARTS class. This informal, cooperative assessment became an important strategy in anticipating and serving the educational needs of students. Soon, HEARTS preservice teachers were working together to devise adaptations for painting (e.g., fashioning stencils for use by two students—one who was visually impaired and one experiencing cerebral palsy—for use in painting) and rearranging classroom furniture (e.g., allowing students in wheelchairs easy access to materials during the mosaic project). This type of group analysis and assessment for student needs allowed us to facilitate social interaction among groups of students and full participation of all learners in HEARTS (Freedman, 2003; Keifer-Boyd & Kraft, 2003).

The Exhibition as Assessment

The greatest instrument for meaningful formal, summative assessment in HEARTS was the Art From the Heart exhibition at the end of the program. Exhibition serves as an effective performance assessment strategy that allowed HEARTS stakeholders to demonstrate "individual and group goal-setting skills," including problem solving and self-reflection competencies, as well as "both personal and group abilities to glean, interpret, and synthesize information from the exhibit and judge its value" (Beattie, 1997, p. 36). Soep (2004a) points out that both assessments and artworks act as histories, or cultural products, that tell the stories of individuals and groups within a particular point in time. Through the vehicle of the Art From the Heart exhibit, HEARTS students and preservice teachers engaged in constructive critique of and self-reflection on their experiences with the program using

individualized questions on Find Cards.[4] Through the exhibit and critique experience, HEARTS participants articulated and shared their ideas pertaining to the exhibit with a diverse audience of family members and friends as a "final phase of instruction" in a "safe environment through 'spontaneity, empathy, and equality'" (James, 1996, p. 153; as quoted in Soep, 2004b, p. 679). In this way, the exhibit acted as a collaborative portfolio of participants' work in HEARTS, evidencing each individual's accomplishments and accountability to their class community (Freedman, 2003).

Portfolio Assessment in the Inclusive Art Class

While the individual art portfolio has long been a tool for authentically assessing the holistic progress of student learning over a period of time in the art class, it is considered a highly attractive alternative assessment for students experiencing special educational needs outside the art classroom setting as well (Boughton, 2004; Downing, 2008; Freedman, 2003). Although the HEARTS exhibition acted as a group portfolio of sorts, an exhibition as a strategy for assessment is not always feasible or necessary. Some of the advantages of the portfolio lie in its flexibility, its ability to serve as a living document that demonstrates the breadth and depth of student progress over time (Boughton, 2004; Downing, 2008; Freedman, 2003). Downing (2008) adds that—if done properly—portfolios are a significant tool in assessing students experiencing different-abilities in that students "do not have to conform to a set process but can demonstrate their skills, strengths, and interests in a variety of ways that tell a lot about them. Furthermore, portfolio assessments apply equally well to all students" (p. 280). To be an effective assessment strategy for students representing a wide range of (dis)abilities, the individual portfolio should:

- Include a wide range of in-progress, preparatory, and final artifacts. These should not only demonstrate studio competencies but should also reveal the "story" of the final artworks—the research, planning, and evolution of a given concept, theme, or work of art. Such items may include finished artworks, sketchbooks, research journals, reflective writings and (self-)critiques, notes, peer or teacher comments, video interviews about the art and its process, photographs documenting the artwork's creation, and other forms of documentary evidences (Beattie, 1997).

- Allow for (structured) student choice making in selecting the artwork and artifacts that will be included in the

---

[4] Chapter 6 discusses and gives examples (in Figure 6.2) of the find-card activity for engaging in critique. Such an activity is easily customized to a student's individual (dis)ability, allowing for the active participation of diverse audiences in an exhibition.

portfolio (Boughton, 2004; Downing, 2008). Downing (2008) points out that the beauty of portfolios is that they are individuated valuations of student progress and, as such, do not need to assess all students' progress in exactly the same way. In their adaptability, portfolios are equitable forms of evaluation.

- Contain the student's self-assessment of his or her work and self-reflection on his or her progress (Boughton, 2004). These, too, may be documented in a variety of ways, according to student preferences and needs; they may be written, digitally recorded or videoed, audio-recorded (e.g., recorded as podcasts), or shared in face-to-face presentations. In assessing their portfolios, students should explain and "defend" their choices of artifacts and artworks that they included.

- Include an instrument for the art teacher to document the student's decision making as demonstration of self-determination (Downing, 2008) and the student's ability to "exercise fully the skills required to perform in the complex ways demanded by the visual arts" (Boughton, 2004, p. 599). Where the student experiencing (dis)abilities is concerned, this type of documentation and data collection is especially important for the art teacher to share with the special educator as a meaningful assessment of the student's authentic learning in the art class. In this way, the art portfolio for the student experiencing different-abilities may become one component of a larger, general portfolio.

Downing (2008) offers that, in authentically assessing the learning of the student experiencing different-abilities, it is important to determine the student's type of curriculum and to begin by asking the right questions according to the goals and objectives of the student's individualized education program (IEP). If the student's different-abilities are severe, it may be that his or her academic curriculum is the functional curriculum;[5] it could also be that the student is included in the general class as a least restrictive environment (LRE) to meet both academic and nonacademic objectives. The same types of non-art-related competencies that we examined earlier as assessment points that art educators often use to evaluate student progress (e.g., participation, effort, and improvement) may also align with functional and other curricular objectives. Some of these might also parallel standards for art education (for examples, see Exhibit 5.A).

Beattie (1997) offers an assessment strategy to account for student ability variance in the art class through the use of a "sliding grading system, which considers effort, progress, and

mastery but weights each component differently depending on the level at which the student is working" to account for "issues of student differences and special abilities" (p. 112). In her model, Beattie offers the three levels of *novice* (with grading categories of effort/progress/mastery, each weighted at the percentages of 40:40:20, respectively, to achieve the final grade), *apprentice* (25:25:50), and *veteran* (10:10:80). She suggests that the art teacher, when recording grades, may note *N, A,* or *V* in the grade book to document students' levels of mastery; students would then advance to the next level once they've attained a specific grade standard in their current levels (Beattie, 1997).

Figure 5.3 is a model of a rubric for assessing art portfolios based on this idea of a sliding scale. With this rubric, the art teacher and student may work together to decide upon the weights for each category.

The portfolio competencies in the rubric in Figure 5.3, which are adapted from the National Standards for Visual Arts (NAEA, 1994), serve as the basis for assessment. For each competency, a student is evaluated on his or her effort, progress, and proficiency; each of these three categories is weighted, depending upon the student's experience in art and upon the level of adaptations or modifications necessary to accommodate special educational needs. Calculating the total of these weighted assessment scores results in the final portfolio score (in this case, a score of 84.7, or a B on a 100 percentile scale). The use of this type of adaptable assessment rubric as a tool in evaluating student work may be beneficial for use with all students in the general art class that includes a wide variance of student (dis)abilities in art.

Shared Assessment

To evaluate is to find value. Evaluating student learning, therefore, is to find valuable processes and pivotal evidence of transformative learning. This assessment perspective differs from measuring toward an endpoint, which may miss finding different ways of learning and knowing. Evaluating contributes toward further learning in discovering obstacles, challenges, and misunderstandings that inform how to change teaching or approach or whether to reevaluate the curriculum. Part of what makes assessment meaningful is how (and if) it is used. While the purpose of assessment is to analyze and indicate student learning, it is also important for evaluating teaching effectiveness so that educators may adjust according to student learning needs where appropriate and necessary. The assessment process for students with special educational needs is not fully realized if the results of the assessments are not recorded and shared. Downing (2008) emphasizes the collaborative nature of reporting on student progress, especially where the student experiencing severe (dis)abilities is

---

[5] See Chapter 3 of this book for more discussion on the functional curriculum.

Exhibit 5.A. Overlap Between Art Education and Special Education Curricular Objectives

It is the third week of classes—almost time for progress reports—and Mr. Mathis, the art teacher, is meeting with Ms. Hughes, the special educator, to talk about Maryanne's progress in the mainstreamed art class. Maryanne, a sophomore in high school, experiences autism with developmental delays but is rather high functioning; she attends the art class with a paraeducator to help accommodate her learning. Her educational objectives in the art class include academic and social domains.

"As we talked about Maryanne at her IEP team meeting a few weeks ago," Ms. Hughes begins, "one of our academic objectives for her this year includes increased opportunities for self-direction and self-determination. That is one of the reasons that we thought the art class might be a uniquely suitable environment for Maryanne this fall."

"Yes," Mr. Mathis replies, "I have really been working with Ms. Marks [the paraeducator] to consciously include and focus on choice-making opportunities for Maryanne, both individually and in peer groups."

Ms. Hughes smiles and opens her notebook computer. "I'd love to hear some examples of that. I am meeting at the end of the week with Maryanne's parents and would really like to share this with them."

"Well," Mr. Mathis says thoughtfully, "The national standards for art education at the high school level require that students are regularly making choices in conceiving of and creating artworks, as well as making intentional decisions about uses of media and techniques. This emphasis on self-expression goes hand-in-hand with the objectives of self-determination and self-direction that you mention." He leans forward as he speaks, "For instance, for Maryanne's first project this year—using color, facial expression, media, and mark-making to convey emotion—students randomly received two emotions, written on paper, from a hat. Then they chose one from those two. I think Maryanne received 'surprised' and 'sad' for her two emotions, and she chose to work with 'sad.'

"We then took digital photos of each student—three photos per student—as they made the facial expression for their word. This took quite a bit of coaching from Ms. Marks; I hadn't anticipated this would be difficult at first, but Ms. Marks assured me that it would be good to try. We ended up pairing Maryanne with another student, Katie, who would make a sad face, and Maryanne would respond with her own. Ms. Marks also asked Katie and Maryanne both to share something sad that had happened to them. (I hoped this would be a good exercise in empathy for Maryanne, too.) To reciprocate, Maryanne and Katie also practiced facial expressions for Katie's emotion—I think it was 'nervous.'

"Anyway, from her three photos, Maryanne chose the one she liked best, the one she would draw. Then Ms. Marks and I helped Maryanne think about sad colors, sad marks, and which art medium would be best to use. She ended up creating her sad self-portrait using oil pastel and dull shades of blue and gray. I thought she produced an appropriately expressive artwork."

Ms. Hughes nods as she types up a few notes. "Your use of visuals, with the facial expression modeling and the choice of photographs, is a very helpful technique for Maryanne's mode of learning. Do keep in mind, though, that she may require several repetitions of a given activity or example before she begins to grasp an idea, so don't get discouraged. Ms. Marks can help you with any challenges there, and so can I." She continues adding a few notes before continuing, "I know it's early yet in the semester, but what are your thoughts on having Maryanne in the class? Does she seem to be benefitting academically and socially?"

"I was a little nervous at first," Mr. Mathis admits, "but Ms. Marks has been a terrific resource. As you know, she's been coming in once a week during my conference period—you even came with her once yourself—so that we can review the art lesson and troubleshoot in advance any challenges or considerations that might not have occurred to me. Because of having her there, I think that everything has gone very smoothly. She's been very good at responding to other students when I'm not readily available, too. We work together to get other students involved with Maryanne, and Ms. Marks has been prompting Maryanne to initiate interactions with students around her, too, even if they're just simple, short conversations. All in all, I think things have gone very smoothly so far, and the art class has worked well for Maryanne."

"Great," Ms. Mathis says as she closes her notebook. "I'll be happy to share this with her parents, and you're welcome to come to that meeting, too, if you like. We'd love to have you there. It's at 4:00 on Thursday."

"I can do that," Mr. Hughes agrees, "And I'll bring her portfolio, too. There's not too much in it yet, but there's the one finished self-portrait, some sketches, and a painting that she's begun. I'll ask Maryanne to choose three or five things for us to have at the meeting."

Figure 5.3. Example of Adjustable Portfolio Assessment Rubric for a High School Art Class.

Student Level: _____ Apprentice (40:40:20) _X_ Practioner (25:25:50) _____ Experienced (10:10:80) _X_ Modified*
*Students with modified curriculum may fall outside the percentages above.

Weight Assignments: _30_ % Effort (10%-40%)　　_50_ % Progress (10%-40%)　　_20_ % Proficiency (20%-80%)*
*Combined total of these should be 100%

Competency	Assessment of Effort, Progress, and Proficiency for Competency		
	E	P	M
Selected examples of art in portfolio evidence student's ability to apply media, techniques, and processes with sufficient skill to carry out intentions and to express meaning.	80	95	75
Effective student choice making is evidenced through use of media, processes, and techniques, as well as in the selection of work to include in the portfolio to evidence breadth and depth of learning in art.	90	95	80
Artwork in portfolio demonstrates an awareness and understanding of art organization principles and structures through the student's use of historical/cultural context, process, and (self) evaluation criteria in creating the art.	85	90	60
Student effectively applied symbols, ideas, and subjects in artmaking and is able to define and defend the use of these in the work.	85	80	60
Artwork exists as a solution to a visual problem through elaboration upon personal direct observation, experience, and/or imagination of the student.	100	85	70
Sum Totals of Effort, Progress, Proficiency:	440	445	345
Average Total of sums for Effort, Progress, Proficiency:	88 (30%)	89 (50%)	69 (20%)
Final Grade (averaged from assigned weights above):	84.7 = B		

Comments: *Good use of color and symbol to convey mood. Watch drying time on paint before layering. Nice work!*

concerned; for this reason, she says, the (art) classroom teacher's involvement in the IEP team, and access to the IEP, is important. Gathering data related to student progress, and the sharing of that assessment data with the special educator and parents, is an essential component of teaching the student experiencing different-abilities, including severe (dis)abilities, in the art class. Such data collection may be in the form of the portfolio rubric, such as in Figure 5.3, but it may also include video documentation of the student working or interacting with others in art class, educator notes from direct observation, checklists, and artworks and other artifacts. The paraeducator who accompanies the student experiencing multiple or severe disabilities may act as an important agent in this data collection as the one who may first notice student progress and whether or not a given modification or intervention is working (Downing, 2008).

For example, a student's social interaction domain of her functional curriculum may have the following objective: "Stacey will successfully initiate a positive and appropriate social interaction with a peer in art class once per day for two weeks." The art teacher may work with the paraeducator in creating class activities that facilitate peer interaction, and the paraeducator may be the one who collects data and documents these interactions to share with the art educator and special educator and the student's parent(s). Likewise, any artwork that is used as an artifact for data collection and assessment "should be clearly dated and contain a brief description of how the student completed the project (under what support conditions) and how much was done independently" (Downing, 2008, pp. 279–280). Here, the paraeducator and art educator would work together, and with the student, to provide relevant information to the special educator and parents as meaningful assessment of the student's authentic learning in the inclusive art class. Figure 5.4 provides one example of a form that the art educator or paraeducator may use to report on the progress of a student who is experiencing moderate to severe different-abilities on a given day in the art class.

Figure 5.4. Example of a Daily Report Form for Student Experiencing Moderate to Severe Disabilities in the Inclusive Art Classroom.

Student's Name: _Robert Diaz_   **Date:** _Oct. 5, 2013_

Person Completing Form (check one):   **Para-educator**   ✔ **Classroom Teacher**

Evaluator's Name: _Cindy Allen_   **Subject/Grade:** _Art/5th_

Please complete below as applicable:

Motor Domain: The student met assignment objectives in the motor domain today.

     Below expectations   Satisfactory   ✔ Exceeded expectations

Example/conditions of activity: _Robert painted the background for his landscape._
Modifications/Adaptations provided: _Two color choices provided at a time; allow background to dry before proceeding; used strap to secure brush to hand._

Academic Domain: The student met class objectives in the academic domain of his or her Individualized Education Program (IEP) today.

     Below expectations   ✔ Satisfactory   Exceeded expectations

Example/conditions of learning activity: _Class discussed near/far (foreground, middle ground, and background) and atmospheric perspective/color_
Modifications/Adaptations provided: _Paraeducator worked with Robert on background/middle ground/foreground using tactile paper cutouts that he could layer to understand concept of near/far_

Social Domain: The student met objectives in the social domain today.

     Below expectations   ✔ Satisfactory   Exceeded expectations

Example/Conditions: _Was agitated when he entered the classroom from an incident in his earlier class but eventually calmed down. Visited appropriately with student next to him about last weekend's hayride and visit to corn maze (student's family owns it and saw Robert there)._

<u>**Select any that apply:**</u>

_____ ✔ Example/artifact of today's work is affixed here. (_digital photo of Robert's painted background_)

_____ ✔ I would like a contact from the special educator: **Phone call**   **Email**   ✔ **Visit**
        The best time(s) to reach me is: _after school, 3:30 p.m._

<u>**Additional Comments:**</u> _It might be good for us to visit briefly in preparation for the upcoming open house/parent-teacher visits. Thanks!_

Such a form should be adaptable and general enough to allow for quick completion during a busy school day, but it should also allow for specific comment and examples where necessary. It should also include the opportunity to request contact between the classroom teacher and special educators if needed. This type of form could be used regularly (e.g., daily, weekly, or biweekly) or as needed and can easily provide a snapshot of what is occurring in the inclusive art class, as well as helpful documentation for the special educator.

Authentic assessment strategies are ones that use meaningful, challenging projects that engage students in substantive activities connected to real-life circumstances (Boughton, 2004; see also Boyd, 2011). Art production—in its potential to connect research, experiential, and affective content to form—has the ability to empower students to reclaim and construct identity and to recognize capabilities in others inasmuch as students create art in order to be understood and to communicate with others (Freedman, 2003, pp. 147–148; see also Ashworth et al., 2010). In the inclusive, communitarian art class, strategies and assessments that respond to individual differences among learners may be beneficial to all learners; thus, "inclusion is [conceptualized] as a response to an increasingly diverse student population. Students with disabilities and non-disabled students become equal members of a learning community where diversity is pre-eminent" (Ashworth et al., 2010, p. 210). Chapter 6 presents the exhibition as formative and summative assessment where all HEARTS students showcase and celebrate diversity within a supportive learning community.

Chapter 6

EXHIBITING TRANSFORMATIVE LEARNING AND TEACHING

In the article "Teaching for Transformation," Patricia Cranton (2002) defines *emancipatory knowledge* as self-awareness through critical self-reflection that frees us from constraints of others' representations of us. Moreover, "the acquisition of emancipatory knowledge is transformative" (Cranton, 2002, p. 64). However, without a communitarian approach to transformative learning and teaching it is difficult to be free from others' perceptions because behaviors, respect, and communication are shaped by these perceptions.

The desire to be free from misperceptions and damaging assumptions is universal. This is why Ricardo Thornton, in the movie about his life with his wife, Donna, two people with cognitive challenges who fall in love, get married, and have a healthy son, proclaim, "We don't need people to tell us about ourselves."[1] Cognitive dissonance, while often invisible, impacts communication, and youth in several other (dis)ability categories, compared with those with mental retardation (i.e., cognitive dissonance), are "less likely to report there is an adult at school who knows and cares about them" (Shannon, 2009, p. 38). According to the *Learning Disabilities Sourcebook* (Shannon, 2009), those labeled as mentally retarded report "feeling not very or not at all useful, not able to deal well with challenges, and rarely or never enjoying life" (p. 38).

In this chapter we tackle the reality of barriers to inclusion practices and how to turn these real and perceived obstacles into surmountable hurdles. As we conclude the chapter and book, we look both back and forward. We look to student and teachers reflections on their experience in the HEARTS program[2] for "aha" moments of change in attitudes toward teaching students experiencing different-abilities. We also look forward to changes in preservice education in which state boards of education recognize and support the federal mandate of a least restrictive environment.

Reality of Inclusion Practices: Breaking Barriers to Inclusion

With the U.S. educational system's aspirations for high achievement of all students, standards defining knowledge, content, and skills per discipline and grade level may seem impossible considering ability variance in the classroom. Teachers are often fearful that disruptions of students experiencing (dis)abilities will impede educational progress of the whole class. "Disability is the social process that turns an impairment into a negative by creating barriers to access" (Davis & Watson, 2002, p. 12).

There are a number of barriers that may impede successful inclusion of students experiencing moderate to severe (dis)abilities within the art classroom setting. Gary Thomas and Georgina Glenny (2005), in the anthology *Ethics and Research in Inclusive Education*, point out that, "despite the avowed unpopularity of the deficit approach in the last quarter of the twentieth century, it keeps returning to haunt special educators. Models of pedagogy persistently seek to find deficiencies in children" (p. 15).

The work of artists is important in changing how we think about pedagogy and the environment of schools. For example, "the social commentary of the novels of Dickens did more, incomparably more, than the early special educators to reform understanding of the nexus of factors which contribute to unhappiness and failure at school. The effects of poverty, alienation, oppression, cruelty and a stultifying curriculum were well understood and explicated by Dickens and stand in sharp contrast to the scientific contributions of his psychological contemporaries" (Thomas & Glenny, 2005, p. 17). More recently, the film *Waiting for Superman*

---

[1] See Exhibit 2.B in Chapter 2 for a discussion of the film *Profoundly Normal* (2003).

[2] See Chapter 4 for a complete description of the program.

(Guggenheim & Chilcott, 2010)[3] has had an impact on societal perceptions of schools in the US. One fertile way for art education to break barriers is to organize art exhibitions locally and online about experiences with (dis)ability.

Certainly collaboration is a key to meeting the individualized educational needs of students experiencing (dis)abilities in the inclusive art class. Find Cards are one way to engage art interpretation and enhance gallery art viewing as a collaborative learning and teaching endeavor. Teams of two or more students collaborate to search for, decide on, and discuss artwork. Awareness of barriers to and benefits of inclusion is another step toward successful inclusion practices. Modifications to policy and procedures and additional education of personnel may minimize many of the barriers to successful inclusion. High standards, including the intent of the National Standards in Art Education (NAEA, 1994),[4] should not be conflated with a call for "greater regimentation" as is too often the case in implementing interpretations of laws, standards, and policies (Bastos & Zimmerman, 2011, p. 6). In the next sections we discuss commonly experienced obstacles to inclusion. We begin by discussing the costs of inclusion given monetary and time constraints.

Time and Money: Inclusion as a Worthwhile Investment

Political and economic challenges as well as sociocultural and physical environments greatly impact the experience of (dis)ability. For example, malnutrition in the first 3 years of a child's life prevents the brain from developing to its natural growth capacity, creating learning difficulties throughout life. Artist Mel Chin—in his project Fundred in collaboration with art teachers throughout the US—draws attention to lead poisoning in the land surrounding schools in communities struggling economically.[5] A first step toward inclusivity is to make sure babies in the school's proximity have adequate nourishment. Like Mel Chin's art project, art educators can facilitate an art project with the community that improves the well-being of all in the community.

The real costs of inclusion are difficult to track because of the variety of aspects involved in educating students with special needs. These often-overlapping aspects may include issues of state, local, and federal funding of programs; costs of transportation, special services, and facilities; and costs of staff development. Janko and Porter (1997) point out that,

while it may be difficult to tell *how* inclusion affects education costs, it is known that it *does* affect those costs. For example, they describe how many school districts implement inclusion programs that they feel will reduce some costs, but they often fail to account for additional costs in transportation and staffing that inclusion may require. They further explain that government agencies have attempted to alleviate some of the financial burden of special education programs, but inclusive programs make it increasingly difficult to track costs:

> Federal and state agencies… learned to save costs by shifting clients, when possible, to other programs for which they may be eligible. It has recently become common practice, for example, for children with disabilities to be enrolled in federal disability programs to reduce fiscal pressures on states. Inclusion contradicts this trend by bringing individuals, programs, and budgets together, by emphasizing collaboration, and by blurring boundaries of agencies and jurisdictions. This is one reason why the costs of inclusion are so difficult to quantify. (Janko & Porter, 1997, p. 28)

Some resources available for students experiencing (dis)abilities for use in the inclusive classroom environment might benefit students who are typically-abled as well. IDEA (2004) provides for such shared benefits through the "permissive use of funds" clause, which states: "Funds provided to the local educational agency under this part may be used for… services and aids that also benefit nondisabled children" (U.S.C. 20 § 1413(a)(4)(A)). Such resources, as described in the permissive use of funds clause, must be in keeping with the IEP of the student experiencing disabilities, and these may include high-technology assistive devices, including computer hardware and software, or supplemental services, such as the provision of a paraeducator. With the provision of a paraeducator, students with different-abilities and students who are typically-abled alike may benefit from the increased instructional attention provided by the addition of staff to the inclusive classroom. One study (Ripley, 1997) on collaborative teaching between general and special educators demonstrated improvements in student learning that were linked to the increased teacher assistance and reduced pupil-teacher ratio inherent within the collaboration model. In this case, educational services provided for students with different-abilities appear to have had the residual advantage of enhancing the learning of the inclusive classroom as a whole.

Some teachers may be concerned with the time commitment needed for an inclusive art class. A HEARTS teacher reflecting on the value of the time she devoted to planning, "found that thoughtful planning and the consideration of adaptive technologies allows for a comfortable learning environment" (V. Eggemeyer, personal communication, June 25,

---

3 The trailer for *Waiting for Superman* is online at www.youtube.com/watch?v=ZKTfaro96dg

4 The National Standards for Visual Arts can be found at http://artsedge.kennedy-center.org/educators/standards.aspx

5 This important art project is described at www.fundred.org

2001). Moreover, as Guay (2006a) points out, art teachers are traditionally isolated and autonomous in their schools, and in creating an inclusive art class this isolation diminishes because of the involvement of stakeholders—students, parents, paraeducators, and special educators—in IEPs. The use of social media such as the National Art Education Association's Special Needs in Art Education Issues Group (SNAE) listserv and other people resources discussed in Chapter 2 provide opportunity for asking, sharing, and creating ideas regarding an inclusive art class.

With or without a paraeducator to assist, art educators need planning time to develop an inclusive art class. Resources, processes, spaces, and materials need to be prepared. When planning periods for special educators and art educators don't coincide, finding time to collaborate becomes especially burdensome; this difficulty is only compounded for elementary school teachers who may serve almost all students on a campus or who may be traveling from school to school (Gerber & Fedorenko, 2006). However, a communitarian approach to differentiated learning involves students teaching each other and learning from each other.

The Challenges of Curriculum Differentiation

> If a teacher is prepared and set up for the different needs of each student there will be more productive and effective results. I have learned it is important to be flexible, patient, and most of all positive. (D. Franklin, HEARTS teacher, personal communication, June 25, 2001)

With the inclusion of students with special needs in the general (art) classroom comes increased variance of abilities, which may lead to instructional demands that teachers may not be prepared to manage (Davis & Watson, 2002; Shannon, 2009). Teaching a class of students experiencing typical-abilities is challenging enough, as is teaching a class of students who are experiencing different-abilities. Combining diverse learners into one class has the potential of creating a class that has both students of high cognitive intelligence and students experiencing severe mental retardation, with a full range of students whose abilities lie between these identifiers.

The job of addressing the educational needs of all students in an inclusive classroom may be overwhelming to the teacher who is trying to balance educational excellence with educational equity (Kauffman, 1995). While appropriate support for education, patience, and creativity may provide for some solutions in educating a class with wide-ranging needs, ability variance in the inclusive class offers a real and common challenge to both teaching and learning. Strategies for addressing this issue are at the core of this book.

Differentiation curriculum development begins by recognizing that all learners are different. Nicole Taylor and John Chacksfield (2005), information communication technology educators specializing in learners with disabilities, advocate that educators need to "create appropriately different learning experiences for mixed ability learners within a curriculum" (p. 14). The nature of tasks can be adjusted through multiple approaches to content, process, and product expectations without diminishing learning goals and by increasing active engagement through relevancy to learning.

As argued in Chapter 2, impairment is not a neutral or apolitical term. Impairments, such as manifested in the term "fidgety children," (i.e., attention deficit disorder), may be a creation of a "medical-technological-pharmaceutical complex" (Davis, 2002, p. 23). This complex weaves and maps to the body sociopolitical identifications that mark what an individual lacks or what is in need of repair. "The social model has stressed that this deficit approach is wrong, because using a wheelchair or Braille or sign language is not inferior to the majority of approaches to mobility or communication, just different" (Shakespeare, 2006, p. 45). As noted in Chapter 2, labels of disabilities may be ensconced in deep institutional and societal racial bias. Donna King, a parent, and educator with a PhD in Curriculum and Instruction from the Pennsylvania State University, recounts how she could not understand why her children, who to her appeared to be typical learners for their age, were labeled as disabled at their school. The activist strategies she developed to challenge the school system is called upon again and again for other children of color, including her grandchildren (personal communication, September 7, 2011). Donna King (2010) developed a dissonance pedagogy that she learned in part from her personal struggles in the face of injustice. She describes how her

> son wrote his senior speech about what it was like to be the only African American male in a college prep English course. His instructor told him to change his speech because it would offend the other students in the class. He refused. She didn't allow him to read his senior speech, and she opted to fail him. My son suffered a long time from that teacher's damaging pedagogical act, but now he is a writer. (King, PDS Journal, 2005, p. 18)

See Exhibit 6.A for Donna King's son's silenced senior speech.

Students can contribute to curriculum differentiation by identifying strengths in themselves and each other and suggesting learning-activity changes that they see as interesting and relevant to their lives. To do so, they need to know this is encouraged and rewarded. This goes against most experiences in schools, which more often reinforce complacency in following rules and procedures to learn specific content.

Exhibit 6.A. Son's Silenced Senior Speech

My son came home from high school and described to me that when he went to his English class, the teacher asked him: "Are you sure you belong here?" The course was a graduation requirement. He looked at his schedule, and said, "Yes, isn't this the college prep English course?" She said it was so he sat down but felt unwelcomed.

For his senior speech in the college prep English course he wrote an essay about his experiences in high school. So, rhetorically speaking, he started his senior speech, "Do you know what it is like to walk into your first class, and the teacher asks, 'are you sure you belong here?'" He wrote about his being the only African American male in a college Prep English course, and the tensions that he endured in this majority class. The English teacher told him to change his speech because it would offend the other students in the class. He refused to change it, and, therefore, she didn't allow him to read his senior speech and she opted to fail him.

As a parent, and an advocate for social justice and inclusive classrooms, I gave him a copy of Langston Hughes's (1951) poem, "Theme for English B,"[1] as a literary healing strategy. Hughes writes: "Will the page that I write be colored or white?" Hughes's poem is about what it is like to be different and to have to validate and claim your positionality and subjectivity. Section 504 of the Rehabilitation Act of 1973, as amended, 29 U.S.C. § 794 provides that "No otherwise qualified individual with a disability in the US... shall, solely by reason of her or his disability, be excluded from the participation in, be denied the benefits of, or be subjected to discrimination under any program or activity receiving Federal financial assistance." While the U.S. federal law legally provides protection from discrimination, I could not protect my son from the act of discrimination by the English teacher toward my son. My son suffered a long time from that teacher's dismissal of him and his writing. However, with role models such as Langston Hughes, he continued to write from his experiences and is now a graduate student at University of Southern California in Los Angeles majoring in professional writing and screenwriting, pending graduation next semester. He went from *victim to victor*. In retrospect, I guess we both did. We are different writers and educational advocates due to how the literary resistance from our dissonant writings have turned into liberatory prose with emancipatory consequences. Hughes poem also inspired me to become an English educator, to teach future teachers, so that no student would be denied a voice. I use this story as a teaching tool to advocate for supportive environments no matter difference.[2]

---

[1] The full poem *Theme for English B* by Langston Hughes (1951) is available at www.mrcoward.com/slcusd/englishb.html

[2] King, Donna. (2010). *A Student Teachers' Perceived Resistance to Teaching Multicultural Education: Will My Pedagogy be "Colored That I Teach?"* (Unpublished Dissertation). The Pennsylvania State University, University Park.

Students actively involved in developing differentiation learn to problem solve by identifying multiple ways to learn, teach, and work together. This is a type of learning that will be useful throughout their lives.

The specialized needs of the student experiencing (dis)abilities may result in disruptions that impede classroom function. Such disruptions could include monopolizing the teacher's time (Gerber & Fedorenko, 2006) or behavioral disturbances that may not only hamper learning but may also create an unsafe environment, as demonstrated by the *Daniel R. R.* and *Ryan K.* cases presented in Chapter 1. The least restrictive environment (LRE) mandate acknowledges that there may be times when the nature of a student's (dis)ability is such that education in the general classroom setting cannot be satisfactorily achieved, even with the provision of appropriate services and aids. IDEA states, however, that the IEP team, when determining placement for the student whose behavior impedes his or her own learning and that of others, must consider appropriate intervention strategies and supports to address the behavior in a general classroom setting. In addition to behavioral issues, though, provision of supplementary services to a student under IDEA may result in a fragmented inclusion/educational experience if the student leaves the class periodically for physical, occupational, or speech therapy. When the IEP team does not understand the value of learning in the art class, disruptions to the student's attendance may occur. It is important for art teachers to communicate to the IEP team the learning goals and communication strategies to meet those goals.

In the art class, as a more variable and typically a more open movement environment, such disturbances can be more likely to occur than in uniformly structured learning environments with less physical activity. This conundrum of disruption and impediment to educational progress can be reshaped into educational benefit with the active sensory and affective engagement of artmaking. Sensory stimulation, reflection time, dialogue, physical movement, and opportunities to try something new without fear of failure because art teachers and student peers value what can be learned through failed attempts are lifelong learning processes that can be nurtured through differentiated curriculum in the art class.

Accessible Exhibitions: Design and Engagement

We advocate a paradigm that not only provides access to educational opportunity or works to compensate for perceived shortcomings resultant from (dis)abilities but also views all students as capable and worthwhile contributors to the class environment, regardless of (dis)ability. One of the HEARTS participants, a graduate student in art education, provides insights from her HEARTS teaching experiences regarding accessibility to educational opportunities through exhibition of student work.

> [On reflecting on practices that should have been used in galleries all along] we should have considered a much larger font for tags to accommodate visitors [who were visually impaired] on a regular basis in the gallery during past semesters…

> Another accommodation was the use of shorter pedestals and no vitrines (which often show a glare) for those visitors in wheelchairs. This should always be practiced in the gallery and in museums. Many museums put important artifacts on taller vitrines (which gives it an air of importance), but this does not allow for younger, shorter visitors to see clearly…

> Utilizing both audio and visual effects through video created an "alive" feeling within the space. Many people view galleries and museums as shrines of art that do not permit loud voices or a lot of movement. This exhibit was bright, alive, and full of energy. (V. Eggemeyer, personal communication, June 25, 2001)

Interpretative accompanying text, placement, multimodal presentations, and activities to foster movement and dialogue are important considerations for creating accessible exhibitions of student artwork. The following are some strategies for accessible exhibitions and engagement in art exhibitions.

Accessibility and Universal Design Principles Toward Difference Design

Ronald Mace, an architect, product designer, and educator coined the term *universal design* to "describe the concept of designing all products and the built environment to be aesthetic and usable to the greatest extend possible by everyone, regardless of their age, ability, or status in life" (National Council on Disability, 2004, p. 5). The Centre for Universal Design (1997) promotes a philosophy with principles for "the design of products and environments to be usable by all people, to the greatest extent possible, without the need for adaptation or specialized design" (cited in Shakespeare, 2006, p. 44). Shakespeare (2006) makes the case that the "principles of Universal Design are unarguable when taken separately, but may create conflict when aggregated" (p. 46). For example,

> Partially sighted people may request large text on white background: people with dyslexia may prefer black print on yellow paper. Some people will prefer rooms to be dim, others will prefer them to be brightly lit. Moreover, different people with the same impairment may require different accommodation[s], because everyone experiences their own impairment differently, and each impairment comes in different forms, and different people have different preferences for solving impairment problems. (Shakespeare, 2006, p. 46)

Barriers to those experiencing different-abilities include inaccessible transportation and educational systems, poor working environments, inadequate health care, and limited access to public buildings and homes. Moreover, people who experience disabilities in the US are disproportionally poor (Russell, 2002).

> Impairment is the rule, and normalcy is the fantasy. Dependence is the reality, and independence grandiose thinking. Barrier-free access is the goal, and the right to pursue happiness the false consciousness that obscures it. Universal design becomes the template for social and political designs. (Davis, 2002, p. 31)

Art educators, in planning exhibitions, should refer to universal design principles and practices (see Aber, 2000), but in doing so need to realize universal design is actualized as *difference design* that considers the particulars of a community of people and the selected public site for the exhibition.

Nonvisual Ways to Experience Visual Art

Artist–educator Linna Muschlitz has curated visual art exhibitions that can be experienced through touch. HEARTS students watched a video of a tactile tour of one of these exhibitions,[6] which heightened their awareness of different ways of knowing and interpreting the meaning of visual artwork. This tactile tour of a gallery exhibition that was not designed for touch, but some artists gave permission for their

---

6 The video, "Alternative Ways to Experience Art: A Tactile Tour" (Keifer-Boyd, 1993), can be viewed at https://streaming.psu.edu/media/?movieId=16136

artworks to be touched, brought awareness to other sensory ways to interpret the artworks. Through associations, memories, symbolism, metaphors, literal grasp of density through sound, and expressiveness through temperature changes and olfactory recognition, one visitor to this exhibition with eyes that do not see in typical ways summarized her gallery experience:

> Frankly speaking, the beeswax painting did not do much for me. The small box sculptures could use more variety to capture my interest. I am intrigued with the heads on metal rods that move and hit each other, the smells from the large woven twig basket form, the temperature differences and hollowness that I could sense by touch and tapping, and especially the relationship between the placard label on burlap next to the metal and sharp glass. My favorite was the aluminum tree with columns surrounding it that we were at first not allowed to touch but thanks to Linna's advocacy we were allowed and did touch. (Gwen, personal communication, 1993)

Creating art that is both visually and tactilely engaging and expressive can have layered meanings through the associative relational aesthetics of touch and vision.

Lysette Ewing (2000) describes her art teaching in which high school students with and without sight are included in the same art class and believes that this enhances everyone's experiences with art. She notes that visual "art is more than visual perception.... [and] the more descriptive the language the better" in exploring the metaphorical meaning of processes, materials, and artworks (Ewing, 2000, p. 86). For example, in learning to translate tactile qualities into metaphor, a student with sight describes her artwork titled "White-Collar World at a High-Rise Price," which she created to convey meaning through its tactile as well as visual qualities:

> I wanted to portray the coldness of the white-collar world. The raised part is supposed to be a building. The base is big, off the table. Fabric covers the base, cotton, which is what all the businessmen wear. The sides are tucked so it's nice and neat. The metal is to represent cold. The box on it represents packaging. The business world is always fast paced. Feel the ridges on this round thing? That represents time. That's what the knobs here are for. Feel how fast paced it is? (Ewing, 2000, p. 87)

Jackie Kolosov creates visual poetry, which she taught HEARTS teachers to use in discussing artwork with HEARTS students and for all to work with for the interpretative exhibition labels. Similar to the tactile tour awareness, visual poetry translates visuals into sounds, words, temperatures, textures,

continuums of dense to hollow to ephemeral, movement, and memories of smells.

Engaging a Diverse Audience

The principles of universal design, accessibility, and alternative ways for encountering art shaped our planning for the HEARTS exhibition as we sought to engage a diverse audience. We used Find Cards (described below) as a strategy toward this engagement and as a way to facilitate reflection and (self-)critique on the HEARTS art and exhibit. The preservice teachers responded to their own universal design efforts with the HEARTS exhibition, as well as to HEARTS members' participation in the experience:

> The students were proud of their work and delighted in the fact that the show was just for them. Tonja had a glow on her face and spoke of her favorite piece, in front of everyone. This was amazing to me. She would never have spoken so boldly or even bragged on her work before. Somewhere inside her the HEARTS program empowered her to believe in herself. I cannot write about this without crying. I never dreamed this class would have such an impact on me. (D. Franklin, personal communication, June 25, 2001)

The challenge for this session was installing an exhibit of artwork that would be accessible to all participants of the program. Other tasks included engaging the participants in meaningful conversation about the artwork displayed. This was facilitated through Find Cards... Pairing participants with other art workshop students to discuss work permitted social interaction, an

Figure 6.1. HEARTS students discuss their works at the Art From the Heart exhibition.

opportunity to analyze artwork, and reciprocal learning for both parties. (V. Eggemeyer, personal communication, June 25, 2001)

When I (Karen) taught at Maude Kerns Art Center in Eugene, Oregon, in the 1980s, I created what I called Find Cards. Each Saturday I taught two classes, from 10:00 a.m. to noon for 5- to 9-year-olds, and 1:00 to 3:00 p.m. for 10- to 16-year-olds. The exhibitions changed each month, and my art lessons connected to the art in the gallery. Students experienced an art exhibition and then made artwork. In the 1970s, I began writing Find Cards for teaching children and youth, and mixed age-groups from 5-year-olds to elders at the Nelson-Atkins Museum of Art in Kansas City. The cards ask the cardholder to work with at least one other person to find what is described on the card. It is a simple idea that involves active searching—moving through space together while looking closely. Since the team has to figure out what it is they are looking for, there is great effort extended in communicating about what the card is asking them to find, as well as motivation to look at the artworks to select one to discuss. When they figure out and find what they are searching for, then there is typically intense dialogue regarding interpretations of meaning.

Teaching teams provided participants with reflective questions on Find Cards (geared, as needed, to the participant's

cognitive level); participants chose a partner and responded to the reflective questions with their partners. A find card begins with a directive or clue of something to "find" in an exhibition and includes a question. Figure 6.2 has six examples of Find Cards that relate to the learning goals and art lessons in the HEARTS program. Find Cards can be developed and modified according to one's curricular goals.

A J. Paul Getty Museum study by Jackson, Fleischer, and Christie (2006)[7] on art-detective cards, describes a similar strategy as the Find Cards. They found that families tended to collaborate, and were active and engaged in the exhibition experience. We too found active engagement with each other and the artwork at the HEARTS Exhibition attended by family, community, students, and teachers. Here are two HEARTS participants' reflections:

> The question and answer collaboration between "typical" students and those experiencing differences helped to reinforce the fact that the goals and objectives of HEARTS were met. [One student] liked [another's] picture of the ghost and he explained the way it made him feel and the different media used in the picture. [Another student] told the "typical" student about slip

_____

[7] A report of the study is at www.getty.edu/education/museum_educators/artdetective_cards.html

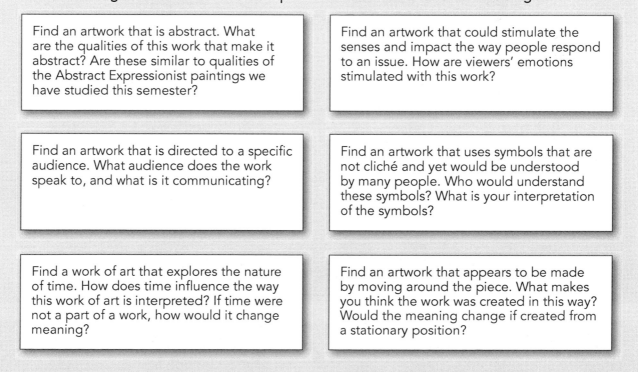

Figure 6.2. Find Card Examples for Interactive Exhibition Viewing.

Find an artwork that is abstract. What are the qualities of this work that make it abstract? Are these similar to qualities of the Abstract Expressionist paintings we have studied this semester?

Find an artwork that could stimulate the senses and impact the way people respond to an issue. How are viewers' emotions stimulated with this work?

Find an artwork that is directed to a specific audience. What audience does the work speak to, and what is it communicating?

Find an artwork that uses symbols that are not cliché and yet would be understood by many people. Who would understand these symbols? What is your interpretation of the symbols?

Find a work of art that explores the nature of time. How does time influence the way this work of art is interpreted? If time were not a part of a work, how would it change meaning?

Find an artwork that appears to be made by moving around the piece. What makes you think the work was created in this way? Would the meaning change if created from a stationary position?

and score and explained how that worked [with clay]. [Still another student experiencing disabilities] used his senses to tell about the tray he made. Each student used some kind of critical thinking or problem-solving strategy. (D. Franklin, personal communication, June 25, 2001)

This exhibit allowed for self-representation through a variety of mediums. Self-expression and cognitive learning were also evident through the find card discussion. There was a lot of interaction between typically- and differently-abled visitor during this reception, which was a part of our HEARTS mission. (V. Eggemeyer, personal communication, June 25, 2001)

The pedagogical approach of the find card activity elicits a sense of student agency in selecting artworks and yet focuses a student team's search and discussion in an open-ended translation of curricular content from the combined translate-ability strengths of the team. Teaching, learning, and assessment are integrated in find card pedagogy.

HEARTS Epilogue and Looking to the Future

We believe that educators should continue to develop reflective practice, that is, thoughtful documentation of teaching, and discussion of the documentation with another teacher, especially those teaching the same students. Reflections on "aha" transformative learning experienced by students who were HEARTS program teachers are examples of reflection on inclusive art education.

Exhibiting Student Reflections on Their HEARTS Experience

The art educator's perception of and attitude toward inclusion can either promote or impede the success of the process (Erickson, 2004; Thomas & Glenny, 2005). One of the HEARTS teachers reflects on the transformation of her attitudes toward teaching students experiencing (dis)abilities:

I had many preconceived notions going into this class about involving students with multiple disabilities in the regular art classroom. I now see that the art classroom is exactly where students with disabilities can develop their creative and expressive capabilities. The HEARTS program has been proof of the endless capabilities of students with multiple disabilities. Art can enable students with special needs to be creative and express their life experiences without feeling threatened. (D. Franklin, personal communication, June 25, 2001)

A teacher's unwillingness to implement modifications or make accommodations for learners with (dis)abilities may have serious ramifications for both the school and the district (Bartlett & McLeod, 1998). Such resistance to inclusion may result from: (a) lack of education in integration strategies; (b) personal bias toward students experiencing (dis)abilities; or (c) a perception that the area of special education is not his or her field of expertise and, therefore, not his or her responsibility. Nonetheless, as Bartlett and McLeod (1998) point out, the IDEA legislation and the courts dismiss the notion that only those certified in special education should be involved in the teaching of those experiencing (dis)abilities.[8]

Even if the art educator is willing to be fully involved in the inclusive education of students with (dis)abilities, however, he or she may not be able if not equipped with the strategies or support system to do so. Preservice and in-service teacher-education experience within the inclusive art class setting is critical in preparing art educators for successful inclusion art classes. With strong educational opportunities, the art teacher has ownership of the learning and is better able to adapt it to various situations and the individuated needs of his or her students once in the classroom. Cates, McGill, Brian, Wilder, and Anderson (1990) offer some strategies for preservice education of special educators that may alleviate apprehension regarding working with students experiencing more severe disabilities. These strategies may be generalized to art educators as well and include providing preservice educators the opportunity to interact with students with varying levels of special needs and encouraging collaboration and shared responsibility between special and art educators in meeting the needs of students with (dis)abilities. Because the special education mandate expects this type of collaboration, the benefits of preparing preservice art educators in cooperative strategies before they even reach the classroom facilitates the education in the LRE as envisioned by the law. The HEARTS program described in Chapter 4 of this book provides one model for such preservice education. Reflecting on the HEARTS experience, one teaching participant noted,

After each actual experience with the students I have felt like the person with the disability. These students have taught me so much, and they have opened my eyes to many new approaches, depending on the individual needs. (D. Franklin, personal communication, June 25, 2001)

While collaboration among the educator team is essential (Downing, 2008; Gerber & Fedorenko, 2006; Kraft, 2001),

---

8 This is evident in the *Rachel H.* decision, as well.

there do exist barriers to cooperative teamwork. Some barriers to collaboration in serving the special educational needs of students in the art class may include teacher attitudes and concerns, as well as lack of preservice educator preparation. The art teacher's investment in the inclusion process may be enhanced with his or her inclusion in IEP development (Kraft, 2001). However, one study (Modrick, 2003) indicates that only 9% of art educators regularly participate in the IEP process, and 60% of art educators have never taken part in IEP development. These numbers are particularly disproportionate if the art class is often the first inclusive class setting for students experiencing (dis)abilities.

Transforming Preservice Art Education

We believe the strategies for inclusion presented throughout this book align with the intent of the federal law and its most recent amendment if interpreted from a communitarian theoretical perspective. Though as of 2013 IDEA is overdue for its next amendment, it competes with other legislation for reauthorization, including No Child Left Behind (2001). Much of the case law surrounding IDEA since its 2004 revision has centered on issues related to due process, such as reimbursement for services or expert witnesses in cases of dispute, so the next reauthorization of IDEA will most likely include some language related to these (Jones, 2011). In fact, Senator Tom Harkin and a bipartisan committee, in looking toward IDEA's future reauthorization, have already drafted the IDEA Fairness Restoration Act (2011), which will allow the prevailing party reimbursement for expert witness fees incurred in enforcing the act. Other funding-related educational matters, though, center on the federal government's budget cuts for education over the next few fiscal years, and these are certainly emerging as concerns for the next reauthorization of IDEA.

Aside from monetary considerations, there are additional issues that may arise as part of the next reauthorization. Education policy researcher Steven Eidelman (2011) suggests that IDEA's next amendments may include more specific points on students' transitions into postsecondary education. In addition, legislative attorney Nancy Lee Jones (2011) anticipates clarified requirements for educational progress under a free appropriate public education (FAPE) and explicit details on what, if any, educational benefit must be clearly stated in a student's IEP. Aside from issues related to due process (such as reimbursement and compensation in cases of dispute), however, early IDEA legislation and related case law have already clearly defined the matter of students' FAPE within the general classroom as the LRE, and these two pivotal concepts have not changed significantly since the law's original enactment.

There is great need for art educators to learn from disabilities studies and to contribute to this research from the art and art education perspective. Reflective participatory action research of communities in art class is one way to advocate for the well-being and lifelong learning practices of all students.

REFERENCES

Aber, H. (2000). *Guidelines for universal design of exhibitions*. Washington, DC: Smithsonian Institution. Retrieved from http://accessible.si.edu/gfude.htm

Alley, K., Goldberger, G. G., & Robinson, R. (Producers), & Graeme, C. (Director). (2003). *Profoundly normal* [Motion picture]. USA: Profound Productions/Randwell Productions.

Allison, A. (2008). *Critical theory and preservice art education: One art teacher's journey of equipping art teachers for inclusion* (Doctoral dissertation). University of North Texas, Denton.

Americans with Disabilities Act of 1990, 42 U.S.C. § 12101 *et seq*. (2008).

Anderegg, M. L., & Vergason, G. A. (1996). Preserving the least restrictive environment: Revisited. In W. Stainback & S. Stainback (Eds.), *Controversial issues confronting special education: Divergent perspectives* (2nd ed., pp. 44–54). Boston, MA: Allyn & Bacon.

Anderson, T., & Milbrandt, M. K. (2005). *Art for life: Authentic instruction in art education*. New York, NY: McGraw-Hill.

Apple, M. W. (1995). *Education and power* (2nd ed.). New York, NY: Routledge.

Arnold, A. (1999). School leadership, the arts, and special education. In A. L. Nyman & A. M. Jenkins (Eds.), *Issues and approaches to art for students with special needs* (pp. 132–141). Reston, VA: National Art Education Association.

Ashworth, M., Bloxham, S., & Pearce, L. (2010). Examining the tension between academic standards and inclusion for disabled students: The impact on marking of individual academics' frameworks for assessment. *Studies in Higher Education, 35*(2), 209–223.

Associated Press (AP). (2004, November 8). NASA studies mega-savant Peek's brain. *USA Today*. Retrieved from www.usatoday.com/news/science/2004-11-08-nasa-rain-man_x.htm

Baladerian, N. (2006). Seven keys to supporting children with disabilities in the child welfare system. In V. Gaylord, T. LaLiberte, E. Lightfoot & A. Hewitt (Eds.). (2006). *Impact: Feature issue on children with disabilities in the child welfare system 19*(1). [Minneapolis: University of Minnesota, Institute on Community Integration.] Retrieved from http://ici.umn.edu/products/impact/191/over4.html

Barber, K. (Producer), & Abrams, A., & Broder, A. L. (Directors). (2002). *Pumpkin* [Motion picture]. USA: MGM.

Bartlett, L., & McLeod, S. (1998). Inclusion and the regular class teacher under IDEA. *Education Law Reporter, 128*, 1–14.

Bastos, F., & Zimmerman, E. (2011). Surprise me! *Art Education, 64*(1), 5–7.

Beattie, D. K. (1997). *Assessment in art education*. Worcester, MA: Davis.

Benard, B. (1995). *Fostering resilience in children*. Urbana, IL: Clearinghouse on Elementary and Early Childhood Education. ED 386 327.

Benin, D., & Cartwright, L. (2006). Shame, empathy and looking practices: Lessons from a disability studies classroom. *Journal of Visual Culture, 5*(2), 155–171.

Billingsley, F. F., Liberty, K. A., & White, O. R. (1994). The technology of instruction. In E. C. Cipani & F. Spooner (Eds.), *Curricular and instructional approaches for persons with severe disabilities* (pp. 81–116). Boston, MA: Allyn & Bacon.

Blandy, D. (1989). As I see it: Ecological and normalizing approaches to disabled students. *Art Education, 42*(5), 7–11.

Blandy, D. (1994). Assuming responsibility: Disability rights and the preparation of art educators. *Studies in Art Education, 35*(3), 179–187.

Blandy, D., Pancsofar, E., & Mockensturm, T. (1988). Guidelines for teaching art to children and youth experiencing significant mental/physical challenges. *Art Education, 41*(1), 60–66.

Block, L. (1998). *Beyond affliction: The disability history project*. Retrieved from www.npr.org/programs/disability

Board of Education of the Hendrick Hudson School District, Westchester County, v. Rowley, 102 S.Ct. 3034 (1982).

Boughton, D. (2004). Assessment and visual arts education. In E. W. Eisner & M. D. Day (Eds.), *Handbook of research and policy in art education* (pp. 585–605). Reston, VA: National Art Education Association; and Mahwah, NJ: Lawrence Erlbaum Associates.

Boyd, J. E. (2011). *A multicultural and social reconstructionist approach to art education: A framework for social justice through art curriculum* (Doctoral dissertation). The Ohio State University. Retrieved from http://etd.ohiolink.edu/view.cgi/Boyd%20Joni%20Etta.pdf?osu1304434369

Bradford, D., & John Hull, J. (2011). Another blinding documentary on Channel 4? *Journal of Visual Culture, 10*(1), 125–133. Retrieved from http://vcu.sagepub.com/content/10/1/125

Brett, A., & Provenzo, E. F. (1995). *Adaptive technology for special human needs*. Albany: State University of New York Press.

Brown, L., Nietupski, J., & Hamre-Nietupski, S. (1976). The criterion of ultimate functioning and public school services for severely handicapped students. In M. Thomas (Ed.), *Hey, don't forget about me: New directions for serving the severely handicapped* (pp. 2–15). Reston, VA: Council for Exceptional Children.

Brown v. Board of Education, 347 U.S. 483 (1954).

Brueggemann, B. J. (2010). The Tango: Or, what deaf studies and disability studies do-do. In S. Burch & A. Kafer (Eds.), *Deaf and disabilities studies: Interdisciplinary perspectives* (pp. 245–266). Washington, DC: Gallaudet University Press.

Burch, S., & Kafer, A. (Eds.). (2010). *Deaf and disabilities studies: Interdisciplinary perspectives*. Washington, DC: Gallaudet University Press.

Burnette, J., & Lokerson, J. E. (2006). Art teachers and special education law. In B. L. Gerber & D. M. Guay (Eds.), *Reaching and teaching students with special needs through art* (pp. 15–25). Reston, VA: National Art Education Association.

Cajori, M. (Producer & Director). (1998). *Chuck Close: A portrait in progress* [Video]. USA: Home Vision Arts.

Campbell, L. (2005). Spiritual reflective practice in preservice art education. *Studies in Art Education, 47*(1), 51–69.

Campbell, L. (2009). Spirituality in holistic art education: Preventing violence among youth in the US. *Journal of Cultural Research in Art Education, 27*, 122–131.

Candlin, F. (2006). The dubious inheritance of touch: Art history and museum access. *Journal of Visual Culture, 5*(2), 137–154.

Capistrano Unified School District v. Wartenberg, 59 F.3d 884 (C.A. 1995).

Carrigan, J. (1994). Attitudes about persons with disabilities: A pilot program. *Art Education, 47*(6), 16–21.

Cates, D. L., McGill, H., Brian, L., Wilder, A., & Androes, T. (1990, April). *Severely and profoundly handicapped students in the regular classroom: It is happening now.* Paper presented at the annual convention of the Council for Exceptional Children, Toronto, Canada. (ERIC Document Reproduction Service No. ED 326 029)

Cedar Rapids Community School District v. Garret F., 119 S. Ct. 992 (1999).

Centre for Universal Design (1997). Retrieved from www.ncsu.edu/www/ncsu/design/sod5/cud/about_ud/udprinciplestext.htm

Certification of Professional Personnel, C Pennsylvania State Board of Educ. §§ 49-1-18 (2007).

Chapman, L. H. (2005). No child left behind in art? *Art Education, 58*(1), 8–16.

Chapman, L. H. (2007). An update on No Child Left Behind and national trends in education. *Arts Education Policy Review, 109*(1), 25–36.

Charlton, J. I. (2006). The dimensions of disability oppression: An overview. In L. J. Davis (Ed.), *The disability studies reader* (2nd ed., pp. 217–227). New York, NY: Routledge.

Chivers, S. (2001). The horror of becoming "one of us": Tod Browning's *Freaks* and disability. In A. Enns & C. R. Smit (Eds.), *Screening disability: Essays on cinema and disability* (pp. 57–64). Blue Ridge Summit, PA: University Press of America.

Chris C. v. Gwinnett County School District, 780 F.Supp. 804 (N.D.Ga. 1991).

Cipani, E. C., & Spooner, F. (1994). *Curricular and instructional approaches for persons with severe disabilities.* Needham Heights, MA: Allyn & Bacon.

Clements, C. (1999). Art education and person-centered futures planning: The dynamic new wave in human services. In A. L. Nyman & A. M. Jenkins (Eds.), *Issues and approaches to art for students with special needs* (pp. 142–154). Reston, VA: National Art Education Association.

Clyde K. and Sheila K. v. Puyallup School District, 35 F.3d 1396 (9th Cir. 1994).

Codina, A. (Producer & Director). (2009). *Monica & David* [Motion picture]. USA: CineMia.

Cooney, J. P. (Producer), & Saleebey, B. S. (Director). (2007). *Rolling* [Motion Picture]. USA: Group in Progress.

Copeland, B. (1984). Mainstreaming art for the handicapped child: Resources for teacher preparation. *Art Education, 37*(6), 22–29.

Corbett, J. (1994). A proud label: Exploring the relationship between disability politics and gay pride. *Disability & Society, 9*(3), 343–357.

Cranton, P. (2002). Teaching for Transformation. *New Directions for Adult and Continuing Education, 93*, 63–71.

Curkovic, F. (2009). *Graphic organisers.* Retrieved from http://artinspired.pbworks.com/w/page/13819592/Graphic-Organisers

Cypress-Fairbanks Independent School District v. Michael F., 931 F.Supp. 474 (S.D. Tex. 1995), *affd.*, 118 F.3d 245 (5th Cir. 1997), *cert. den.* 118 S.Ct. 690 (1998).

Danforth, S. (2007). Disability as metaphor: Examining the conceptual framing of emotional behavioral disorder in American public education. *Educational Studies, 42*(1), 8–27.

Danforth, S. (2009). *The incomplete child: An intellectual history of learning disabilities.* New York, NY: Peter Lang.

Daniel R. R. v. State Board of Education, 874 F.2d 1036 (5th Cir., 1989).

Darke, P. (1997). Everywhere: Disability on film. In A. Pointon & C. Davies (Eds.), *Framed: Interrogating disability in the media* (pp. 10–14). London, England: The British Film Institute.

Davis, J., & Watson, N. (2002). Countering stereotypes of disability: Disabled children and resistance. In M. Corker & T. Shakespeare (Eds.), *Disability/postmodernity: Embodying disability theory* (pp. 159–174). New York, NY: Continuum.

Davis, L. A. (2000). More common than we think: Recognizing and responding to signs of violence. *Impact: Feature issue on violence against women with developmental or other disabilities 13*(3). [Minneapolis: University of Minnesota, Institute on Community Integration].

Davis, L. J. (2002). *Bending over backwards: Disability, dismodernism, and other difficult positions.* New York: New York University Press.

Davis, L. J., & Smith, M. (Eds.). (2006). Disability–visuality [Themed issue]. *Journal of Visual Culture, 5*(2), 131–136.

DePaul University American Sign Language Project. (n.d.). Retrieved from http://asl.cs.depaul.edu

Dewey, J. (1938). *Experience and education.* New York, NY: Macmillan.

Dias, S., & Chadwick, P. (2009). *Disability social history project.* Retrieved from www.disabilityhistory.org

Dickens, C. (1843). *Christmas Carol.* London, England: Chapman & Hall.

Dickens-Smith, M. (1995). *The effects of inclusion training on teacher attitude toward inclusion.* (ERIC Document Reproduction Service No. ED 381 486)

Dillon, S. (2011, September 23). Obama turns some power of education back to states. *The New York Times.* Retrieved from www.nytimes.com/2011/09/24/education/24educ.html?_r=1&scp=2&sq=nclb&st=cse

Disability Movies (2010–2011). *Disability movie stereotypes and clichés.* Retrieved from http://disabilitymovies.com/disability-movie-cliches/

Disabled World. (n.d.). *Computer assistive technology demonstration.* Retrieved from http://videos.disabled-world.com/video/185/computer-assistive-technology-demonstration

Downing, J. E. (2008). Are they making progress? Assessing the skills of students with severe and multiple disabilities in general education classrooms. In J. E. Downing (Ed.), *Including students with severe and multiple disabilities in typical classrooms* (3rd ed., pp. 261–286). Baltimore, MD: Paul H. Brookes.

Draves, W. (2000). *Teaching online.* River Falls, WI: LERN Books.

Duncan, B., & Berman-Bieler, R. (2000–2007). *Disability World.* Retrieved from www.disabilityworld.org

Duncum, P. (2010). Seven principles for visual culture education. *Art Education, 63*(1), 6–10.

Duquette, C. (1990). Exceptional children: Right to an education, appropriate education and equality of treatment. *B. C. Journal of Special Education, 14*(3), 278–286.

Education for All Handicapped Children Act of 1975, 20 U. S. C. §§ 1401 et seq. (1975).

Education of the Handicapped Act of 1970, Pub. L. No. 91-230, 84 Stat. 175 (1970).

Eidelman, S. M. (2011). The reauthorization of IDEA 2004 and its impact on postsecondary opportunities for people with intellectual disabilities. *Think College Insight Brief, Issue No. 7.* Boston, MA: University of Massachusetts Boston, Institute for Community Inclusion.

Eisenhauer, J. (2007). Just looking and staring back: Challenging ableism through disability performance art. *Studies in Art Education, 49*(1), 7–22.

Eisenhauer, J. (2008). A visual culture of stigma: Critically examining representations of mental illness. *Art Education, 61*(5), 13–18.

Eisenhauer, J. (2010). "Bipolar Makes Me a Bad Mother": Performative Dialogue about Representations of Motherhood. *Visual Culture & Gender, 5,* 28–34.

Elementary and Secondary Education Act Amendments of 1974, Pub. L. 93–380, 88 Stat. 580 (1974).

Elementary and Secondary Education Act of 1965, Pub. L. No. 89-10, 79 Stat. 27 (1965); amended by Title VI, Pub. L. No. 89-750, 80 Stat. 1204 (1966).

Ely, S. (2000). *What is assistive technology? A basic guide for individuals with disabilities and their families.* Bloomington, IN: Indiana Institute on Disability and Community.

Eraclides, G. (2000). *Teachers' needs in supporting students with a disability in the classroom: A research report.* Introductory paper presented to the Box Hill Institute, Melbourne, Australia. (ERIC Document Reproduction Service No. ED 456 273)

Erevelles, N., & Kafer, A. (2010). Committed critique: An interview with Nirmala Erevelles. In S. Burch & A. Kafer (Eds.), *Deaf and disabilities studies: Interdisciplinary perspectives* (pp. 204–221). Washington, DC: Gallaudet University Press.

Erickson, M. (2004). Interaction of teachers and curriculum. In E. W. Eisner & M. D. Day (Eds.), *Handbook of research and policy in art education* (pp. 467–486). Reston, VA: National Art Education Association; and Mahwah, NJ: Lawrence Erlbaum Associates.

Ewing, L. (2000). Art in the dark: A nonvisual learners' curriculum. In D. E. Fehr, K. Fehr & K. Keifer-Boyd (Eds.), *Real-world readings in art education: Things your professors never told you* (pp. 83–89). New York, NY: Falmer Press.

Expansion of Teaching in the Education of Mentally Retarded Children Act of 1958, Pub. L. No. 85-926, 72 Stat. 1777 (1958).

Family Educational Rights and Privacy Act (FERPA). 20 U.S.C. § 1232 (2010). (to be codified at 34 C.F.R. pt. 99).

Fedorenko, J. (1996). *Integrating art in the special education curriculum through university and community school collaboration: Implication for teacher preparation* (Unpublished doctoral dissertation). The Ohio State University, Columbus, OH.

Fehr, D. E. (2008). Developing arts education policy at the federal level: The first ten months of the National Education Task Force. *Studies in Art Education, 49*(4), 381–384.

Feminist Cyberspaces. (2011). *A teaching resource wiki.* Retrieved from http://adarocks.wikispaces.com

FeministFrequency. (2009). *The Bechdel Test for women in movies.* Retrieved from www.youtube.com/watch?v=bLF6sAAMb4s

Ferguson, S. (Producer), & Jackson, M. (Director). (2010). *Temple Grandin* [Motion picture]. USA: HBO Films.

Finerman, W. (Producer), & Zemeckis, R. (Director). (1994). *Forrest Gump* [Motion picture]. USA: Paramount Pictures.

Forlin, C. (1997). *Re-designing pre-service teacher education courses: An inclusive curriculum in new times.* Paper presented at the annual conference of the Australian Association of Research in Education, Brisbane, Australia. (ERIC Document Reproduction Service No. ED 425 583)

Forlin, C. (Ed.). (2010). *Teacher education for inclusion: Changing paradigms and innovative approaches.* Abingdon, England: Routledge.

Freedman, K. (2003). *Teaching visual culture: Curriculum, aesthetics, and the social life of art.* New York, NY: Teachers College Press. Reston, VA: National Art Education Association.

Freire, P. (1990). *Pedagogy of the oppressed.* New York, NY: Continuum.

Friend, M., & Cook, L. (2006). *Interactions: Collaboration skills for school professionals* (5th ed.). Boston, MA: Allyn & Bacon.

Gardner, H. (1996). The assessment of student learning in the arts. In D. Boughton, E. W. Eisner & J. Ligvoet (Eds.), *Evaluating and assessing the visual arts in education: International perspectives* (pp. 131–155). New York, NY: Teachers College Press.

Gartin, B. C., & Murdick, N. L. (2008). Individualized education program. In E. L. Grigorenko (Ed.), *Educating individuals with disabilities: IDEIA 2004 and beyond* (pp. 337–359). New York, NY: Springer.

Gelzheiser, L. M., McLane, M., Meyers, J., & Pruzek, R. M. (1997). *Do general and special education teachers foster peer interactions of students with disabilities?* (Government Document No. A 57.2:B 541101). Albany, NY: The University at Albany. (ERIC Document Reproduction Service No. ED 408 757)

Gerber, B. L. (2006). Troubleshooting the art lesson. In B. L. Gerber & D. M. Guay (Eds.), *Reaching and teaching students with special needs through art* (pp. 27–39). Reston, VA: National Art Education Association.

Gerber, B. L., & Guay, D. M. (Eds.). (2006). *Reaching and teaching students with special needs through art.* Reston, VA: National Art Education Association.

Gerber, S. A., & Fedorenko, J. (2006). Building collaborative partnerships. In B. L. Gerber & D. M. Guay (Eds.), *Reaching and teaching students with special needs through art* (pp. 161–176). Reston, VA: National Art Education Association.

Gething, L. (1994). The interaction with disabled persons scale. In D. S. Dunn (Ed.), Psychosocial perspectives on disability [Special issue]. *Journal of Social Behavior and Personality, 9,* 23–42.

Giangreco, M., & Broer, S. (2005). Questionable utilization of paraprofessionals in inclusive schools: Are we addressing the symptoms or the causes? *Focus on Autism and Other Developmental Disabilities, 20,* 10–26.

Giangreco, M., Feldman, S., & Broer, S. (2001). *A guide to schoolwide planning for paraeducator supports.* Burlington, VT: University of Vermont, Center on Disability and Inclusion.

Go2Web20. (n.d.) Retrieved from http://go2web20.net

Greer v. Rome City School District, 950 F.2d 688 (11th Cir. 1991).

Grigal, M. (1998). The time-space continuum: Using situational supports in inclusive classrooms. *Teaching Exceptional Children, 30*(6), 44–51.

Grigorenko, E. L. (Ed.). (2008). *Educating individuals with disabilities: IDEIA 2004 and beyond.* New York, NY: Springer.

Guay, D. M. (1993). Normalization in art with extra challenged students: A problem-solving framework. *Art Education, 46*(1), 58–63.

Guay, D. M. (1994). Cross-site analysis of teaching practices: Visual art education with students experiencing disabilities. *Studies in Art Education, 34*(4), 222–232.

Guay, D. M. (1999). A way in: Strategies for art instruction for students with special needs. In A. L. Nyman & A. M. Jenkins (Eds.), *Issues and approaches to art for students with special needs* (pp. 17–33). Reston, VA: National Art Education Association.

Guay, D. M. (2006a). Special needs students in the art room: A journey. In B. L. Gerber & D. M. Guay (Eds.), *Reaching and teaching students with special needs through art* (pp. 3–13). Reston, VA: National Art Education Association.

Guay, D. M. (with Gerlach, K.). (2006b). Clarifying roles for paraeducators in the art room. In B. L. Gerber & D. M. Guay (Eds.), *Reaching and teaching students with special needs through art* (pp. 189–206). Reston, VA: National Art Education Association.

Guggenheim, D. (Director), & Chilcott, L. (Producer). (2010). *Waiting for superman* [Motion picture]. USA: Box Office Mojo.

Guthrie, J. W. (1980). An assessment of educational policy research. *Educational Evaluation and Policy Analysis, 2*(5), 41–55.

Hallahan, D. P., & Kauffman, J. M. (1995). Toward a culture of disability. In J. M. Kauffman & D. P. Hallahan (Eds.), *The illusion of full inclusion: A comprehensive critique of a current special education bandwagon* (pp. 59–74). Austin, TX: Pro-ed.

Hakim, D. (2011, June 5). Abused and used: A disabled boy's death, and a system in disarray. *New York Times.* Retrieved from www.nytimes.com/2011/06/06/nyregion/boys-death-highlights-crisis-in-homes-for-disabled.html?pagewanted=1&_r=2&nl=nyregion&emc=ura1

Haraway, D. (1991). *Simians, cyborgs and women: The reinvention of nature.* New York, NY: Routledge.

Harter. L. M., Scott, J. A., Novak, D. R., Leeman, M., & Morris, J. F. (2006). Freedom through flight: Performing a counter-narrative of disability. *Journal of Applied Communication Research, 34*(1), 3–29.

Higgins, K., & Boone, R. (Eds.). (1997). *Technology for students with learning disabilities: Educational applications.* Austin, TX: Pro-ed.

Honig v. Doe, 484 U.S. 305 (1988).

Hurwitz, A., & Day, M. (2007). *Children and their art* (8th ed.). Belmont, CA: Thomson Higher Education.

IDEA Fairness Restoration Act Bill, S. 613, 112d Cong. (2011).

Individuals with Disabilities Education Act Amendments of 1997, 20 U.S.C. §§ 1401 *et seq.* (2000).

Individuals with Disabilities Education Act Amendments of 1997 Regulations, 34 C.F.R. §§ 300 *et seq.* (1999).

Individuals with Disabilities Education Act of 1990, 20 U.S.C. §§ 1401 *et seq.* (1990).

Individuals with Disabilities Education Improvement Act of 2004, 20 U.S.C. §§ 1401 *et seq.* (2004).

Individual with Disabilities Education Improvement Act of 2004 Regulations, 34 C.F.R. §§ 300 *et seq.* (2006).

Information Technology Technical Assistance and Training Center (n.d.). Section 508. Retrieved from www.ittatc.org

Iscovich, M. (Producer), & Marshall, G. (Director). (1999). *The other sister* [Motion picture]. USA: Mandeville Films.

Jaeger, P., & Bowman, C. A. (2005). *Understanding disability: Inclusion, access, diversity, and civil rights.* Westport, CT: Praeger.

Jacklin A., Robinson, C., O'Meara, A., & Harris, A. (2007). *Improving the experiences of disabled students in higher education.* York, England: The Higher Education Academy. Retrieved from www.heacademy.ac.uk/assets/York/documents/ourwork/research/jacklin.pdf

Jackson, A., Fleischer, D., & Christie, C. A. (2006). *Evaluation of the J. Paul Getty Museum's art detective cards program.* Retrieved from www.getty.edu/education/museum_educators/artdetective_cards.html

Jackson, M. (Director). (2010). *Temple Grandin.* [Motion picture]. USA: HBO Films.

James, P. (1996). The construction of learning and teaching in a sculpture studio class. *Studies in Art Education, 37*(3), 145–159.

Janko, S., & Porter, A. (1997, March). *Portraits of inclusion through the eyes of children, families, and educators.* Seattle, WA: University of Washington, Early Childhood Research Institute on Inclusion.

Johnson, M. (Producer), & Levinson, B. (Director). (1988). *Rain man* [Motion picture]. USA: MGM.

Jones, N. L. (2011, May 12). The Individuals with Disabilities Education Act (IDEA): Selected judicial developments following the 2004 reauthorization [Web log post]. Retrieved from http://education-legislation.blogspot.com/2011/05/individuals-with-disabilities-education.html

Karten, T. J. (2005). *Inclusion strategies that work: Research-based methods for the classroom.* Thousand Oaks, CA: Corwin Press.

Karten, T. J. (2008). *Embracing disabilities in the classroom: Strategies to maximize students' assets.* Thousand Oaks, CA: Corwin Press.

Kauffman, J. M. (1985). The regular education initiative as Reagan-Bush Policy: A trickle-down theory of education of the hard-to-teach. In J. M. Kauffman & D. P. Hallahan (Eds.), *The illusion of full inclusion: A comprehensive critique of a current special education bandwagon* (pp. 125–155). Austin, TX: Pro-ed.

Kauffman, J. M., & Hallahan, D. P. (1995a). Full inclusion in historical context: Introduction to part I. In J. M. Kauffman & D. P. Hallahan (Eds.), *The illusion of full inclusion: A comprehensive critique of a current special education bandwagon* (pp. 3–4). Austin, TX: Pro-ed.

Kauffman, J. M., & Hallahan, D. P. (1995b). Toward a comprehensive delivery system for special education. In J. M. Kauffman & D. P. Hallahan (Eds.), *The illusion of full inclusion: A comprehensive critique of a current special education bandwagon* (pp. 157–191). Austin, TX: Pro-ed.

Kaufman, A. K. (2008). Policy of law of Individuals with Disabilities Education Improvement Act of 2004: Attempting no student left behind to the extent enforceable. In E. L. Grigorenko (Ed.), *Educating individuals with disabilities: IDEIA 2004 and beyond* (pp. 39–59). New York, NY: Springer.

Keifer-Boyd, K. (Producer, Director, & Editor). (1993). *Alternative Ways to Experience Art: A Tactile Tour* [Video available at https://streaming.psu.edu/media/?movieId=16136]. USA: University of Oregon.

Keifer-Boyd, K. (2000). By the people: A community-based art curriculum. In D. E. Fehr, K. Fehr & K. Keifer-Boyd (Eds.), *Real world readings in art education: Things your professors never told you* (pp. 155–165). New York, NY: Falmer Press.

Keifer-Boyd, K. (2003). Participatory art pedagogy: Informed by feminist principles. Retrieved from: http://judychicago.arted.psu.edu/?page_id=78

Keifer-Boyd, K. (2007). From content to form: Judy Chicago's pedagogy with reflections by Judy Chicago. *Studies in Art Education, 48*(2), 133–153.

Keifer-Boyd, K. (2012). Feminist web 2.0 pedagogy: Collaborations that sustain difference. In C. Bitzer, S. Collingwood, A. Quintana & C. Smith (Eds.), *Feminist cyberspaces: Pedagogies in transition*. Newcastle upon Tyne, England: Cambridge Scholars Press.

Keifer-Boyd, K., & Kraft, L. M. (2003). Inclusion policy in practice. *Art Education, 56*(6), 46–53.

Keifer-Boyd, K., & Maitland-Gholson, J. (2007). *Engaging visual culture*. Worchester, MA: Davis.

Keifer-Boyd, K., & Smith-Shank, D. (2006). Speculative fiction's contribution to contemporary understanding: The handmaid art tale. *Studies in Art Education, 47*(2), 139–154.

Kibbler, J. H. (1991). The Education of the Handicapped Act: The floor of opportunity. *Journal of Juvenile Law, 12*, 26–34.

King, D. (2010). *A study of student teachers' perceived resistance to teaching multicultural education: Will the pedagogy be "colored that I teach?"* (Unpublished doctoral dissertation). The Pennsylvania State University, University Park.

Knight, W. B. (2006). Using contemporary art to challenge cultural values, beliefs, and assumptions. *Art Education, 59*(4), 39–45.

Knight, W., Keifer-Boyd, K., & Amburgy, P. M. (2004). Revealing power: A visual culture orientation to student-teacher relationships. *Studies in Art Education, 45*(3), 270–273.

Kraft, L. M. (2001). *A historical/legal analysis and case study of a high school art classroom as a least restrictive environment for students experiencing disabilities*. (Doctoral dissertation, Texas Tech University). Retrieved from *Dissertation Abstracts International, 62*, 02A (Accession No. AA13005249)

Kraft, M. (2006). Art education and disability: Re-envisioning educational efficiency. *The Journal for Social Theory in Art Education, 26*, 302-320.

Kunjufu, J. (2005). *Keeping Black boys out of special education*. Chicago, IL: African American Images.

Langtree, I., & Langtree, L. (2006). *Famous people with disabilities*. Retrieved from www.disabled-world.com/artman/publish/article_0060.shtml

Lazarus, E. (1989). Equality and excellence education in arts. *Design for Arts in Education, 90*(6), 30–32.

Levin, M. R., & Shank, A. (Eds.). (1970). *Educational investment in an urban society: Costs, benefits, and public policy*. New York, NY: Teachers College Press, Teachers College, Columbia University.

Lewis, R. (1993). *Special education technology: Classroom applications*. Pacific Grove, CA: Brooks/Cole.

Lindstrom, J. H., Tuckwiller, E. D., & Hallahan, D. P. (2008). Assessment and eligibility of students with disabilities. In E. L. Grigorenko (Ed.), *Educating individuals with disabilities: IDEIA 2004 and beyond* (pp. 197–225). New York, NY: Springer.

Loesl, S. D. (1999). Art education for students with disabilities: Practical strategies for successful inclusion. In A. L. Nyman & A. M. Jenkins (Eds.), *Issues and approaches to art for students with special needs* (pp. 55–62). Reston, VA: National Art Education Association.

Lokerson, J. E., & Joynes, A. C. (2006). Students with learning disabilities. In B. L. Gerber & D. M. Guay (Eds.), *Reaching and teaching students with special needs through art* (pp. 83–106). Reston, VA: National Art Education Association.

Lombardi, T. P., Nuzzo, D. L., Kennedy, K. D., & Foshay, J. (1994). Perceptions of parents, teachers, and students regarding an integrated education inclusion program. *High School Journal, 77*(4), 315–321.

Longmore, P. (n.d.). *Institute on disability dateline*. Retrieved from http://bss.sfsu.edu/disability/dateline.html

Majchrzak, A. (1984). *Methods for policy research*. Newberry Park, CA: Sage.

Mandel, J. V. (Producer), & Rubin, H. A., & Shapiro, D. A. (Directors). (2005). *Murderball* [Motion picture]. USA: Paramount.

Mark A. v. Grant Wood Area Educational Agency, 795 F.2d 52 (8th Cir. 1986).

Martin, J., Jorgensen, C. M., & Klein, J. (1998). The promise of friendship for students with disabilities. In C. M. Jorgensen (Ed.), *Restructuring high schools for all students: Taking inclusion to the next level* (pp. 49–70). Baltimore, MD: Paul H. Brookes.

Mason, M. (1990). Disability equality in the classroom—A human rights issue. *Gender and Education, 2*(3), 363–366.

Matalon, D. (Producer), & Hallström, L. (Director). (1993). *What's Eating Gilbert Grape?* [Motion picture]. USA: Paramount Pictures.

McMillan, J. H., & Schumacher, S. (1997). *Research in education: A conceptual introduction*. New York, NY: Addison-Wesley.

Melvin, D. H. (1995). The desegregation of children with disabilities. *DePaul Law Review, 44*, 599–671.

Microsoft Office. (2011). *PowerPoint blog: Are your presentations accessible?* Retrieved from http://blogs.office.com/b/microsoft-powerpoint/archive/2011/03/01/are-your-presentations-accessible.aspx

Mills v. Board of Education of the District of Columbia, 348 F. Supp. 866 (D. D. C. 1972).

Mitchell, D., & Synder, S. (2003). *Narrative prosthesis: Disability and the dependencies of discourse*. Ann Arbor: University of Michigan Press.

Modrick, J. E. (2003). Guest columnist, Special Needs in Art Education, *NAEA News, 45*(6), 16.

Moore, S., & Jeffries, C. (2006). *Art, disability, and expression exhibit of VSA arts: Disability culture.* Retrieved from www.vsarts.org/prebuilt/showcase/gallery/exhibits/disability/disabculture.html

Mostert, M. P. (1998). *Interprofessional collaboration in schools.* Needham Heights, MA: Allyn & Bacon.

Mouth Foot Painting Artists (MFPA). (2003). MFPA website. Retrieved from www.mfpausa.com

NASA Accessibility. (2009). Retrieved from www.nasa.gov/accessibility/section508/sec508_overview.html

National Arts and Disability Center (NADC). (1998–2011). Retrieved from http://nadc.ucla.edu/Gallery.cfm

National Art Education Association. (1994). *National Standards for Visual Arts.* Reston, VA: National Art Education Association.

National Center for Accessible Media (NCAM). (2009). Retrieved from http://ncam.wgbh.org/invent_build/web_multimedia/tools-guidelines

National Council on Disability. (2004). *Design for inclusion: Creating a new marketplace.* Retrieved from www.ncd.gov

National Institute of Art and Disabilities (NIAD). (2011). *NIAD art center: Empowering artists with disabilities.* Retrieved from http://niadart.org

Nelson, H. L. (2001). *Damaged identities: Narrative repair.* Ithaca, NY: Cornell University Press.

Nelson, R. (Producer & Director). (1968). *Charly* [Motion picture]. USA: ABC Pictures.

No Child Left Behind/Elementary and Secondary Schools Act. 20 U.S.C. §§6301 *et seq.* (2001).

Nordlund, C., Speirs, P., & Stewart, M. (2010). An invitation to social change: Fifteen principles for teaching art. *Art Education, 63*(5), 36–43.

Nussbaum, M. C. (2010). *Not for profit: Why democracy needs the humanities.* Princeton, NJ: Princeton University Press.

Oberlander, K. (2011). *Art of Possibility® Studios.* Retrieved from http://artofpossibilitystudios.wordpress.com/2011/06/

Oberti v. Board of Education of the Borough of Clementon School District, 995 F.2d 1204 (3rd Cir. 1993).

Office of Special Education and Rehabilitative Services (OSERS). (1995). *Individuals with Disabilities Education Act Amendments of 1995: Reauthorization of the Individuals with Disabilities Education Act (IDEA).* Washington, DC: U.S. Department of Education.

Office of Special Education Programs (OSEP), U.S. Department of Education. (2007). *Alignment with the No Child Left Behind Act.* Retrieved from http://idea.ed.gov/explore/view/p/%2Croot%2Cdynamic%2CTopicalBrief%2C3%2C

Orr, D. (2005). Minding the soul in education: Conceptualizing and teaching the whole person. In J. P. Miller, S. Karsten, D. Denton, D. Orr & I. Kates (Eds.), *Holistic learning and spirituality in education* (pp. 87–100). Albany: State University of New York Press.

Ostrove, J., & Oliva, G. Identifying allies: Explorations of deaf-hearing relationships. (2010). In S. Burch & A. Kafer (Eds.), *Deaf and disabilities studies: Interdisciplinary perspectives* (pp. 105–119). Washington, DC: Gallaudet University Press.

Patston, P. (2011). *International guild of disabled artists and performers.* Retrieved from http://igodap.org

Patterson, L. (2010). Unlikely alliances: Crossing the deaf and hearing divide. In S. Burch & A. Kafer (Eds.), *Deaf and disabilities studies: Interdisciplinary perspectives* (pp. 144–161). Washington, DC: Gallaudet University Press.

Pennsylvania Association for Retarded Children (PARC) v. Commonwealth of Pennsylvania, 343 F. Supp. 279 (E. D. Pa. 1972).

Pennsylvania State Board of Education. (2006, June 28). *Certification of Professional Personnel.* Chapter 49-2. Retrieved from www.education.state.pa.us/portal/server.pt/gateway/PTARGS_0_2_381986_0_0_18/Chapter%2049%202%20June%2028%202006%20JEB%20.pdf

Peters, M. A. (2007). The body also has a history: A critical aesthetics for arts education. In L. Bressler (Ed.), *International handbook of research in arts education* (Part 2, pp. 1161–1171). Heidelberg, Germany: Springer.

Pilkington, E. (2009, December 22). The real Rain Man dies of heart attack in home town of Salt Lake City, aged 58. *The Guardian.* Retrieved from www.guardian.co.uk/world/2009/dec/22/kim-peek-rain-man-dies

Pointon, A., & Davis, C. (1997). *Framed: Interrogating disability in the media.* London, England: British Film Institute.

Polk v. Central Susquehanna Intermediate Unit 16, 853 F.2d 171 (3rd Cir. 1988).

Rehabilitation Act of 1973, Section 504 Regulations, 34 C.F.R. § 104.1 *et seq.*

Reid, D. K., & Knight, M. G. (2006). Disability justifies exclusion of minority students: A critical history grounded in disability studies. *Educational Researcher, 35*(6), 18–23.

Ripley, S. (July 1997). *Collaboration between general and special education teachers* (Report No. EDO-SP-96-5). Washington, DC: ERIC Clearinghouse on Teaching and Teacher Education. (ERIC Document Reproduction Service No. ED 409 317)

Rosenthal, J. (Producer), & Schumacher, J. (Director). (1999). *Flawless* [Motion picture]. USA: Tribeca Productions.

Russell, M. (2002). What disability civil rights cannot do: Employment and political economy. *Disability and Society, 17*(2), 117–135.

Sabol, F. R. (2004). The assessment context: Part one. *Art education policy review, 105*(3), 3–9.

Sabol, F. R. (2010). No Child Left Behind: A study of its impact on art education. Reston, VA: National Art Education Association.

Sacramento City Unified School District Board of Education v. Rachel H., 14 F.3d 1398 (Ninth Cir., 1994).

Schemo, D. J. (2004, May 13). State approved education measures. *The New York Times*, p. 23A.

Schiller, M. (1999). Access to art education: Ethical and legal perspectives. In A. L. Nyman & A. M. Jenkins (Eds.), *Issues and approaches to art for students with special needs* (pp. 7–16). Reston, VA: National Art Education Association.

Section 504 of the Rehabilitation Act of 1973, 29 U.S.C. § 794 *et seq.*

Section 508 of the Rehabilitation Act, 29 U.S.C. § 794 d. (1998). Retrieved from http//:section508.gov

Sells, D., & Shepard, J. (1998). *Fostering resilience in special education students.* Spokane, WA: Gonzaga University. (ERIC Document Reproduction Service No. ED 425 576)

Semmel, M. I., Gerber, M. M., & Macmillian, D. L. (1995). A legacy of policy analysis research in special education. In J. M. Kauffman & D. P. Hallahan (Eds.), *The illusion of full inclusion: A comprehensive critique of a current special education bandwagon* (pp. 39–57). Austin, TX: Pro-ed.

Shakespeare, T. (2006). *Disability rights and wrongs*. New York, NY: Routledge.

Shannon, J. B. (2009). *Learning disabilities sourcebook (Health reference series)*. Detroit, MI: Omnigraphics.

Sheldon, K. (1996). "Can I play too?" Adapting common classroom activities for young children with limited motor abilities. *Early Childhood Education Journal, 24*(2), 115–120.

Simpson, C. G., McBride, R., Spencer, V. G., Lowdermilk, J., & Lynch, S. (2009). Assistive technology: Supporting learners in inclusive classrooms. *Kappa Delta Pi Record, 45*(4), 172–175.

Skiba, J. R., Poloni-Staudinger, L., Simmons, B. A., Feggins-Azziz, R. L., & Chung, G. C. (2005). Unproven links: Can poverty explain ethnic disproportionality in special education? *The Journal of Special Education, 3*, 130–144.

Skylar, A. A., Higgins, K., & Boone, R. (2007). Strategies for adapting WebQuests for students with learning disabilities. *Intervention in School and Clinic, 43*(1), 20–28.

Smith-Shank, D. L. (Ed.). (2004). *Semiotics and visual culture: Sights, signs, and significance*. Reston, VA: National Art Education Association.

Snell, M. E. (2002). Using dynamic assessment with learners who communicate non-symbolically. *Augmentative and Alternative Communication, 18*, 163–176.

Soep, E. (2004a). Assessment and visual arts education. In E. W. Eisner & M. D. Day (Eds.), *Handbook of research and policy in art education* (pp. 579–583). Reston, VA: National Art Education Association; and Mahwah, NJ: Lawrence Erlbaum Associates.

Soep, E. (2004b). Visualizing judgment: Self-assessment and peer assessment in arts education. In E. W. Eisner & M. D. Day (Eds.), *Handbook of research and policy in art education* (pp. 667–687). Reston, VA: National Art Education Association; and Mahwah, NJ: Lawrence Erlbaum Associates.

Special Education Services and Settings, 19 Texas Education Code (TEC) § 89.63(c)(1) (1996).

S. Rep. No. 168, 94th Cong., 1st Sess. 1425 (1975).

Steckelburg, A., & Vasa, S. F. (1988). *Preservice and in-service training program to prepare teachers to supervise and work more effectively with paraprofessional personnel*. Paper presented at the 66th Annual Convention of the Council for Exceptional Children, Washington, DC, March 28-April 1. (ERIC Document 297510)

Stokrocki, M. (2004). Contexts for teaching art. In E. W. Day & M. D. Day (Eds.), *Handbook of research and policy in art education* (pp. 439–466). Reston, VA: National Art Education Association; and Mahwah, NJ: Lawrence Erlbaum Associates.

Taylor, N., & Chacksfield, J. (2005). *ICT for learners with special needs: A handbook for tutors*. London, England: David Fulton.

Taylor, P. G., Carpenter, B. S., II, Ballengee Morris, C., & Sessions, B. (2006). *Interdisciplinary approaches to teaching art in high schools*. Reston, VA: National Art Education Association.

Taylor v. Board of Education, 649 F.Supp. 1253 (N.D.N.Y. 1986).

Texas Education Agency (TEA). (2000, September). *State plan for fiscal years 1994–1996 Under Part B of the IDEA* [Online]. Retrieved from www.tea.state.tx.us/special.ed/stplan/

Texas Education Agency (TEA). (1996, September). *Subchapter D: Special education services and settings*. (19 TEC §89.63(c)(1)). Retrieved from http://ritter.tea.state.tx.us/rules/tac/ch089d.html

Texas Education Agency/Education Service Center 20 (TEA/ESC 20). (Revised 2009, December). *The least restrictive environment: Question and answer document*. Retrieved from http://portal.esc20.net/portal/page/portal/doclibraryroot/SpEd%20Stwd%20AGC%20Left%20Nav/LRE-QA.pdf

Texthelp Systems Ltd (2011). *Welcome to texthelp systems*. Retrieved from www.texthelp.com/theRSAorg (2010). Retrieved from www.youtube.com/watch?v=zDZFcDGpL4U

Thirteen/WNET (Producer), & Lignetti, J. (Director). (1996). *People in motion part 2: Breaking the silence barrier: Inside the world of cognitive disabilities* [Motion picture]. (Available from Films for the Humanities and Sciences, P.O. Box 2053, Princeton, NJ, 08543-2053)

Thomas, G., & Glenny, G. (2005). Thinking about inclusion: Whose research? What evidence. In M. Nind, K. Sheehy, J. Rix & K. Simmons (Eds.), *Ethics and research in inclusive education: Values into practice* (pp. 9–27). New York, NY: Routledge Falmer.

Thompson, C. (2000). Drawing together: Peer influences in preschool-kindergarten art classes. *Visual Arts Research, 25*(2), 61–68.

Thunder-McGuire, S. (1999). Narrative accounts of experience, context, meaning, and purpose. In A. L. Nyman & A. M. Jenkins (Eds.), *Issues and approaches to art for students with special needs* (pp. 99–108). Reston, VA: National Art Education Association.

Turnbull, A. P., Turnbull, H. R., Shank, M., & Leal, D. (1995). *Exceptional lives: Special education in today's schools*. Upper Saddle River, NJ: Prentice-Hall.

Turnbull, H. R. (1991, October). *The communitarian perspective: Thoughts on the future for people with developmental disabilities*. Paper presented at the meeting of the North Carolina Developmental Disabilities Planning Council, Raleigh, NC.

Turnbull, H. R., Brotherson, M. J., Czyzewski, M. J., Esquith, D. S., Otis, A. K., Summers, J. A., Van Reusen, A. K., & DePazza-Conway, M. (1983). A policy analysis of "least restrictive" education of handicapped children. *Rutgers Law Journal, 14*(489), 489–540.

Tusler, A. (Ed.). (2011). *About disability website: Bibliography*. Retrieved from www.aboutdisability.com/bib.html

United Nations. (2006). *Unite to end violence against women*. Retrieved from www.un.org/en/women/endviolence/situation.shtml

United Nations (2006). *Unite to end violence against women. United Nations Secretary General's campaign*. Retrieved from www.un.org/en/women/endviolence/pdf/VAW.pdf

United Nations (2013a). *Enable: Development and human rights for all*. Retrieved from http://www.un.org/disabilities/default.asp?id=210

United Nations (2013b). *United Nations convention on the rights of persons with disabilities*. Retrieved from www.un.org/disabilities/convention/conventionfull.shtml

U.S. Department of Education. (2007). *Building the legacy: IDEA 2004*. Retrieved from http://idea.ed.gov/explore/view/p/%2Croot%2Cdynamic%2CQaCorner%2C2%2C

Verstegen, D. A. (1994). Efficiency and equity in the provision and reform of American schooling. *Journal of Education Finance, 20*(1), 107–131.

Vincent, L. J., Salisbury, C., Walter, G., Gruenwald, L. J., & Powers, M. (1980). Program evaluation and curriculum development in early childhood/special education: Criteria of the next environment. In W. Sailor, B. Wilcox, & L. Brown (Eds.), *Methods of instruction for severely handicapped students* (pp. 303-328). Baltimore, MD: Paul H. Brookes.

Virtual Ability Island. (2011). Retrieved from http://virtualability.org

Vygotsky, L. (1978). *Mind and society: The development of higher psychological processes.* Cambridge, MA: Harvard University Press.

Vygotsky, L. (1986). *Thought and language.* Cambridge, MA: MIT Press.

Weishaar, M. K. (2008). The law and reality: Understanding the Individuals with Disabilities Education Improvement Act. In E. Grigorenko (Ed.), *Educating individuals with disabilities: IDEIA 2004 and beyond* (pp. 63–83). New York, NY: Springer.

Welch, A. R. (1998). The cult of efficiency in education: Comparative reflections on the reality and the rhetoric. *Comparative Education, 34*(2), 157–175.

Wendell, S. (1989). Toward a feminist theory of disability. *Hypatia, 4*(2), 104–124.

Wexler, A. (2002). Painting their way out: Profiles of adolescent art practice at the Harlem Hospital Horizon art studio. *Studies in Art Education, 43*(4), 339–353.

Wexler, A. (2009). *Art and disability: The social and political struggles facing education.* New York, NY: Palgrave.

Wikipedia. (2011). *List of free software for audio.* Retrieved from http://en.wikipedia.org/wiki/List_of_free_software_for_audio

Wilson, A. T. (2011). Human rights of women and girls with disabilities in developing countries. In D. Bergoffen, P. R. Gilbert, T. Harvey & C. L. McNeely (Eds.), *Confronting global gender justice: Women's lives, human rights* (pp. 231-244). New York, NY: Routledge.

Wilson, C., & Wright, L. (1994). Enhancing access to knowledge. In J. I. Goodlad & P. Keating (Eds.), *Access to knowledge: The continuing agenda for our nation's schools* (Rev. ed., pp. 223-236). New York, NY: College Entrance Examination Board.

Wolfe, D. (1988). Opening up assessment. *Educational Leadership, 45*(1), 24–29.

Wright, W. D. (Preparator). (July 2005). *U.S. Department of Education (USDOE) commentary and explanation about proposed regulations for IDEA 2004.* Retrieved from www.wrightslaw.com/idea/law.htm

Yell, M. L. (1998). *The law and special education.* Upper Saddle River, NJ: Merrill.

Zederayko, M. W., & Ward, K. (1999). Art class: What to do when students can't hold a pencil. *Art Education, 59*(4), 18–22.

Zimmerman, E. (1994). How should students' progress and achievements in art be assessed? A case for assessment that is responsive to diverse students' needs. *Visual Arts Research, 20*(1), 29–35.

GLOSSARY OF COMMON ACRONYMS

FAPE   Free Appropriate Public Education

HEARTS   Human Empowerment Through the Arts

IDEA   Individuals with Disabilities Education Act

IEP   Individualized Education Program

LEA   Local Education Agency

LRE   Least Restrictive Environment

NCLB   No Child Left Behind Act

NSVA   National Standards for Visual Arts

SEA   State Education Agency

LIST OF FIGURES AND EXHIBITS

ABOUT THE AUTHORS

Michelle Kraft is Professor of Art Education at Lubbock Christian University (LCU) in Lubbock, Texas. Prior to that, she taught art at Dunbar High School and Dunbar Junior High School in the Lubbock Independent School District, working extensively with students experiencing a range of (dis)abilities. Kraft has authored and coauthored several journal articles and book chapters, including in *Matter Matters: Art Education and Material Culture Studies*, edited by Paul Bolin and Doug Blandy (National Art Education Association, 2012), *Visual Arts Research, The Journal for Social Theory in Art Education, The Journal for Cultural Theory in Art Education, Visual Culture & Gender,* and *Art Education.* She is the recipient of several grants and teaching awards. She is active in the National Art Education Association and in the Texas Art Education Association (TAEA), and has presented at numerous conferences at state and national levels. She has served as chair of the Higher Education Division of TAEA and as editor of TAEA's peer-refereed journal, *Trends in Art Education.* Kraft has been a reviewer for a number of journals, including *The Journal for Social Theory in Art Education, Visual Arts Research,* and *Visual Culture & Gender.* In addition to teaching, she has served as department chair and is currently the Assistant Dean for the Hancock College of Liberal Arts and Education at LCU.

Karen Keifer-Boyd, Professor of Art Education and Women's Studies at The Pennsylvania State University, has coauthored *InCITE, InSIGHT, InSITE* (NAEA, 2008), *Engaging Visual Culture* (Davis, 2007); coedited *Real-World Readings in Art Education: Things Your Professors Never Told You* (Falmer, 2000); and served as editor of the *Journal of Social Theory in Art Education* and guest editor for *Visual Arts Research.* In 2005, she cofounded the journal *Visual Culture & Gender.* Her research is translated into several languages and focuses on feminist methodologies for teaching critical and creative inquiry with dynamic/interactive technologies. Keifer-Boyd has been invited to present her research in Austria, Finland, Germany, Hong Kong, South Korea, Taiwan, Turkey, and Uganda. She has been honored with leadership and teaching awards including USSEA Ziegfeld Award for 2013: 2012 Fulbright Award as Distinguished Chair of Gender Studies at Alpen-Adria-Universität Klagenfurt in Austria, 2006 Fulbright Award for research in Finland, the National Art Education Association (NAEA) Women's Caucus Connors Teaching Award in 2005, the Texas Outstanding Art Educator in Higher Education Award in 2001, the Chi Chapter of Phi Beta Delta (Honor Society for International Scholars) in 2001, and the Arts Administrator of the Year NAEA Award for the Pacific Region in 1994. Keifer-Boyd is an NAEA Distinguished Fellow Class of 2013, and served as president of the NAEA Women's Caucus from 2010—2012, coordinator of the NAEA Caucus on Social Theory and Art Education from 1999–2001, and is the Coordinator of the Judy Chicago Art Education Collection at Penn State.

INDEX